The Life and Times
Of
Thomas of Ercildune

'The Rhymer'

Elizabeth Barton
2017

The Life and Times Of Thomas of Ercildune

'The Rhymer'

By

Elizabeth Burton

ISBN 1 861431 63 9

Printed by Llanerch Press Ltd, 2012

Front Cover

Thomas and the Fairy Queen

Miniature costume figures made by Anne
Carrick

From the exhibition at Smailholm Tower

Depicting the 'Border Ballads'

From

Sir Walter Scott's 'Minstrelsy of the Scottish
Border'

Photo by Peter Brown

Taken on the wall-walk at Smailholm Tower

The Three Eildons taken from Scott's View
One of the few viewpoints where all three
hills can be seen simultaneously.

Foreword

Being born and raised in the village of his birth, I have lived my life in an area which has, for nearly eight centuries, been associated with Thomas the Rhymer. I grew up accustomed to names such as 'The Rhymer's Stone,' 'Rhymer's Mill,' 'Rhymer's Football Team', 'Rhymer's Tower Filling Station', and Rhymer's Tower Coffee Shop', without giving too much thought to their origins. Street names such as 'Thorn Street', 'Thornfield Crescent', and 'Thorn Bank,' house names of 'The Thorn', and 'Thorn Cottages', which relate to the famous *'Rhymer's Thorn Tree'* of Thomas's prediction, I once took for granted.

It was not until recent years, when I began to take an interest in my local history and heritage, that I became aware of the influencial impact of 'The Rhymer' on our legendary and literary history; this being right here on my doorstep. I began to take an in- depth look at the life and legend of Thomas the Rhymer and was enlightened, and fascinated by my findings; the results of which are contained in the following chapters.

While I have endeavoured to keep the information on Thomas's life as authentic as possible, due to the shortage of factual information regarding the life of Thomas of Ercildune, I have relied on the credibility of accounts by the early writers of the fourteenth and fifteenth century, local writers of the nineteenth century and local knowledge passed down through many generations. From the scant amount of available information, I have printed what I believe to be as accurate an account as is possible to achieve with regard to the bizarre life and legend of Thomas of Ercildune.

A Tale of Fact & Folklore

Preface

Nearly eight hundred years have passed since Thomas the Rhymer lived in Ercildune in the Merse. The Merse is in the area of Scotland known today as the Southern Uplands. Approximately four miles southwest of Ercildune are the Eildon Hills; a landmark as famous as it is unique. It was on the lower slopes of the north Eildon that Thomas, in his youth, *"beheld a Lady gay come riding o'er the fernie brae."* The consequences of his encounter with this mysterious lady are epitomised in a rhyming tale, with which the name of *Thomas the Rhymer* is most commonly associated. In Scottish folklore, the 'Ballad of Thomas the Rhymer' tells of his meeting with The Queen of Fair Elfland at the Eildon Tree. According to legend, Thomas returned to Ercildune, after a seven year absence, bestowed with the gift of prophecy. Therereafter, he lived a mysterious life for many years, until his final, and by all accounts, rather bizarre departure from the land of mortals.

In more recent times, this mystical part of Scotland has inspired many famous poets; Sir Walter Scott, James Hogg, John Leyden, and John Veitch to name a few. In medieval times it was no different, the poetic ballads relating to the area go back many centuries.The countryside is one of outstanding natural beauty; gentle rolling hills provide an easy ramble for walkers, while trout and salmon stocked rivers attract anglers from far and near. Forlorn ruins of keeps and castles enthrall the historians, while capturing the imagination of the casual tourist. Off the beaten track, there are quaint little villages which reflect an era far removed from the twenty- first century.

In the nineteeth century, Sir Walter Scott said *"I can stand on the Eildon Hills and point out forty-three places famous in war and verse."* These few words sum up the history, legends, and literature associated with the area in which Thomas was born.

Back in the thirteenth century, the area surrounding Thomas's birthplace would present an entirely different picture to that of today. In place of acres of cultivated terrain, there would be dense forests of oak and birch. The creatures that prowled the forests would include wild boar, and wolves; however, the forests were believed to be inhabited by less earthly creatures, whose presence instilled a far greater fear into the hearts of mortals.

Nestling at the foot of the Eildon hills was the new Cistercian monastery of Melrose. Nearby, the river Tweed meandered through the valley on its way to the sea. On a hillside to the east, the promontory, on which the old monastery of Mailros once stood, was carpeted with lush green grass, and stood out like a haven amid the intimidating darkness of the surrounding forests.

The landscape has changed considerably over the past few centuries, progress made in lifestyle, agriculture, and habitat all having a dramatic visual impact, yet nature's creations have remained virtually unchanged in that time.

The aura of mystery and magic is almost tangible in the vicinity of the Eildon Hills. Elsewhere, the restless spirits of a persecuted race hover on the zephyrs which swirl through the valleys; they are not visible like the crumbling ruins, but their legacy reflects the Border Land's troubled past with a similar poignancy. Within a thirty mile radius of Thomas's home town, visible reminders of the area's history are in abundance; skeletal remains of fortified castles, peel-towers precariously perched atop rocky crags, some in a ruinous state, others sympathetically restored to their former glory, antiquities discarded by the Romans when they retreated from our island, and the fragmented ruins of once majestic, monastic Abbeys.

Visitors from home and abroad absorb the history, while basking in the natural beauty and tranquillity of the area; however, the peaceful ambience of the Border Lands of today belies its troubled past. For many centuries, the plaintive cries of the bereaved resounded round the hills and echoed through the valleys, as loved ones were massacred defending the land of their birth.

From the indigenous tribes of pre-Roman times, through the Wars of Independence, to the more recent raids of the Border Reivers, these lands witnessed scenes of bloodshed and carnage. The heart-rending tales, handed down orally from one generation to the next, formed the basis of the culture and traditions of the *Lowlanders* of today.

During the early years of Thomas's life there was peace in the lowlands of Scotland, albeit fragile and transient. It was a period in history when battles were raging with the Norsemen, the crusades to the Holy Land were ongoing, and the latter years of Thomas's life saw the beginning of the first Scottish War of Independence. It was also a time of a profound belief in the powers of the supernatural. The traditions and superstitions, inbred in the ancient Celtic tribes, were indelibly imprinted in the hearts and minds of their descendants.

Thomas's life is thought to have spanned eight or nine decades, a remarkable achievment in such volatile times, yet for some reason, as yet unexplained, his name is not recorded in any of the monastic chronicles, nor is it mentioned in any history books covering the period. There is no shortage of books telling of the prophecies attributed to Thomas, his adventure with the Fairy Queen is immortalised in music and verse, but the factual evidence of his life is virtually non-existent. His time on earth was shrouded in mystery, his final disappearance from the mortal world is legendary, yet his posthumous fame has stood the test of time.

In the following chapters I have looked at the period in which Thomas lived, the politics, culture, language, and the basis of the superstitions of the time, whilst including the literary works of Thomas.

The first written evidence of his prophecies came to light soon after his disappearance; it has been suggested as early as 1306. From that time, until the present day, the legend of Thomas the Rhymer has continued to influence authors and musicians alike.

The prophecies included herein are not the entire collection of those attributed to Thomas; however, they are sufficient to warrant his status as one of the world's most renowned prophets.

Included in Chapter 5 is my version of the 'Ballad of Thomas the Rhymer,' complete with the prophecies as told by the Fairy Queen, transcribed into modern

English.

Despite his fame being largely relegated to the annals of myth and folklore, Thomas was a person of great importance, both in his own time, and in the following centuries. Even now, he continues to intrigue the people of the twenty -first century; his *Romance* still captures the imagination. Thomas of Ercildune played an important part in Scotland's history; not least for his legacy to its literary heritage.

"Mysterious Rhymer, doomed by fate's decree,
Still to revisit Eildon's lonely tree."
Sir Walter Scott

Was Thomas an ordinary mortal
with an extraordinary gift?
Or was he "not of this world",
as the Gaels believed?

E.B

Acknowledgments

I wish to express my sincere thanks to the following people, each of whom have, in one way or another, contributed to the enhancement of the contents of this book.

First and foremost, To Hugh MacKay, for undertaking the laborious task of verifying the historical data and correcting my errors, I extend my heartfelt thanks and sincere gratitude. Hugh's comprehensive knowledge of literature is astounding; it is thanks to his patience and guidance that the manuscript eventually reached the stage where it was ready for publication.

To Alex Blair, whose infinite wealth of local knowledge never ceases to amaze me, who always went the 'extra mile' when I asked for help, thank you from the bottom of my heart. I will be eternally grateful to you for passing on the detailed information, safely stored in your head for the past eighty years; it is now down in print.

To Jim Richardson-Learmont, for his help with regard to the Lermontov/Learmont connection; Jim allowed me to access a personal letter from a member of the Russian Lermontovs. The two exchanged correspondence after each had researched the link between the two surnames. Jim also followed the book's progress avidly from start to finish; I hope he is impressed with the end result.

To Dr Brian Moffat, whom I contacted when I began my research, for allowing me to include extracts from your meticulously detailed accounts of the history of Soutra Aisle, I extend my sincere thanks. Dr Moffat has dedicated twenty-six years of his life to researching the history of Soutra Aisle.

I would also like to acknowledge the kindness of John and Christine Dever, owners of Ercildoune Homestead in Australia, for allowing me to print the information regarding the Australian / Ercildoune, Scottish / Ercildoune - Learmont connection, contained in their website.

Angela Lemaire is a local author, artist, and printmaker, her passion for the legend of Thomas the Rhymer being on a par with my own. Angela and I have remained in regular contact with regard to Thomas for many years now. I wish to extend my sincere thanks to Angela for allowing me to print the 1652 version of the ballad contained in her book entitled 'The Journey of Thomas the Rhymer.'

To Ronnie Black, for supporting me over the years with regard to my promotion of the legend of Thomas of Ercildoune, also for granting me permission to use the information you had collated on Thomas, especially with regard to the Gaelic connections and traditions, I extend my thanks and gratitude.

To Mathew Withey, curator at 'Abbotsford' home of Sir Walter Scott, for allowing me to access Scott's private collection of literary works, thus enabling me to authenticate, and clarify the Scott/Rhymer connection. It also enabled me to include some of Scott's works associated with Thomas the Rhymer, for this I convey my sincere thanks.

The geophysical survey of the Rhymer's Tower ruin was carried out by G.U.A.R.D. - Glasgow University Archaeological Research Division, on behalf of Historic Scotland. It is thanks to their kind permission that I was able to include, in chapter eleven, an extract of the information contained in the survey.

'Hadrian's Wall Path,' compiled and written by Mark Richards and published by Cicerone, is a comprehensive, illustrated guide to walking the entire route of Hadrian's Wall. It is with the kind permission of the author and publisher that I was able to include, in chapter1, the information on the construction of Hadrian's Wall. Thank you both.

I would also like to thank publishers Birlinn Ltd., not forgetting the editor Ronald Black, for granting me permission to quote the tale, included in chapter 4, from the 'Gaelic Otherworld.'

The information contained in this book has many sources, one of them being a book entitled *'The Romance and Prophecies of Thomas of Erceldoune'* by James A.H.Murray. My grateful thanks are hereby conveyed to Llanerch Press who published a facsimile reprint of this book in 1991 and granted me permission to source much of my information from this book.

To Val Miller, for providing me with information on the 'Rhymer's Stone Project,' of which she is the founder, I extend my thanks and gratitude. Val also very kindly lent me the photograph which appears on the front cover of this book.

With regard to the front cover photograph, I would like to thank Peter Brown who took the photograph of the costume figurines at Smailholm Tower, and kindly gave his permission for the photograph to be used on the front cover; I absolutely love it.

Last, but not least, thank you to my family, who, for the past year have shown the utmost patience and understanding when meals were not ready on time, when I hogged the computer for hours on end, and when I ushered them hastily out the door to allow me to "get on with my book." Hopefully, life at home will now return to normal and visiting family and friends will once again be received hospitably.

INDEX

Chapter I

The Birth of Alba

He signed his name 'Thome Rymor de Ercildune', the signature can be found in a Charter of the mid-thirteenth century, to which he bore witness. Apart from this document, and another signed by his son and heir c1299, there is very little historical evidence to prove his existence. However, in spite of this, the legendary and literary legacy of the life and works of Thome de Ercildune continue to captivate the population of the modern world.

Thomas, as he became known, was born early in the thirteenth century in the part of Scotland known as the *Southern Uplands.* These lands witnessed many battles, both before and after the first boundaries of Scotland were tentatively created. In the years leading up to the thirteenth century, the country known today as the *British Isles* saw many changes. The land was invaded and occupied by Romans, Anglo-Saxons, Normans, and Norse in the first Millennium AD; religion, language, and rulers, also changed frequently during this time. The boundaries of Scotland, similar to those which exist today, were established just a few centuries before Thomas was born.

The earliest evidence of human habitation in Scotland was originally thought to have dated from 8500 BC, however, recent archaeological discoveries prove beyond doubt that Scotland was occupied by *Upper Palaeolithic* humans whose habitation of Scotland goes back to the end of the *Old Stone Age.* This pre-dates earlier evidence of human occupation in Scotland by 3000 years.

The earliest inhabitants of lowland Scotland were nomadic cave-dwelling tribes; their survival was dependant on hunting and gathering. In pre-Roman times, the individual Celtic tribes occupying the southern territory from east to west, and as far north as *The Firth of Forth,* were known collectively as *The Britons.* The Britons' occupied lands which stretched from Cornwall in the south, to the Firth of Forth in the north.

As far back in time as the Iron Age, this land was known as the land of the *Brit,* or *Britons.* The Britons spoke a language identified as *Brythonic,* this being one of two *Celtic* insular languages; the other being *Goidelic.* Despite much debate and controversy, it has been generally accepted by the modern scholars that at this point in time the language of the *Picts* in the north was also a *Brythonic* language, although distinct from the language of the Britons.

Shortly after the birth of Christ the island of Great Britain was invaded by the Romans. The Roman legions forged north, their intention being to conquer, and ultimately *civilise* the barbaric tribes, however, they underestimated the defiance and tenacity of the early settlers and met with fierce resistance. In 78AD, the Roman army, led by Governor *Gnaeus Julius Agricola* reached the habitat of the northern Britons. *Cornelius Tacitus,* historian of the Roman Empire, and son-in-law of Agricola, wrote in his history about the tribes of the area. Tacitus named the tribe which occupied the lands to the north and south of the river Tweed as the *Votadini,* the names of *Selgovae,* and *Novante* were given

4

to the tribes occupying the lands to the west, and the name of *Damnonii* was given to the tribe occupying the lands around the river Clyde. These tribes belonged to a much larger group, known collectively as the *Celts*. The roots of the Celtic people go back to the continent of Europe, long before Britain became an island. The Romans gave Latin names to the indigenous tribes; they also gave the Latin name of *Britannia* to the southern part of the island, while they referred to the land north of the Forth as *Caledonia.*

Hadrian Aelius succeeed *Governor Agricola* and came to Britain in 117AD. Hadrian gave instructions for a great wall to be built from coast to coast cross-country to protect his empire. The wall, although not intact, is still in place today and extends from the Solway Firth at *Bowness* (Maia), to *Wallsend* on the Tyne (Segedunum); a distance of eighty-four miles. In its heyday the wall was between seven and nine (Roman) feet wide and ten to fifteen feet in height. The numerous forts, which were built along the entire length of the wall at approximately five mile intervals, reached a much greater height. The building of the wall began in 122AD; the main part of its construction taking ten years to complete. During this time, fifteen thousand men from three legions, namely XX Valeria, V1 Victrix, and 11 Augusta, were employed in its construction. *Hadrian's Wall,* as it became known, remained intact as an effective frontier for approximately three hundred years.

The Romans created an extensive Empire while occupying this island; it stretched as far north as the *'Land of the Picts,'* or *Pictland* as it was once known. The Romans gave the Latin name of *Picti* to this large northern tribe. *Picti* translates as the *speckled* or *painted* people; the name is thought to derive from their habit of adorning their skin with elaborate body art. The name of 'Picti' was eventually shortened to *Pict*. The Picts were known to be a strong, large limbed, fearless race; a fiery, red-haired race, who for many centuries defended their lands and culture relentlessly.

The southern lands eventually succumbed to the power and influence of the Roman legions; the Picts, however, did not succumb to the might of the Romans, but succeeded in maintaining their independence and culture - for the time being at least. The Picts attempted to expand their kingdom further south on several occasions; however, their quest to gain more territory was in vain, on each occasion they were driven back into the northern territory by the Roman troops.

In 142AD, Emperor *Antoninus Pius* gave orders for a wall to be built at the northern frontier of their Empire in Britannia. This later became known as the *Antonine Wall*. The wall, which took approximately twelve years to build, ran from the mouth of the river *Forth* in the east, to a point near Dumbarton on the *Firth of Clyde* in the west. Being a turf wall, rather than stone built, it was not as impressive as 'Hadrian's Wall', however, with its length of approximately forty miles, and its height similar to that of Hadrian's Wall, its construction is still considered to be an incredible feat of skill and dexterity.

The Romans also created a network of roads throughout their Empire; one being named the "*Via Regia,*" which translates as the "Royal Road", now more commonly known as "*Dere Street*". The road, approximately 180 miles in length, stretched from York in the south, to the boundary of the Roman Empire in the north, namely the Antonine wall; the route of this road is still visible to this day.

During the period when the Romans occupied the lands between the two great walls, the site of the Roman headquarters and supply base was at Newstead; here, Governor Agricola established a fort in 79AD. Newstead is situated near the lower slopes of the north Eildon; the area which would later become associated with the legend of Thomas and the Fairy Queen. The name of this large Roman fort was *Trimontium;* the Latin, *Trium Montium,* translates as 'three mountains.' A granite altar stone now marks the site of this once extensive Roman fort and the sites of many Roman camps and forts can still be found in the locality. Excavations in the late twentieth century uncovered the site of a Roman amphitheatre near Newstead. The site is in a hollow near the banks of the river Tweed and is visible from a viewing platform. An interpretation board provides a brief history of the period of Roman occupation in the area, and also includes information on the influence it continues to have on the area today. The Trimontium site is easily accessible on foot, either by a short walk from Newstead, or from the A68 near the Leaderfoot Viaduct. Newstead is reputed to be the oldest inhabited village in Scotland.

It is known that the Romans used Eildon's north peak as a signal station; however, the north Eildon played a significant part in the lives of the indigenous tribes long before the Romans came to these shores. The Eildon Hills were once volcanic, their unique formation being a natural creation of the evolution of the earth's

7

landmass. The alignment is such, that from certain viewpoints, the hill to the southwest is completely obscured by the other two; a feature which filled the ancient tribes with fear and awe. To these superstitious people, this was a living mountain, sacred, and worthy of great respect.

The middle Eildon, standing at a height of 1,385ft, is the highest and most conical in shape, the hill to the southwest is the lowest. Near the summit of Eildon hill north is a plateau, with three concentric rings or ramparts still visible in the twenty-first century. Excavations here have revealed the remains of an ancient settlement, or hill fort. At the end of the Bronze Age, approximately 700 BC, this settlement is believed to have been inhabited by 3,000 to 4,000 people; it is also thought to be the largest settlement to exist in Scotland in prehistoric times. Not only is the site exposed to the elements, but neither is there any nearby access to water; the wells being a long way down at the foot of the hill. It is impossible for us to comprehend the logic, and reason for a settlement of this size in such a location. Research by archaeologists has provided evidence to suggest that the site was not inhabited on a permanent basis, but only used periodically throughout the year.

Medieval gatherings were commonplace in Celtic culture; these being held for a variety of reasons, some of which included, merry-making, serious discussions, and feasting. The meetings and celebrations usually lasted for a month at a time, and were known to be held at the four cross quarter days.

The *Beltane* festival, which celebrated fertility and the

blossoming of spring, was held at the beginning of May. The *Lughnasadh* (Lammas) festival was held at the beginning of August, this festival celebrated the ripening of crops and fruit – harvest time. The festival of *Samhain,* which was also known as the *"festival of the dead"*, was held at the beginning of November. Samhain was a time when the spirits of the departed were close at hand, the time we now call Hallowe'en; the start of the *Celtic New Year* was also celebrated at this time. The fourth festival, *Imbolc,* celebrated the lactation of the ewes, a time of new-born lambs, and a general rebirth of the earth after the dark, unproductive days of winter. Imbolc was held around the beginning of February, the Christian equivalent is called *Candlemas*. Undoubtedly, the Eildon Hills were used as a meeting place, at least four times annually, to celebrate the Celtic festivals.The Celtic belief being, that at the time of the four cross quarter days, the *otherworld* and the *mortal* world were at their closest, making transition between the two possible; Thomas allegedly met the *Queen of the Otherworld* at the beginning of May, the time of the *Beltane* festival. The twice yearly solstices, which occur around the middle of June and December, and the twice yearly equinoxes, which occur around the middle of March and September in our calendar year, were also times of celebration for the ancient Celts. Until the arrival of the Romans, and the subsequent introduction of Christianity, these pagan fire-festivals were held regularly by the ancient tribes. The Roman occupation of the British Isles lasted approximately four centuries, following their withdrawal many of the lowland inhabitants reverted to their paganistic beliefs and rituals.

In the middle of the fifth century, approximately 430 AD, the *Anglo-Saxons* from the continent of Europe crossed the dividing sea and landed in the southern part of *Britannia*. The Anglo-Saxons were a *Germanic* race, consisting mainly of Angles, Saxons and Jutes; eventually they made their way north to the land of the Britons. It was around this time, that the Picts in the north were about to be confronted with an enemy more persistant and formidable than the Romans.

At their closest point, the shores of Northern Ireland are only twelve miles in distance from the shores of the Western Isles of Scotland. Approximately 498AD, a member of the *Scotti* tribe, by the name of *Fergus Mor mac Eirc*, came across the sea, with a small band of men, from the county of Antrim. Fergus Mor (*Mor - in Gaelic -meaning big, or great),* was reputed to be of royal descent and originated from the Kingdom of *Dal Riata*. Since they came in small numbers and landed on the remote islands of *Islay* and *Jura*, these invading tribesmen- the *Gaidheil*- would not pose much of a threat to the Picts initially; however, through time, they came with increasing numbers and landed on the mainland of Argyll where they established a permanent base.

Eventually the Scotti tribe established a fort on a rocky outcrop at *Dunadd* on the Kintyre peninsula. Fighting between the two tribes of the *Picts* and *Scots* continued for many years. However, the formidable Picts, whom the Romans had failed to conquer, would not exist as a separate race for much longer.

In the sixth century, the Scots established the *Kingdom*

of Dalriada; this kingdom extended from County Antrim in Ireland to the western coast of Argyll and included the Inner Hebridean islands. At the height of Dalriada's power - from c574AD to c606AD - their ruler was *King Aedan mac Gabrain.*

In c563AD, St. Columba, accompanied by twelve monks, came to these western shores from Ireland. They landed on the small island of Iona, which is situated in the stormy waters of the Atlantic Ocean off the west coast of Scotland. However, unlike the Scotti tribe, they came in peace. St. Columba was the founder of a Benedictine monastery on this tiny island, it is said he was sent as a penance for troubles he caused in Ireland.

Iona Abbey continues to be a place of great importance in the Christian world today, and remains a focal point for pilgrims. King Aidan of Dalriada -*Aedan mac Gabrain*- (son of Gabrain), was inaugurated at the monastery on Iona by St. Columba, and for many years it was the site of the inaguations of future kings of Scotland; their bodies also being interred here. The outcome of St. Columba's Christian faith gradually rippling around the land was that Christianity flourished and Paganism was suppressed.

The Lia Fail, or *Cloch na Fail,* was used for the inaugurations of future Kings of the Scots, first at *Dunadd,* then later at *Scone.* The Stone, now known as *The Stone of Destiny,* is thought to have originated in the Holy Land but came to Scotland's shores from Ireland. In Celtic mythology, the *Lia Fail* is also known as the sacred stone of the *Tuatha de Danann,* an ancient civilisation. The Stone of Destiny continues to be regarded as an iconic part of Scottish history.

11

The *Kingdom of Strathclyde* remained in the hands of the *Britons* at this time, their capital being at *Dumbarton,* or in Gaelic, *Dun Breatainn,* which translates as *Fort of the Britons.*

King Ida was the first recorded King of *Bernicia.* In 547AD, under his leadership the Angles encroached on the lands which the Romans had abandoned to the native Britons. The Anglo-Saxons' persecution of the lowland Cymric tribes continued for many years. At a site in the Yarrow Valley, ancient *Standing Stones* mark the graves of the fallen, some of the stones date from the sixth century AD. One such stone, known as '*The Yarrow Stone,*' is a *Christian* monument which marks the grave of two Chieftans; the inscription on the stone is in Latin.

In 593AD, *Aethelfrith* became King of *Bernicia,* he was the grandson of *King Ida* and renowned as the greatest Saxon antagonist of the northern Cymric tribe. According to the words of the *Venerable Bede "he was like a ravening wolf. He devoured his prey in the morning, and divided the spoils in the evening."* By now, the once extensive territory of the *Cymry,* known as *Manaw Gododdin,* was shrinking. Meanwhile in the north, the *Kingdom of Dalriada* was expanding eastwards, *King Aidan* forged south towards the central belt, into the territory held by *King Aethelfrith.* In the year 603AD, King Aidan confronted King Aethelfrith with a sizeable army of mixed tribes, loyal to the Christian cause of St Columba, but was defeated at the *Battle of Degsaston.* The precise location of this battle-site has not been ascertained, however, *Bede* reported it to be in *Liddesdale* on the north side of the *Cheviot Hills.*

In the aftermath of this battle, the map of the four kingdoms showed that the boundaries of the *Kingdom of Strathclyde* had shrunk significantly. Following the *Battle of Chester* - which, according to *Bede* took place in the year 603AD, but according to the *Annales Cambriae* is dated 613AD - *the Britons* from the northern territories were defeated by the army of King Aethelfrith. This resulted in the northern Britons becoming completely segregated from their *Welsh* kinsmen. For a short period after this defeat, the *Britons* were compelled to relinquish their quest to repossess the southern lands, now held by the *Angles*.

Invasions of the old *Kingdom of the Britons* continued relentlessly. The small group, which remained in their diminished kingdom, retreated to the safety of the higher ground above the rivers Tweed, Ettrick, Teviot, and Yarrow.

This was a critical time for the Cymric race, as the Picts and Scots from the land north of the Firth of Forth (*the 'Mare Frenessicum'*), the Gaels from the west, and the Angles from the south, converged on the land once occupied by the Romans.

The laments and ballads, written down by the survivors of the Cymric tribe, epitomise the desolation of a defiant race, and serve to provide us with a glimpse of their futile struggle to defend their precious land.

The *Cymri* continued to retain their independence, and their diminished kingdom, for nearly two hundred years after this time. According to *Professor John Veitch,* it was during this period that they created *The Catrail,* a defensive frontier, to protect the last remnants of their kingdom. He also concluded this to be the limit of their kingdom for two hundred years, since the map of the *Monastic Church* from the eighth century showed the boundary to the east had not changed for this length of time.

It is known that the Britons used *vallums,* or *turf walls* as a means of protection against repeated invasions. The use of *palisades* (stakes), on a wide V-shaped ditch with precipitous sides, was known to be an effective means of defence.

Along the entire length of the Catrail - approximately forty-eight miles - are the remains of numerous forts, camps, and dwellings. These camps and forts are of *British,* rather than *Roman,* origin. The route of the Catrail begins at *Peel Fell,* one of the peaks in the *Cheviot* range of hills on the border between Scotland and England, and terminates at a spot on the *Gala Water* near *Torwoodlee,* in the Scottish Borders.

According to Professor Veitch who, during the nineteenth century, had walked its entire length many times, it ran at times like a circuit, zig-zagging and sometimes doubling back. He noted that the line was more noticeable in some places than others. Where it crossed a stream, it followed a direct route northwest rather than deviating and taking an easier route. Where it crossed high ground, it ran at mid-brae level rather than taking an easier route lower down.

The remains of an imposing British fort on its route were once clearly visible at the crossing of the *Allan* water, roughly two miles above its junction with the river *Teviot.* Professor Veitch also noted that in the late nineteenth century, the line of the *Catrail* was clearly visible at *The Rink,* in a wood at *Holybush,* and again at

Mossilee; these locations being within a few miles of its culmination at *Torwoodlee* near Galashiels. The site of an old hillfort can still be seen at *The Rink,* the old earthworks of the Catrail are also visible here.

This deep ditch with precipitous sides, and running in a northwesterly direction for a distance of nearly fifty miles, has caused controversy among researchers. Its purpose, when it was created, and by whom, has been the subject of much debate; with recent scholars suggesting an iron-age date. However, *Professor Veitch,* writing in the nineteenth century, concluded that the most obvious purpose was one of defence. The Cumbric tribes were in dire need of a defensive frontier to defend this last small remnant of their once vast kingdom. Suggestions of it being a Roman road, or indeed any road, were refuted by Veitch, since the *Catrail* bears no resemblance to the known roads of either the Romans or the later inhabitants of these lands; these being straight flattened tracks, while the *Catrail* is a deep trench, with no other apparent logical explanation for its unorthodox route.

Despite views to the contrary, I like to think of Professor Veitch's theory as being credible and have a tendency to believe his reasoning for its purpose. In his book entitled, "History and Poetry of the Scottish Border" 1893, he explains his reasoning behind the name *Catrail;* the prefix *Cat* is both *Welsh* and *Saxon.* The Cornish/Armorican *Cad* defines as *battle,* and the affix *treyle,* means to *turn.* The prefix *cad* is still used in many placenames in the area today, *Cadrona,* and *Cademuir* (Cadmore), both being in Peebleshire. *Cadmore,* meaning *great battle,* was reputedly the site of one of the battles of *King Arthur,* and is situated between the *Lyne water* and the river *Tweed* in Peeblesshire.

Gildas lived in the period from c516AD to around 570AD; he was reputed to be the son of a *Prince of Strathclyde.* Gildas wrote his history c560AD named, *"The Historia and Epistola of Gildas."* According to Gildas, the historical King Arthur battled on the lands of *Strathclyde,* as well as fighting the *Saxons of Wessex.* Place names with connections to *Arthur* can be found in the lowlands of Scotland today, and as far north as the old *Kingdom of Strathclyde.* An article, which was included in the *'Gentleman's Magazine'* in 1842, suggested that all twelve of the battles of King Arthur were fought in *the Kingdom of the Cymric tribes.* In the words of Professor Veitch, *"Mr W. Skene, a sagacious and educated person, elaborated on this article."* The theory being, that the first battle, according to *Nennius,* was fought *"in ostium fluminis quad dicitur Glein."* This is said to be on the border between Ayrshire and Lanarkshire. The sites of the subsequent eleven battles have names which suggest that they were fought between the *River Tweed,* the southernmost line of the *Cymric,* and *Llanerch* (Lanark) in the west. The final battle was the Battle of Badon Hill in 516AD, (the *Obsessio Badonici Montis),* or *Mons Badonis.* The *Mons Badonis* was originally thought to be near *Bath* in England. However, *Dr Guest* states, that according to the *Brutes,* after the battle of *Bouden Hill* (Badon Hill) in 516AD, King Arthur gave the district he recovered from the *Saxons* to three brothers, namely *Urien, Llew* and *Arawn. Urien* was given *Mureif,* a district beyond the *Antonine Wall, Llew* was given *Lodoneis* or Lothian, and

Arawn was given *Yscotlant,* or *Prydyn,* the northernmost part of the reclaimed land, as far north as *Stirling.* King Arthur was the Christian hero, the *Dux Bellorum* of the *Cymric* tribe who were being driven out of their homeland. The two opposing leaders, *Arthur* and M*odred* were both slain at the final battle of *Camlon,* or Camelon in 537AD.

The W*elsh/*C*umbric* poems of the era link King Arthur with the *Cymric Kingdom of Strathclyde,* the placenames having connections with the area. The *Latin* historians corroborate this connection, along with the idea of King Arthur as *Guledig, King Arthur the Blessed,* guarding the southern defence against the combined forces of the *Picts* and *Anglo-saxons.* A *Cromlech,* consisting of two tall slender upright stones with a flat stone laid on top, locally known as *'Arthur's Table,'* stood on a haugh near the river Tweed, just two miles from *Merlin's* grave. Above the haugh is a conical hill-top called the *Height of the Lour,* a formidable pre-historic fort was once situated on its summit. However, despite all the evidence to substantiate the theory that most of the twelve battles of King Arthur took place in the lowlands and central regions of Scotland in the sixth century, the subject remains controversial.

In the mid seventh century, St Aidan established a monastery on the banks of the river Tweed, just a few miles downstream from the site of the old Roman fort of Trimontium. St. Aidan was accompanied by twelve Saxon monks from the monastery at Lindisfarne; Lindisfarne, or *Holy Island,* is situated off the east coast of Northumbia. A three mile long causeway was built in 1954 to link the Island to the mainland. St. Aidan,

17

originally from Ireland, was the first Bishop of the monastery on Lindisfarne. St. Aidan travelled many miles inland from Lindisfarne to establish the new monastery on the banks of the river Tweed. The area at this time was still under Anglo-Saxon rule; the kingdoms of Diera and Bernicia having united to form the new *Kingdom of Northumbria.* Eata was one of the young monks trained by St Aidan; he later became the first Abbot of this new monastery on the banks of the River Tweed.

St. Columba, like all the monks who came from Ireland, spoke the Gaelic language. The name given to this monastic location was *Mailros,* or, as it was originally known in Gaelic, *Am Maol Ros.* The definition of *Maol* in Irish Gaelic is *bald,* but in Scottish Gaelic it defines as *promontory. Ros* is Gaelic for *rose;* the rose is the symbol of the Virgin Mary to whom all Cistercian monasteries are dedicated. *Promontory* is defined as *a piece of high ground jutting into the sea.* The site on which the monks chose to build the monastery is a mound of high ground, encompassed on three sides by a horseshoe bend in the river Tweed - *a promontory.* In the words of the late Reverend W.S. Crockett; *"The promontory of Old Melrose sat like an oasis amidst the surrounding forest, its green grass and golden broom a welcoming sight."*

The name of 'Old Melrose' still exists today, while there are few traces left of the old monastery, the mound where it stood is still clearly visible. The *golden broom* continues to bloom on the hillside, and still, in the hustle and bustle of the twenty-first century, the surrounding area, called '*Scott's View*' in memory of Sir Walter Scott, is a haven of peace and tranquillity. The

18

three peaks of the *Eildon Hills* can be seen simultaneously from this spectacular viewpoint, forming the centrepiece of this panoramic vista which overlooks the site of Old Melrose, enthralling locals and visitors alike.

In the year 651AD, while tending his sheep near the Leader River, a young shepherd boy had a vision of a soul being carried heavenwards by Angels. When told of St. Aidan's death, which occured on the night of his vision, the young boy took this to be a calling to the monastic life. The young shepherd boy made his way to the monastery at Mailros, vowing to dedicate the remainder of his life to Christianity. The Prior of the abbey, St. Boisil, was at the entrance as the boy arrived. Upon seeing Cuthbert, it is said that he exclaimed, *"Behold a Servant of the Lord"*. The young shepherd boy did indeed devote the remainder of his life to Christianity, later becoming known as Saint Cuthbert.

St. Boisil, like many people of the time, had the gift of second sight, correctly predicting his own death from a plague which would ravage the Abbey, while predicting that Cuthbert would recover after being struck down by the same plague. Saint Cuthbert went on to become Prior of Mailros after the death of St Boisil. The town of nearby *St.Boswells* takes its name from St. Boisil of Mailros, likewise, the name of St. Cuthbert lives on in the area today. A local walking trail, which starts at Melrose and finishes at Lindisfarne, is known as *St. Cuthbert's Way*. St. Cuthbert went on to become Prior of Lindisfarne in 664AD, and died there in 687AD. It is written that when St. Cuthbert's coffin was opened, eleven years after his death, there was no sign of decomposition on his body; St. Cuthbert later became known as Northumbria's most revered Saint.

> *"After many wanderings past,*
> *He chose his lordly seat at last,*
> *Where his Cathedral, huge and vast,*
> *Looks down upon the Wear;*
> *There, deep in Durham's gothic shade,*
> *His relics are in secret laid."*

Another story associated with the monastery of Mailros is the tale of a man called *Drythelm*. In the year 696AD, during a serious illness, *Drythelm* was thought to have died. However, he awoke from a deep coma and told his friend Hemgils of a dream, or vision, which had occurred whilst in his comatose state. As related by St Bede in his *Ecclesiastical History, Drythelm* is taken on a journey. He is transported to the realm of the spirits, where he is subjected to heat, cold, flames, and snow. First he is taken to a place where fiends are chanting, wailing, and mocking, the noise is deafening. Suddenly, he is left alone in the darkness; this is the place known as *purgatory*. He then becomes aware of a light in the darkness, shining bright like a star. He is guided by forces unknown towards the light, but can see only a high wall with no visible access to the other side. On reaching the wall, he is transported to the top, whereupon he can see a field where flowers are growing, the sweet fragrance of which fills his nostrils; this being in sharp contrast to the acrid stench from the fires which he had previously encountered. In the field the light is intense, he can see people dressed in white clothing, rejoicing; this is the entrance to heaven, where the souls of the righteous congregate to await permission to enter. Drythelm wishes he could stay in this place forever. He is told that he can return and be reunited with the blessed souls, on the condition that he lives the remainder of his time on earth in righteousness and simplicity. Drythelm then awakes to find himself back with his kin, firmly believing that he has spent the night in the abode of the deceased. Following his vision, Drythelm, like Cuthbert joined the monks at the monastery of *Mailros*. For the remainder of his time on earth he would stand daily in the waters of the river *Tweed*, fully clothed. Each day he could be seen standing in the river, praying, and singing psalms.

He continued this ritual in winter when the river was almost completely frozen over. He did not change out of his wet clothing, but let them dry on his body. When asked; *"do you not feel the cold,"* he replied, *"I have seen greater cold."*

Meanwhile, further north in Caledonia, the Picts and the Scots were becoming integrated, marriage between the two warring tribes now being a common occurence. At this time, the tribes of the Picts, Scots, and the Britons were under the control of the King of Northumbria, until 685AD, when *Eagfrid* was killed in the *Battle of Dunnachton*. The Pictish *King Bridei of Fortriu* led the northern tribes in this battle; the defeat of the army of King Eagfrid secured lasting independence from Northumbria for the Picts. Before his last fateful battle, *Eagfrid* granted the town of Carlisle, including the area within a fifteen miles radius, to his friend and counsellor, *Cuthbert of Lindisfarne.*

In the year 759AD, Aethelwold, also known as Moll, was leader of the Northumbrian forces. The following year, the outcome of a fierce battle in the vicinity of the Eildon Hills saw a victory for the Saxons under his leadership; this year also saw the death of the Pictish *King Unnust.*

At the latter end of the eighth Century, the Danes and Norwegians, otherwise known as the Vikings, first approached the shores of Scotland in their longboats. The first Viking landing on Scottish shores was known as *"The siege of Strathclyde."* The north, west, and east coastlines of the British Isles were subsequently under continuous invasions by the Vikings for the following five centuries.

In 793AD, the east coast of England was once again under seige by the Vikings, the priory at Lindisfarne was seized, and many monks were killed. The Vikings rampaged and pillaged inland leaving scenes of devastation in their wake; the Viking invasions also continued in the north. In 839AD, a battle between the northern tribes and the Vikings saw many Pictish royals being killed; this ultimately resulted in the language and culture of the Picts being lost forever.

In this time of confusion *Alpin of Kintyre* stepped into the breach. Alpin was the son of *King Eochaid 1V Rinnamail,* King of the Scots, and *Unuisticc,* Princess of the Picts. Alpin's reign was shortlived however; he was killed less than two years later, in 841AD, during a battle with the Picts.

Following the death of his father, *Kenneth MacAlpin (Coinneach mac Ailpein),* became the first *King of the*

Picts and Scots. He united the two kingdoms of *Dalriada* and *Pictland,* which ultimately led to the formation of the *Kingdom of Alba;* Scottish Gaelic – *Rioghachd na h-Alba.*

Alba *(pronounced Alaba),* being the word the Gaels used, and do to this day, for Scotland. During his reign, Kenneth MacAlpin introduced the first of the *Scottish Laws.* He claimed new lands eastwards, forging south to the central belt, through Strathclyde, and as far south as the river Tweed. He invaded the territory which was previously held by the Anglo-Saxons. The raids by the army of Kenneth MacAlpin resulted in the defeat of the Anglo-Saxons in this area; the monastery at Mailros was destroyed during these raids. The monastery was rebuilt, but never regained the status it held when first established by St Aidan. It did however, continue to be a place of sanctity and pilgrimage for many years; the vision of the ascetic Drythelm playing an important part in its popularity. A chapel, dedicated to St. Cuthbert, remained on the site for many centuries. The body of St. Cuthbert was carried to Mailros by the monks from Lindisfarne during the Viking raids on the east coast; this being nearly two centuries after his death. His body was then moved to different locations for seven years, before finding its final resting place at Durham Cathedral.

King Edgar of England lived from c943AD until c975AD, his adviser was known by the name of Dunstan. Following the advice of Dunstan, King Edgar gave the northern part of Northumbria, from *Tweed* to *Forth* (Merse and Lothians), to *Kenneth III,* King of the Scots.It was around this time that the boundaries of a new nation were established, and have remained virtually unchanged to this day; this was the birth of Alba.

....

Chapter 2

A Land of Change

In 1018, the Scottish King Malcolm II (*Maol Chaluim mac Choinnich*) invaded Northumbria, where a battle was fought on the south side of the river Tweed at *Carham.* This resulted in the Northumbrian army being defeated; following which, the entire district north of the River Tweed became part of Scotland. The government hub for a relatively united Scotland at this time was centred in *Mynyd Agned;* the *Castrum Puellorum,* now known as *Edinburgh,* or in Gaelic, *Dun Eideann.* The theory that Edinburgh was named after the Northumbrian King Edwin has been refuted by recent scholars. The name of *Din Eidyn* was first recorded during the period of the Kingdom of Gododdin c600AD; the word *Din* being Celtic for hillfort, the Gaelic *Dun* being its equivalent. On the Scottish throne at this time was King Malcolm III, who, backed by English allies from Northumbria, was responsible for the death of MacBeth at the battle of *Lumphanan* in Aberdeenshire in 1057. Scotland prospered under the rule of Macbeth for seventeen years, before he was cruelly murdered by the eldest son of his predecessor, King Duncan.

King Malcolm III founded the *House of Canmore,* a dynasty of Kings and Queens who ruled Scotland for nearly one hundred and fifty years. The Gaelic for Canmore is *Ceann Mor;* Ceann, translates as head or chief, and Mor, translates as big or great. Malcolm's first wife *Ingebjorg* was of Norwegian descent, his second wife *Margaret* was the sister of *Edgar,* heir to the throne of

England; however, Edgar was denied the chance of becoming King due to the Norman invasion of England.

At the *'Battle of Stamford Bridge'* in 1066, the army of King Harold of England repelled an invasion of northern England by the Vikings. Three weeks later, a decisive battle, which resulted in the *Norman Conquest* of England, took place on October 14th 1066, at *Senlac Hill,* approximately six miles from the town of Hastings. William I, Duke of Normandy (also known as William the Conqueror), invaded England with an army consisting of Normans, Bretons, Flemings and French. King Harold was killed during this battle, and his army defeated. This resulted in William, Duke of Normandy becoming King William I of England. The defeat saw a dramatic change for the people of England, not least in the culture and language. A Norman/French influence crept into the language, and was, for almost four centuries to follow, the language spoken in the courts and by the nobility.

At this time, King Malcolm III was King of *Alba,* until his death in 1093. Three of Malcolm's six sons from his marriage to Margaret went on to become kings of Scotland, namely Edgar, Alexander1, and David1. Margaret's influence brought many new customs to Scotland; she also introduced English words to the mainly *Gaelic* speaking people. Queen Margaret later became known as *Saint Margaret of Scotland* for her patronage of the Scottish church. Margaret died at Edinburgh Castle, shortly after the death of her husband. Their son Edgar (*Eagar mac Mhaol Chaluim*), who was in his teens when his Father died, ruled Scotland until his death in1107. His younger brother, and heir to the throne, Alexander (*Alasdair mac Mhaol Chaluim*- son of Malcolm), became King Alexander 1st of Scotland. His domain however, was confined to the central part of Scotland, since the northern areas were under Norse rule at this time. After his death in 1124, King Alexander's younger brother, David1 (*Daibhidh mac Mhaol Chaluim*), was successor to the throne. In *The Treaty of Durham,* 1139, David was recognised as king of an independent Scotland by King Stephen of England. King David1 later commissioned a church to be built within the grounds of Edinburgh Castle in memory of his Mother. It is known today as *Saint Margaret's Chapel (Caibeal Naomh Mhairead.)*

King David I was instrumental in promoting Christianity throughout Scotland. In 1136, French Cistercian monks from Rievaulx Abbey in Yorkshire were invited by King David 1 to establish a monastery in lowland Scotland. The site they chose for this monastery was a place called *'Little Fordel;'* which was just three miles upstream from the site of the first Celtic monastery at Mailros. This new monastery, once considered the finest and richest of its kind, was situated in a valley of the river Tweed, at the foot of the three peaks of *Trium Montium.* The monks named this monastery *Melrose;* there are various theories for the choice of the name. It could simply be an Anglian version of the old Celtic name of *Mailros,* however, Mell is also an old Scots word for *amalgamate* or *blend,* which the masons would use while building the abbey. Mell is also the Scots word for a hammer; the rose being the symbol of the Virgin Mary. The site of the old Celtic monastery at Mailros, first established by St. Aidan in the mid seventh century, later became known as *'Old Melrose'*.

St. Waltheof, stepson of David I, and uncle of King Malcolm 1V, was the second Abbot at the new abbey of Melrose. He was considered to be one of the most psychic of the monks at Melrose Abbey; a variety of miraculous events being attributed to him during his lifetime. St. Waltheof died on August 3rd 1159 and when his coffin was opened, eleven years after his death, there was no sign of decomposition on his body. In 1206, his tomb was reopened and his body was found to be still in a pristine condition. However, when the tomb was reopened in 1240, his bones had been reduced to ash.

The reign of King David 1 brought about a change for the better in the culture and lifestyle of the people of Scotland. He encouraged and enabled the poorer classes to become educated, created burghs, and introduced the feudal system. The feudal system allowed the more opulent in society to possess land and property which otherwise they could not afford. The land effectively belonged to the king, or the wealthy nobles, but for a payment of land rent, or feu duty as it was known, the Lairds and Barons could construct their impressive stone - built tower houses, with a few acres of land included in the lease.

The burgh of *Berwick* was the first of the great Scottish burghs. Berwick was captured by the English, and continued to change hands between Scotland and England for many years.

By 1130, King David1 had established burghs at Stirling, Perth, Scone, Haddington, Aberdeen, Dunfermline, and Edinburgh. Roxburgh was another of the four major Scottish burghs; the castle here being an

28

important fortified Scottish stronghold in earlier times. In 1193, Margaret, daughter of King William 1 of Scotland, was born at Roxburgh Castle, as was King Alexander III.

The Burghs, or walled towns, had privileges of trade and commerce, they also had *common lands* and a shared bond with the other *burgh towns* in the loyalty to their kingdom, and the supervision of its defence.

During his reign, King David oversaw the expansion of religious houses, and was responsible for the establishment of fifteen new churches throughout Scotland. Included in those are the border abbeys of Melrose, Kelso, and Jedburgh. Dryburgh abbey was founded in 1150, by *Hugh de Moreville,* Constable to King David I. Hugh de Moreville was also known as *Lord of Lauderdale. Modan,* an Irish Culdee Saint, established a sanctuary at the spot known as *Dryburgh* c522AD; prior to this, the ancient druid priests performed their pagan rites here. Dryburgh's original name of *Darach Bruach* is Gaelic for the *bank,* or *grove of oaks.*

King David I ruled a relatively peaceful Scotland until his death in Carlisle in 1153. His successor, until his death at Jedburgh Castle in 1165, was King Malcolm1V.

It was around this time that the remaining *Britons of Strathclyde* were last referred to as a separate race. *The Britons,* while retaining their language and culture, had merged peacefully into the melting pot of mixed races in the new *Lowland* Scotland. Although the last generations of *Cumbric,* or *Welsh* as they were previously known, were absorbed into the general population of the southern lands of Scotland, an empathy with the *Welsh* culture is retained. Throughout the poetic literature of the border lands, there is a continuation of their thoughts and spirits, reminders of their struggle to survive as a race, remaining forever in the hills and valleys of the area.

A mix of languages was spoken in southern Scotland at this time. Latin was spoken by the scholars, Welsh (Cumbric), French, Quant Inglis, and Gaelic, were also spoken.

Modern *Scottish Gaelic* is very similar to *Irish Gaelic;* it also resembles *Manx Gaelic.* The language of the Welsh, Cornish, and Bretons (from Brittany in France), have similarities to the Gaelic, these lands all being inhabited by the *Celts.*

Today, *Scottish Gaelic* is more commonly associated with the highlands and islands, yet in earlier times it was also spoken in the lowlands, as well as in the southwest of Scotland. Many placenames of Gaelic origin remain today in lowland Scotland, proof of a Gaelic speaking community in the area many centuries ago. *Auchen* is Gaelic for field, the village of Auchencrow in the Lammermoor hills of Berwickshire in the Merse being one example of a placename with Gaelic origins, *Annaid,* or *Annat,* is Gaelic for church, Annat's Hope in Peeblesshire in the Scottish Borders being another.

A story told in *"Poems from Maitland MS",* by Mr Pinkerton, *Complaynt of Scotland;* the editor, *"Being told of a tradition of a hunter who raised a mighty boar, and pursued him from his lair in the Yarrow Valley up to St Mary's Loch, where he was slain at a place called Muichra, he was curious to examine the source of the name, it means the place of the boar, in Gaelic";* the modern Scottish Gaelic word for a pig is *Muc. Gaelic* is a

Celtic language, it was brought to Scotland by the *Gaidheil* (settlers from Ireland), but its earliest roots began in Central Europe.

King William (*Uilliam mac Eanrig*), who was the brother of King Malcolm 1V, and grandson of King David1, was crowned at Scone in 1165. He was a powerful ruler, his reign of fifty years being largely spent in conflict with English Kings. King William bought back lands from King Richard; these lands had previously been taken from Scotland by King Henry II. King Richard of England was in desperate need of funding for his crusade to the Holy Land. During his reign, King William also increased the number of burghs, the concept of which was established by King David1. King William was nicknamed *'The Lion'* after his death, it is uncertain if this was attributed to his fearlessness in battle, or for the fact that he adopted the ensign of the rampant red lion on a yellow background; this he was allowed to do under the terms of the *Laws of Heraldry.* The ensign was originally used as the *Royal Coat of Arms,* and as such could only be used by Royalty. It was used as the official ensign of the *Kingdom of Scotland* until the *Union of the Crowns* in 1603. It was later incorporated into the *Great Seal of Scotland,* today it is part of the *Royal Standard of the United Kingdom.* At one time, the use of the flag other than by reigning monarchs would result in severe punishment; however, it is now considered to be the second national flag of Scotland and is used to represent the country at many social events.

King William was also founder of the Abbey at Arbroath, where, in 1320, during the period of *Robert the Bruce;* the *Declaration of Arbroath* was signed by the Scottish nobles. After having three daughters, all of whom married English nobles, his wife eventually bore him a son; he would later be crowned King Alexander II.

William was only twenty two years old when he was crowned at *Scone* on the *Stone of Destiny*. His reign of fifty years was remarkable and unprecedented in such volatile times. He died in 1214, and is buried in the grounds of the abbey he founded at Arbroath. Alexander II was only sixteen years old when, following his Father's death, he became heir to the throne of Scotland.

....

Chapter 3

13th Century Lowland Scotland

Following the death of his father, a very young and naïve King Alexander II undertook the burden of maintaining a relatively stable Scottish kingdom. Lowland Scotland was peaceful at this time, at least in comparison to centuries past. The children of the nobility were being educated at the local Abbey's cloister schools. Daily life for the poorer families revolved around farming; with crops, livestock, and goods being traded at the local markets. The nearby ports, such as Berwick and Edinburgh, provided means of international commerce. After many centuries of conflict - the lands of their forefathers being subjected to protracted invasions - the last remnants of the Cumbric tribes lived peacefully alongside the others of mixed race. The people of these lands, whose ancestors fought each other for many centuries, had a new identity. The population was united, not by individual tribal names, but by nationality. The *Gaels,* with their mix of Irish blood, from the north and west, the *Norman/Saxons,* a mix of French and Anglian, from the south and east, and any stray *Norse* settler, were collectively classed as *Scots.*
Since the nomadic tribal groups of Europe had retained their individual identities for many centuries, nationality was a fairly new concept in the thirteenth century. However, the deep-rooted *Celtic* traditions, inherited from their ancestors, were steadfastly adhered to by the remaining Celts.
A small hamlet, known as *Ercildune,* nestled in a valley

beside the Leader water in the southernmost part of Scotland, the area known as *The Merse*. Ercildune was situated on the border between the *Britons* former *Kingdom of Strathclyde*, and the old *Anglo-Saxon Kingdom of Bernicia*. Around the year 1220, a son was born to a family of nobility in the little hamlet of Ercildune, he would later become known worldwide as *Thomas the Rhymer*.

The family lived in a substantial stone built tower house, which was situated near the east bank of the Leader water. Very little is known about the ancestry of Thomas, but it is generally believed that the family owned the tower house prior to his birth. It is possible, but not proven, that the title of Laird Learmont was inherited from his Father since the ownership of tower houses and land was restricted to the nobility at that time.

Ercildune was a place of great importance in medieval times, not least during the reign of King David 1. In the words of W.S. Crockett in his book entitled 'The Scott Country,' first published in 1902, "David, the Sair Sanct, subscribed in June, 1136, *apud Ercheldon,* the Foundation Charter of Melrose Abbey, and his son Prince Henry, in 1143, subscribed here, the Confirmatory Charter of the same Abbey."

The Anglo-Norman names of the men who witnessed this charter are as follows: *Moreville, Somerville, De Arden,* and *Lindsay.* However, other witnesses are described as *"men from that land."* The lands are *Melrose, Eldun* (Eildon) *Derne-wic* (Darnick) *Gattunshalech* (Gattonshaugh) *Gattunesside* (Gattonside) *Seleschirche* (Selkirk) and *Trauequair*

34

(Traquair). Most, but not all, of these *'local'* witnesess have Saxon names: *Gospatrick, Earl of Dunbar; Ulfchill, son of Eilaf; Eilaf, son of Huctred; Maccus, son of Undwain; Huctred, son of Sioth; Huctred, son of Gospatrick; Orm, son of Eilaf; Eilaf, son of Gospatrick; Eduf, son of Norman; Osolf, son of Edive; Osolf, son of Elfston; Robert Brus Meschin; Radulf, son of Turstain; and Roger, nephew of the Bishop.*

It is possible that on the two occasions, when the Melrose Abbey foundation charter was signed in Ercildune in 1136 by King David I, and later confirmed by his son Prince Henry in 1143, the Royals would stay at the residence of the Earl of Dunbar in Ercildune.

The name of *Thomas Rymour* (*Old Gaelic –Tomas* Reumhair), would become linked to *Ercildune* and the area surrounding the peaks of *Trimontium* for many centuries. Thomas is regarded by many as an enigma; this could be due to the fact that the details of his life are scant, and mysterious. While this is true, sufficient written evidence of his life and work survive to ensure continued interest and curiosity.

The true surname of Thomas has been the subject of debate for many years. Throughout history, he has been known by many names; *Tomas de Ercildune, Thomas the Rhymer, True Thomas, Sir Thomas,* and *Laird Learmonth,* with variants in the spelling. Surnames were not in common use at this time, which is apparent from the signatures in the charter of the *Foundation of Melrose Abbey,* the offspring were simply known as, *'son of,'* the christian name of the father. In *Gaelic,* placing *mac* before the father's Christian name signified the son of that person. However, nearly a century later, in the

35

Bemersyde Charter, c1260, which bears the signature of *Thome Rymor de Ercildune,* most of the signatures represent their place of abode.

The following evidence would appear to substantiate the theory of the Learmont surname being linked to Thomas. In 1527, *Hector Boece,* a Scottish Philosopher living from 1465 until 1536, vouched for Thomas's surname being Learmont. *Nisbet the Herald,* in work dated 1702, refers to Thomas as; *"Sir Thomas Learmont of Earlston in the Merse."* Alexander Nisbet was born in1657 and lived in Berwickshire from that time until 1725. He was the author of "A System of Heraldry;" his ancestors can be traced back to the twelfth century and were descendants of *Gospatric,* Earl of Northumbria. A memorial to Alexander Nisbet can be found in Greyfriars Kirk in Edinburgh.

The following quote is taken from the introduction to the edition of 'Sir Tristrem' by Sir Walter Scott;

"An interesting discovery in old papers lodged in the Clerk of Session regarding genealogical memoirs links the name of Learmont to Thomas of Ercildoune.

The papers were once the propery of the Learmonts of Balcomie in Fife. It is written in the hand of a seventeenth century scribe. If the information is accurate, with regard to the contract of marriage, it provides valuable information on the name and lineage of Thomas of Ercildoune. The documents provide the genealogy of the Honourable and Ancient name of Leirmont. It states that the name came from France. "The Chief of the the name was the Laird of Ersilmont in the Mers, whose predescessor, Thomas Leirmont lived in the reign of Alexander III. On(e) of whose sons married Janet de

Dairsie. The house of Dairsie bears a rose in the base as a difference. The house of Dairsie is now extinct, only Leirmont of Balcomie in Fife is chief now; whose predescessor was master of howshold to King James 1V. Dairsie was left to the second brother, so upon this account, Balcomie is holden of the King, and Dairsie of the Archbishop of St. Andrews, so the house of Balcomie bears the simple coat of arms without the rose in the base, as a destinction from Dairsie."

It has been suggested that the Learmont name may have come from the female side, perhaps through the marriage to an heiress of the Learmont family.

Following his bequest to the monks of Soltra, which included the family home and its lands of nearly ten acres, the son and heir of *Thomas Rymor de Ercildune,* himself *Thomas de Ercildune,* would lose the right to be called *de Ercildune.* It has been suggested that Thomas, the son, may have adopted the Learmont surname at this time. It has been suggested by previous writers that the surname of Thomas was Rymor or Rimour. If that was the case, then the son and heir would have taken the name of Rimour or Rymor also. For many centuries, the *Learmont* families worldwide, while researching their family tree, have produced evidence to substantiate their lineage from *Thomas Learmont* of Ercildoune. Whereas, the same cannot be said for the families of *Rimour,* or *Rimeur,* although there is documented evidence of families bearing the name having stayed in the area, and the deceased being interred in the old cemetery in Earlston. According to an account by Mrs C. Wood, a native of Earlston; "a plan of the churchyard from 1842 showed sixteen graves with the name Learmont, eleven of which lay in a row, the oldest being dated 1564." A *'right of sepulture'* was still claimed in Earlston churchyard in the nineteenth century by the *Learmont* family. This would appear to substantiate the general opinion that Learmont was the family name; alternatively, it was adopted by his immediate descendants shortly after the death of 'The Rhymer'. A deed in the title of the *'Learmonts of Wedderburn'* indicates that this branch of the family was descended from Thomas of Ercildune. As catalogued by the Historical MSS. Commission;

"Instrument of Sasine, dated 14th March 1583, in favour of Thomas Learmonth, son and heir apparent of John Learmonth of Erslington, in those two acres of Erslington which formerly belonged to the deceased Thomas Rymour, lying in the town and territory of Erslington, Earldom of March, and Sheriffdom of Berwick, and which the said John had resigned, proceeding upon a precept granted by Sir Alexander Henryson, Master of the Hospital of Trinity College Church, Edinburgh, dated 7th April 1576."

The name of *Learmont* is thought to have originated in England in the twelfth century, first being spelt *Leuremue*, and then later having derivations in the spelling such as Learmonth, Learmouth and Leirmouth. The name *Leuremue* is of French origin, the French influence being prominent in England following the Norman Conquest.

The name of Rymor, or *'The Rhymer,'* as it later became, would undoubtedly be linked to Thomas's profession as a bard, the word coming into the English language from medieval Scottish Gaelic. The word 'Bard' describes a professional poet or musician; *bard* in modern Gaelic is defined as *poet.* The bards were highly revered in medieval times and were employed by reigning monarchs and the nobility. Thomas was also known by the name of *'True Thomas;'* the Fairy Queen supposedly gave Thomas the gift of *"a tongue which would never lie"* as a token of their encounter.

One writer from the seventeenth century claimed that the home of Thomas the Rhymer is near Crail in Fife. This is most definitely not the case, as the *Bemersyde Charter,* the *Soltra Charter,* and written accounts by the early scribes prove beyond any reasonable doubt that his birthplace and home was Ercildune in the Merse.

In the early thirteenth century the hamlet of Ercildune would consist of a few scattered huts made out of wattling, with heather, or straw used to thatch the roofs. The canes and twigs, used to make the wattling, would be plentiful in the dark, dense forests which surrounded the settlement. The daub, used to hold fast the lattice-work of twigs, was made from damp clay, or animal dung. This process was similar to the lath and plaster of later years. These were eco-friendly constructions, built using locally sourced materials.

Just a short pony-ride away, to the east of the residence of Thomas, was a castle owned by the Earl of Dunbar. From an early age, until the year 1286, Thomas was known to be a regular visitor to this residence of the Earls of Dunbar. To reach the Earl's castle, Thomas would negotiate the old track which skirted the peat-bog, and ran alongside the *Trufford Burn,* a tributary of the Leader. The Earl of Dunbar's main residence was his ancestral seat of *Dunbar Castle,* a fortified stronghold with a vantage point overlooking the North Sea, some thirty miles away. The present Earl, similar to his ancestors and successors, regarded the castle in Ercildune as his "*country retreat.*" It was used regularly by the Earls of Dunbar and March as a *hawking seat,* a shooting lodge of the time, where they, and their noble friends would indulge in sport by day, and spend the evening feasting and making merry.

Thomas regularly made the journey along the old track to visit the 7th Earl, his wife the Countess of Dunbar, and their family. The tower house to the west, owned by Thomas, Laird of Ercildune, and the castle to the east, owned by the Earl of Dunbar, would be imposing structures compared to the flimsy little huts of the villagers; they would be status symbols of wealth and power. The two men of nobility would host grand banquets; their guests would include, among others, the reigning monarchs of the time.

Until his death in 1248, *Patrick II* was the 6th Earl of Dunbar. At this time Thomas would be in his youth, however, it is known that he frequented the castle during this time; the rumour being that he was smitten by *Lady Bethoc,* the beautiful young daughter of Patrick II and his first wife.

Patrick, the eldest son of the 6th Earl was heir to the title of Earl of Dunbar, and he became Patrick III, 7th Earl of Dunbar following the death of his father in 1248. The family of Dunbar were known to have played an important role in the life and times of Thomas, the reasons for this are uncertain. It has been suggested they may have been related in some way, it is also possible that the Earls owned the feudal land on which

40

Thomas's property stood; for many centuries the Earldom of Dunbar owned the feudal lands from Dunbar castle to the English border. It is almost certain that Thomas's lands were not owned by the Crown, since there is no documentation from the period to support this.

The previous Earls of Dunbar, including the 6th and 7th Earls, were known to be *valiant knights* who fought alongside their King in many battles. They were a family of great renown, having descended from Royalty, the fact that Thomas frequented the castle, for whatever reason, speaks volumes for his high status in the local community at this time.

The descendants of the Earls of Dunbar, and the Earls of March and Dunbar as they became known in later years, continued to own these lands until 1436. They were all descended from Cospatric, Earl of Northumbria, who died in 1166. Cospatrick, like Thomas, took the name, *de Ercildune*. Following the death of the 7th Earl in 1289, the 8th Earl and succeeding Earls took the new title of *Earl of March and Dunbar.*

Ercildune was situated in a natural valley through which flowed the river *Leader.* To the south of the river Leader, the sombre peak of *Arciol Dun* would dominate the skyline as it still does today. It is a landmark, similar to the Eildon Hills, which can be clearly seen from all directions. Three concentric rings, which signify the remains of an old *British* fort, are still visible near its summit of 1003ft. *Arciol Dun* means *look- out,* or *prospect hill,* it has been generally accepted that the name of Ercildune was derived from its name. The 'Black Hill' and the 'Eildon Hills', are known to be

41

volcanic, the bedrock of these hills are solid black whinstone, a residual effect of the molten lava from which they were formed. The lower hills in the area are formed from softer red sandstone. The caves, used by the early settlers, can still be seen in these sandstone hills, and also on the river banks of the Jed, the Teviot, and the Ale. This beautiful, pink-tinged stone was used in the construction of the older houses, Churches, and some of the Abbeys in the area.

The entire landmass of Britain was at one time under the ocean, the cliff-tops around the east Berwickshire coast near St Abbs, being at one time the sea-bed. The last great ice-age in Scotland reached its peak 20,000 years ago, at this time the land was completely covered in a sheet of ice. The temperature has risen and fallen several times since; the last *mini* ice–age lasted for approximately seventy years and occured between 1645 and 1715. The landscape of today has been carved by the glaciation from the last great ice-age; however, prior to that, the evolution of the land over millions of years formed the basis of our present landscape.

In the thirteenth century, the landscape of lowland Scotland would be quite similar to that of today, with undulating lowland, rolling hills, and the occasional, now extinct, volcanic peak dotting the skyline in every direction. The climate at this time was warmer than that of today. However, unlike today, extensive forests of oak and birch would encompass as far as the eye could see. The Ettrick forest, where William Wallace planned his attacks on the English army, was nearby, as was the great forest of Jed. To the northeast, the land rose steeply towards the Lammermuir hills, as it did to the northwest, to what is now known as the *'Southern Upland Way'*. Directly to the east lay *'The Merse,'* a flat fertile plain which stretched all the way to the sea.

A variety of languages was spoken in lowland Scotland at this time. The plains of Berwickshire, still known today as *The Merse*, were inhabited by a variety of people, with *a blend of tongues,* which eventually formed the basis of the *English* language. The influence of the Gaels from the north and the west, ensured that Gaelic was still spoken, but this, like the old *Welsh* language of the *Cymri,* was gradually dying out. *Latin and Middle English (Scots)* would be used by the scholars; the Anglo-Normans would still speak French. Thomas, being educated, would almost certainly understand Latin, the *Bemersyde Charter* bearing his signature is written in Latin. The prophecies of Thomas were written in *Quante Inglis* (Scots), and it is generally accepted that he had the Gaelic.

The influence of the Norman/Scandinavians who remained in Scotland at this time, came from the Viking settlers. The Vikings had colonised the province of Normandy in the ninth century. The population of lowland Scotland in the thirteenth century was a melting pot of mixed races. Until the beginning of the first *Scottish War of Independence* the inhabitants of lowland Scotland were still regarded by the *Highlanders* as Saxons; however, after the start of the wars, the *Lowlanders* were accepted by the *Highlanders* as being *Scottish.* The Gaelic word, *Sasunnach,* the term used for the *Saxons* by the Gaelic speaking highlanders, included any non-Gaelic speaking lowlander. Today, the word *Sassenach,* a derivation of the Gaelic spelling, is

43

commonly used by the Scots for an English person. The placenames which remain in the area today are a mix of Gaelic,Anglo-Saxon, Scandinavian and Norman/French. At the time of Thomas's birth, and during his early years, King Alexander II (*Alasdair mac Uilleam* –*son of William*), was the reigning monarch. King Alexander II was born at Haddington, approximately twenty miles, as the crow flies, from Earlston. King Alexander II invaded northern England in 1215, resulting in King John (*the bad*) bringing his army north to wreak havoc on the towns of Berwick and Roxburgh; Berwick, at this time, being on the Scottish side of the border.

In 1221, Alexander, now twenty three years old, married Joan, sister of King Henry of England, Joan was only eleven years old when she married King Alexander. Unfortunately, Joan's marriage to the king was not to last, she died in 1238 at the young age of twenty eight, leaving no heir to the throne. King Alexander's second marriage to Marie de Coucy, the daughter of a nobleman, took place at Roxburgh castle on May 15th 1239; the marriage produced a son and heir two years later in 1241.

King Alexander II was a good politician and considered to be a stable and reliable monarch, his marriage to Joan reconciled Scotland and England for a short time. In 1237, the two countries negotiated an exchange of lands in the *Treaty of York*. Following this treaty, the boundary between Scotland and England was defined much as it is today, one difference being that Berwick remained in Scotland for the time being. Apart from the ongoing invasions of the northern islands by the *Vikings*, life in Scotland was relatively peaceful during the reign of King Alexander II. He died from natural causes on the Island of Kerrera on July 8th 1248; his body was interred in the gounds of *Melrose Abbey* at his request. King Alexander II was fifty one years old when he died, having ruled Scotland for thirty five years. His son *Alexander III*, born seven years earlier at *Roxburgh Castle*, was crowned King of Scotland on July 13th 1248. The true reason behind the friendship between Thomas of Ercildune and King Alexander III is lost in the mists of time. Many stories tell of Thomas being a confidante of the king, being knighted by the king, and of Thomas collecting feu duty throughout Scotland on the king's behalf. Thomas, being a bard, may have been employed by the king in the role of personal adviser. The role of the bard in medieval times was not a menial position; on the contrary, it was a highly skilled profession. During his lifetime, Thomas is known to have travelled the length and breadth of Scotland; the written proof is contained in accounts by the early writers, and in his prophecies. According to Blind Harry - *The Minstrel* - Thomas was a regular visitor to the religious house of Fail, and a friend of the Minister there; the head of all *Trinitarian* establishments are known as Ministers. Fail, also known as Failford Abbey, was in the Parish of Tarbolton in South Ayrshire. The date of its foundation, and by whom, are controversial, however, it is thought to have been founded in 1252, by Andrew Bruce. Despite being partially destroyed by fire in 1349, Fail continued to be in use until 1562; the ruins remained until 1952, when they were completely removed. Fail was a Trinitarian house, run by the order of the Red Friars, and dedicated to Saint Mary, with the *Mother*

45

House being noted as Saint Mathurian in Paris. The reason for Thomas's frequent visits to this particular monastery has not been ascertained, however, it is documented by *Henry the Minstrel* that "Thomas was a regular visitor to Fail and a friend of *The Minister* there." An extract from a rhyme to that effect is as follows;

"Thomas Rimour into the fail was then,
With the mynystir, quhilk was a worthy man:
He uyst oft to that religious place;
The people demyt of wit mekill he can;

The Monks of Melrose apparently owned lands neighbouring those of Fail, which made rivalry over lands and wealth between the two orders a common occurence. It is apparent from his written works that Thomas was well educated - not a common trait of the time. It is possible that Thomas may have furthered his education with the help of the Clerics at Fail monastery. *Soltra,* a medieval hospital, was conveniently situated beside the old Roman, *Royal Road.* This road stretched northwards, skirting the range of hills - now called Soutra – which separate the *Merse* from the *Lothians.* The Roman road linked the south with the north, in its place today the modern A68 links Scotland and England. The route of the old Roman road, now known as Dere Street, can still be seen at this, and various other locations. The site where the hospital of Soltra once stood is now a popular visitor attraction, with the added bonus of spectacular views.

Soltra, founded in c1164, was in use as a hospital until the seventeenth century, being run by the *"Master and*

Brethren" of the Augustinian order. It was dedicated as, 'The House of the Holy Trinity at Soutra.' In the twelfth, and early thirteenth century the hospital was wealthy and powerful, its income funded by its vast estates, these being spread over twenty square miles. The information provided by the old charters tells us that the role of the medieval hospital was vast and varied. Included in these were, taking care of the sick, the poor, and the aged, as well as providing food and shelter to the traveller. Being situated beside the main route linking the north with the south, there would be many a weary traveller knocking at the door. The heyday of the medieval hospital was in the fourteenth century, at this time it was funded mainly by donations from wealthy patrons, *or their heirs.* Thomas's ancestral home, which included lands of almost ten acres, was bequeathed to the monks of *Soltra* by his *son and heir,* Thomas de Ercildune. Despite extensive investigations, I can find no justifiable reason why the bequest was made to this particular establishment. It is possible that Thomas, or a member of his family, may have received treatment at the hospital, for which the house was repaid generously. In the early thirteenth century, the Lindsay family were the chief patrons of a nearby mansion house, known then as *Coldingknowe,* which included extensive lands surrounding Ercildune. They were a family of great wealth and stature in the neighbourhood. The mansion house of Coldingknowe was less than a mile away from the residence of the Rhymer. A local rumour states that a secret underground tunnel linked the dungeons of *Coldingknowe* to the vaults beneath the tower of *The Rhymer* at Ercildune. Thomas however, was not intimidated by the owner's wealth and grandeur, he put a curse on the house of Coldingknowe, *"for now and evermair."*

A *Charter* of *The Lindseys,* preserved in the *Durham Archives,* is as follows, *Carta W.de Lidessi de Fauope ixta Ledre ante 1165 to the monks of Melrose,* witnessed by; *Swano de Ercedun, and Cospatricio de Ercedun.* In another charter, it is documented that *William de Lindsei de Ercildoune* granted the church at Ercildune to the *Priory of Coldingham.*

There were two Cospatrics - father and son - second and third respective Earls of Dunbar, ancestors of Earl Patrick, 7ᵗʰ Earl of Dunbar who owned the castle in Ercildune in Thomas's time. *Petrus De Haga* (the surname later becoming Haig), originally from Normandy, was the founder and first occupier of another mansion house, just a few miles to the south of Ercildune. This mansion house, which includes a large estate, is called *Bemersyde;* it has been continuously inhabited from the twelfth century to the present day by the *Haig* family, as prophesied by Thomas.

The new Cistercian abbeys of Melrose, Dryburgh, Kelso, and Jedburgh were only a short distance away. Thomas was known to frequent the religious houses and abbeys; he would also ride to the lower braes of the Eildon hills, known as *Huntlee Bankes,* to find inspiration for his poems. To reach the abbeys, the Eildon Hills, and Huntly Banks, Thomas had two rivers to negotiate, namely the river Leader, and the river Tweed. A ford crossed the river Leader just a few yards upstream from the home of Thomas, the spot is still known today as *Craigsford,* where a bridge now crosses the Leader water. At ninety four miles long, the Tweed is the fourth longest river in Scotland, has strong undercurrents, and deep pools. The fords would allow a safe crossing of the river Tweed, *Monksford* and *Abbotsford* being two examples of names still in use today. The monks from the abbeys of Melrose and Dryburgh would use these fords, as would the nomadic tribes many centuries before.

The Crusades to the Holy Land were ongoing during the early part of Thomas's life. In 1248, Earl Patrick II (6th Earl of Dunbar), led an army of Scots to Jerusalem to fight alongside King Louis 1X of France. While on this crusade, Earl Patrick II died in Egypt, on 28th June 1248. Nothing in the chronicles of the period suggest that Thomas took part in any of the crusades, nor is there any proof that Thomas was involved in later battles fought on home soil. Although there is no doubt that Thomas was a skilled swordsman, the existing evidence regarding his persona portrays him as a man of peace, a romantic nature-lover, involved in the literary arts, rather than on the battlefield.

Due to his youth, the young King Alexander III was considered an easy target to usurp. In 1255, there was an unsuccessful conspiracy, led by *pro-English* Scots, against the young king. In the interim, between the death of his father and King Alexander III taking complete control of the nation's government - a period of fourteen years - the politics of the time were unstable and volatile. In 1262, the young king *came of age,* and subsequently, aided by the support of his loyal followers he established a stable government and a secure nation for the people of Scotland until his untimely death in

1286. Thomas was reputed to be a staunch supporter, and a trusted ally of King Alexander III, unfortunately, the same could not be said for his friends and neighbours, the Earls of Dunbar.

The following account, which has been handed down through many generations, was related to me by a senior Earlston resident, *"Lady Bethoc, daughter of the 6th Earl of Dunbar, accompanied Thomas on many of his missions, these being undertaken on behalf of King Alexander III. One of these "missions" lasted for seven years. Thomas and Lady Bethoc also met secretly at the idyllic spot near the waterfall at Boglie Burn (Goblin Brook), on the foothills of the Eildon Hills."*

Although Thomas was classed as *landed gentry*, he would not be considered eligible to court an Earl's daughter. A small village near Earlston, known today as Bedrule, was apparently once known as *'Bethoc's Rule.'*

The local rumour goes on to say that Lady Bethoc bore a son to Thomas, however, she died at a young age some time before Thomas; her death left Thomas distraught.

Could Lady Bethoc be the inspiration for Thomas's rhyme, which tells of the *Beautiful Lady on a White Horse near the Eildon Tree?*

•••••••••••••••••••

Chapter 4

Celtic Mythology

At the beginning of the thirteenth century, the lower slopes of the Eildon hills would be covered in dense woodland, small brooks would cascade from the three summits. The climate was known to be much wetter and warmer at this time; the forbidding forests would exude danger, opportunity, and enchantment. The area surrounding the Eildon Hills would be an awe-inspiring, yet intimidating place to visit at this period in time. Legendary tales of rituals by the Druid Priests and their followers, combined with the superstitions of the Eildon Hill's secret powers would still be fresh in the minds of the locals.

Over the centuries, a few of the inhabitants who dwelled in the vicinity of the *Eildon Hills* were linked to miraculous and visionary events; the names of *Waltheof, Cuthbert, Drythelm, Merlin, Arthur, Michael Scot,* and *Thomas the Rhymer,* all being associated with *visionary tales.* According to legend, Thomas acquired his prophetic gift following his return from a seven year absence. According to Thomas, this time was spent serving the Fairy Queen in the '*otherworld.*'

To be able to *create* - whether it is in artisitic, musical, or literary form - requires a certain degree of *vision, imagination and insight.* However, a vision, which resulted in Thomas disappearing for seven years, was incomprehensible, even for this period in time when superstitions were prevalent. The fact that Thomas returned with prophetic powers would be even more astounding to his kith and kin. Thomas would be ridiculed by some, and feared and shunned by many. It is little wonder that he was regarded as being, *"not of this world."* Thomas's *insight* into the future was surreal, and remained unrivalled until the birth of the French apothecary and seer *Nostradamus,* in the sixteenth century.

Due to the accuracy of his predictions, there is little doubt that Thomas possessed this gift. As said by *Archbishop Spottiswood "Whence or how he came to have this knowledge can hardly be ascertained, but sure it is that he did divine and answer truly of many things to come."* John Spottiswood was born in West Lothian in 1565; he was Archbishop of St. Andrews, Archbishop of Glasgow, a church historian, and High Chancellor of Scotland. John Spottiswood died in 1639, and is interred in Westminster abbey. His endorsement of the credibility of Thomas's predictions is a mark of respect from a man of such veneration.

My belief is that Thomas lived his life in a way similar to that of the ancient Celtic tribes, in tune with nature, his mind open and receptive, both to the natural and supernatural world. A man, who by means as yet incomprehensible, had knowledge of the future events which would subsequently unfold. Over a period of almost eight hundred years, most of Thomas's prophecies have come to fruition, as for the ones at present unfulfilled, we can only wait and wonder.

Although Christianity was well established as a religion in the early thirteenth century, our predecessors worshipped the *Gods of Nature* for many thousands of years before the birth of Christ. Neolithic man was more

52

in tune with the natural world, the elements, such as fire, and water. Folklore tales from around the world tell of mythological fire creatures and water spirits. Anglo-Saxons legends tell of the spirits of the hills, the fields, the water, and the sea. Europe and Scandinavia have similar legends which tell of the spirits of the *otherworld*. Scotland is no different, here the water spirit is known as the *Kelpie*, or water horse; these are said to inhabit the lochs and rivers.

The *Fairy*, or *Banshi*, was the supernatural being associated with the Celtic culture. These spiritual creatures, with amazing powers, were to be feared and respected. The word *Fairy* is derived from *Middle English, the old French* spelling being *Faerie*, other spellings are *Fayerye, Feirie and Faery*. Definitions of the word are given as, fate, spirit, or enchantment. Tales connected to the *little people* describe them as being dressed in green, and very elusive; however, they are also said to be quite tall, very beautiful, and extremely intelligent.

Within a few miles of the spot where Thomas encountered the *Fairy Queen* there is a spot known locally as *The Fairy Dean,* or *Elwand Glen,* now known locally as Ellwyn Glen. Sir Walter Scott called this place *"A refuge of the Elfin race."* This spot is in a valley where the Allan water meets the river Tweed, between Galashiels and Melrose. At the head of this glen is another, by the name of *Glen Dearg,* the Gaelic translation being *The Red Glen.* The Pavilion is to the east of Elwyndale, the site of the old abbey of St. Colm, being at nearby Colmslie. This entire area was known at one time to be a place of spiritual activity by the creatures from the otherworld, tales of *Fairy Paths* and *Fairy Stones* well known in the locality.

During this time, when there was a belief in magic, witchcraft, and prophets, the superstitions associated with the spirits from the otherworld were accepted as being perfectly normal and rational. Today, we still speak of *fairy lights,* and *fairy godmothers,* but no-one now believes in *Fairies.* To admit to having a belief in the supernatural world today would be considered unusual, however, I know of several people who have this belief. The ancient mythological tales, and the legends surrounding the inhabitants of the otherworld still fascinate the population of our modern, *enlightened* society. I believe that many people living in our *scientifically orientated* world of today still secretly wonder about the powers of the supernatural world. Numerous books, still current, with connections to the *supernatural* and the *spirits* from the *otherworld,* occupy a large corner of the market in our modern literary society.

The Celtic Fairies supposedly had the ability to *abduct* mortals from *middle earth* and spirit them away to the otherworld. In the present day, there are many instances where folk simply vanish without trace. It is acceptable to believe that they may have been abducted by *Aliens* from outer space, yet to consider that they may have been abducted by the *Fairy Folk* is too bizarre to even contemplate. However, in medieval times, and for centuries previous, this belief was strong, and accepted without question.

The Faeries were the more genteel of the species, having a love of music and poetry, whereas the Dwarfs and

Elves were more fiendish and temperamental. The *Brownies* were much uglier than the fairies, being grotesque dwarf-like creatures. They were said to inhabit every farmhouse in Scotland, the owners firmly believing that the luck of the house would run out if the *Brownies* deserted the house. According to legend, one Brownie, after tiring of living at a farm called *Bodsbeck* in Ettrick and moving to the neighbouring farm of *Leithenhall,* transferred the good luck from one house to the other. The German spirits were called *Kobold,* from which the English *Goblin,* and Scottish *Bogle* is derived. They were known to lurk in the dark caverns and huge rocks, whereas the Faeries frequented the wooded glades, and hills. The Scandinavian Dwarfs, called *Trows* or *Trollds,* were the impish fiends who dwelled in the lakes and rivers.

As written in 'Popular Rhymes, Fireside Stories and Amusements of Scotland,' published by William and Robert Chambers, Edinburgh 1842;

"Even as recent as the nineteenth century it was still believed that he who has the courage to rush upon a fairy festival and snatch from them their drinking cup or horn, shall find it provides him with a cornucopia of good fortune, if he can bear it across a running stream." In the nineteenth century, a goblet was still carefully preserved in Eden Hall in Cumbria, which supposedly had been seized at a banquet of the Elves, by one of the ancient Musgrave family. Or, as others have said, by one of their domestics who had seized it in the manner described. The Fairy Train had then vanished crying aloud; "If this glass do break or fall, Farewell the luck of Eden Hall." Another story, relating to the superstitions associated

with the Faeries, is one regarding the *Ploughmen of Clydesdale*. *"They would repeat a rhyme several times on turning at the end of the ridges; Fairy, fairy, bake me a bannock and roast me a collop, and I'll give you a spurtle of my gad end. It is said that they would find the fare waiting for them at the end of the fourth furrow."*

The ancient tales and legends of these *otherworld* creatures inspired musicians, poets, and authors alike. Shakespeare wrote about the entrances to the *Fairy Kingdom* being *"in places of wilderness."*

The legend of the *Loch Ness Monster* is famous both near and far. This tale continues to draw visitors to Scotland, Loch Ness being one of the most important destinations on the tourists' itinerary. Some sincerely believe they have spotted the monster, while many others spend a great deal of time waiting and watching, camera at the ready.

A poem called *'The Mermaid,'* by *John Leyden,* is included in *The Minstrelsy of the Scottish Border* by *Sir Walter Scott;* it is a *Gaelic Traditional Ballad* relating the bizarre love affair between *MacPhail of Colonsay* and the *Mermaid of Corryvreckan.* Corryvreckan is a notorious channel of water off the west coast of Scotland, between the tips of the islands of Jura and Scarba. Once the channel is safely negotiated, it leads out to the wild waters of the Atlantic Ocean; however, the crossing should not to be attempted by the inexperienced mariner. In a tale akin to the *Ballad of Thomas the Rhymer,* the poem describes how *MacPhail,* while negotiating the crossing, is carried off by the mermaid to a deep coral cavern under the boiling cauldron of the notorious gulf. When the mermaid takes on her mortal form MacPhail is spell-bound by her beauty, however, he is forbidden to see her with her *scaly tail*. MacPhail eventually tires of her, and pleads to be allowed to return to his true love on Colonsay. MacPhail is imprisoned by the mermaid for several years before eventually being allowed to return to his own world. One line from the poem reads, "*The sea- snake heaves his snowy mane.*" According to *Olaus Magnus;* "In *Norwegian* folklore, a *gigantic serpent* two hundred feet long, and twenty feet thick, swam in the waters around the coastline off Bergen. The sceptics dismissed this tale as another '*Loch Ness Monster'* tale, until 1808, when a creature of this description was washed ashore on one of the *Orkney Isles* off the northern coast of Scotland."

The *Druids* worshipped the divine sanctity of the forests, and regarded them as places of spiritual dwelling. The conversion to Christianity saw large areas of forest being cut down to quell resistance from the nature worshippers. In the year 567AD, the '*Council of Tours'* castigated the *Britons* for worshipping the natural elements such as water, fountains, and stones. The city of *Tours,* situated on the Loire River in France, was considered to be the seat of Christianity in the days of the medieval Roman Catholic Church.

It is known that gifts were offered to appease the Gods of nature, by the Druids. These rituals took many forms, but often it was done by dropping metal into water, the tradition of throwing coins into a well, or fountain, stems from this ancient rite. Post Roman times saw many wells being sealed, however, a gift was offered to pacify the water spirits before this took place.

In Neolithic times, the natural world was thought to be

full of spirits. The Gaels held a superstitious reverence for the mountains and rivers, the names of many Scottish mountains being proof of these ancient superstitions. *Beinn-breach* translates from Gaelic as the spotted or speckled mountain, while *Tom na h-Iubhraich,* pronounced Tom-na-hurich, translates as *The Hill of the Yew Wood,* where, in Gaelic tradition, Thomas is still thought to sleep. This spiritual belief also existed in the Orient and throughout Western Europe. *Annat* or *Andate* was the Goddess of Victory; she was worshipped by the *Assyrians* and the *Persians,* the placename of Annat still exists near Torridon, which is in Wester Ross in the highlands of Scotland. In the lowlands, the *Charter of James V1* to the town of Peebles preserves the name of *Annat's Hope* near the town.

The *Merlin* of Upper Tweeddale was also known as *Merlin the Wild.* He was thought by some to be the son of the devil, capable of assuming the form of spirit, or earthly creature. The sixth century *Cymric* Merlin, bard, seer and wizard, was known as Merdwinn Wylit *(Tumulus Merlini).* Similar to many of the early prophets and wizards, his knowledge and foresight was more than ordinary folk could comprehend. After the battle of *Arfderydd,* or Arthuret (which is north of Carlise), Merlin went a little bit crazy. The aftermath of the battle, which destroyed all that Merlin held dear, left Merlin without the will to live. He was accused of being possessed by demons, and shunned by his fellow mortals. In a fragile state of mind, he retreated to the sanctuary of the forests to seek the solitude of nature, his appearance becoming less like a human and more like a wild aminal. Only one person stood by him, his

58

friend Kentigern; the Gaelic *Ceanntigearn* defines as Chief Lord. Kentigern went on to become patron saint of Glasgow; he also founded the kirk at Stobo in Peeblesshire, thought to be the earliest ecclesiastical structure in Tweeddale.

When his friend Kentigern died, Merlin was overcome with grief, and his mind became completely deranged.

He was accused of molesting a local woman, which rendered him an object of fear and loathing in his local community. He was probably innocent of this crime, however, his fellow humans, believing he was *"not of this world"*, plotted his death. Had he been alive today, he would have received counselling, instead of which he was stoned and tortured by local shepherds. While trying to escape, he slipped on the steep river bank; his body was impaled on a stake as he fell into the river Tweed. Merlin predicted his own death in exactly the manner in which it occurred. Merlin's grave is marked, and can still be seen on the banks of the Powsail burn, beside a thorn tree, near to the spot where he met his death. This location is also mentioned in one of Thomas's prophecies.

A tale relating to *Waldhave,* as he lay alone on a morning in May, is written in a similar manner to the Ballad of Thomas the Rhymer;

Upon Loudon Law a lone as I lay
Looking to the Lennox, as me leif thought.
The first morning of May, medicine to seeke
For malice and melody that moued me sore.

The story, as told in *'The Romance and Prophecies of*

Thomas of Erceldoune,' tells of the strange sight Waldhave beheld as he lay on *Loudon Law.* A voice is heard, and then a weird figure is seen pursuing hares and foxes across the hill. On seeing Waldhave, the apparition focuses his attention on the man, rather than the animals, and assaults him with a club. Waldhave draws his sword and wrestles the beast to the ground, refusing to let him up until he swears *"to do him no harm."* As the figure stands up, Waldhave is filled with amazement at the sight he beholds, describing it thus;

He was formed like a freike, all his foure quarters,
And then his chin and his face haired so thick,
With haire growing so grime, fearful to see.

In reply to Waldhave enquiring his name and nature, he answers that he *"drees his weird"* (endures his fate), in that wood, and goes on to say that he is offended by Waldhave questioning his appearance. He relates a few prophesies and finishes with the words;

Go musing upon Merlin if thou wilt
For I mean no more, man, at this time.

The account is very similar to the meeting of Merlin and Kentigern many centuries earlier, as told by John of Fordun. It is said that Thomas, like Merlin, still *"drees his weird"* in the *otherworld* under the Eildon Hills.

In medieval times and for many centuries previous, *'second sight'* and the role of the prophets was commonplace. Many of the Saints from the abbeys were known to have performed miracles. St. Boisil had the gift of second sight, as did St. Bede, and Waltheof.

Michael Scot the wizard was born c1175 and died c1235; he was the son of Sir Richard Scot and was born in the family home at the castle of *Balwearie* in Fife. He was first educated at *Oxford,* before going on to *Paris,* and *Toledo* in Spain. He was credited with being a brilliant alchemist, an astrologer and astronomer, as well as being accomplished in linguistics. Michael Scot was fluent in Arabic, and translated several of the works of the Greek philosopher *Aristotle* from Arabic into Latin, complete with commentaries. He was regarded as a philosopher of great importance at the court of the Holy Roman Emperor. Much of his later life was spent living in the border lands, beside the Eildon Hills and the river Tweed, where tradition says he performed his magic by *Oakwood,* and *Fairy Carterhaugh.* Doctors of the thirteenth century held Michael Scot in the highest regard. He was referred to in works by *Dante;* his literary work is still preserved to this day. Upon his tomb being opened many years after his death, it is written that the body of Michael Scot, similar to that of St. Cuthbert, showed no sign of decomposition.

It is written in rhyme;

> *"Before their eyes the wizard lay,*
> *As if he had not been dead a day.*
> *His left hand held a book of might,*
> *A silver cross was in his right."*

More words of spiritual vision about the wizard;

> *"I buried him on St Michael's night,*

61

When the bell toll'd one, and the moon was bright,
And I dug his chamber among the dead,
When the floor of the channel was stained red,
That his patron's cross might o'er him wave,
And scare the fiends from the wizard's grave."

Michael Scot is said to have died at the abbey of *Home Cultram* and to have been buried there, however, Sir Walter Scott believed in the tradition that his body is interred in the grounds of Melrose abbey.

A traditional ballad relates to a band of Scottish soldiers during the Stewart period. They were well acquainted with the tales of the wizard's powers and by chance spent a night at his birthplace, which unnerved them somewhat;

"What gars ye gaunt my merrie men,
What gars ye look sae eerie,
What gars ye hing your heids sae sair,
In the castle o' Balwearie?"

Michael Scot, like *Thomas, King Arthur,* and *Merlin,* is remembered not for his true genius, but sadly relegated solely to the annals of myth and fantasy.

The *otherworld* supposedly exists below our *middle earth,* the inhabitants of which can live alongside mortals without being seen. In Celtic mythology it has many names, *Tir nam Beo,* which translates from Gaelic as the land of the living, or *Tir nan Og,* land of the young. There are numerous names for this world where there is no death or ill-heath, it is almost timeless, and one day in our time can last for a hundred years in this place of utopia.

Legends in Greek, Welsh, and Irish mythology have a common thread linking them. They all tell of a meeting between a beautiful woman and a mortal of her choosing. In Celtic mythology, the meeting takes place at the entrance to the otherworld, this usually being beside a thorn tree. The mortal is immediately infatuated with this ethereal creature and becomes her lover. After intercourse has taken place, the once beautiful young woman is transformed into a creature which resembles an old hag. The mortal however, is now compelled to leave the land of his birth behind and embark on a journey to the otherworld. In some instances, the journey can take place in a glass boat, sailing across many seas until another kingdom is reached, or in others, by mounting a white horse and riding for many days and nights. On reaching the Fairy Kingdom, the hag is restored to her former beauty. The mortal is forbidden to speak to anyone other than his mistress for the duration of his stay in her kingdom; otherwise he will never be allowed to return to his own country. To the mortal, the entire episode seems to have occurred in the space of a few days, however, if the mortal is allowed to return to middle earth - often he is not - he will discover that he has been gone for many years and his life will be changed forever.

The number associated with many similar tales is seven - a magical number in folklore - in the case of Thomas, legend tells that he was absent from Ercildune for seven years.

In Irish mythology, the *Sidhe* were *Faery Folk* believed to be descended from the *Tuatha De Danann* - people of the

Goddess Danu - an ancient civilisation who were believed to possess the gift of immortality. It is said they were driven under the hills to seek refuge, the mounds under which they lived were called *Sidhe Mounds*. The Sidhe race was said to be distinct from humans, yet they allegedly interacted with humans for thousands of years in pre-Christian times. The Faery folk could move quickly from place to place and could assume different forms, they were also highly intelligent. In Scottish Gaelic, na *Daoine* translates as *The Fairies*.

The *Eildon Hills* are sometimes called 'the hollow hills.' This *otherworld* under the hills can be *visited* by *mortals* just as our world can be accessed by *them*. The spring festival of the *Latha Bealltainn,* which we now call *May-Day,* was a sacred ritual celebrated in pre-Christian Celtic times when the sun was mid-way between the *spring equinox* and the *summer solstice*. The town of Peebles, in the Scottish Borders, has a *Beltane Queen* in conjunction with its *common-riding* celebrations; these are held in June each year. In 1621, James V1 granted a charter to the burgh of Peebles, stating that the *Beltane Fair* was to be held on May 3rd and to be called *"Beltane Day"*. The ancient *Druid* rite of passing between two fires which were placed close together, ensured good health and prosperity. A *Beltane Fire Festival* is held annually at the end of April on *Calton Hill* in Edinburgh.

At the time of the *Latha Bealltainn,* the otherworld and the mortal world are at their closest, making transition between the two possible. According to Celtic mythology, the mortal who has been chosen to enter the kingdom of the Faeries has the ability to flit between the two worlds at will. Thomas is thought to have revisited mortal earth

64

on at least two occasions, one such visit is told in the story of *Canonbie Dick*. The tale, included in the appendix to the general preface of 'Waverly' vol.1, by Sir Walter Scott, gives an account of Dick's encounter with a mysterious stranger.

The meeting took place on a moonlit night while Dick was crossing *Bowden Moor* near Melrose, not far from the old home of Thomas of Ercildune; Bowden moor lies at the foot of the magical Eildon Hills. Dick, a local horse-dealer, was walking home from the local horse fair with a large number of horses. As he trudged across the lonely moor, he was approached by a stranger, this in itself being an unusual occurrence for Dick since he was well acquainted with all the local folk. Dick thought the cloaked stranger appeared to take on an unearthly, ghost-like appearance, but concluded it was just the shadows, cast by clouds fleetingly obscuring the moon, playing havoc with his imagination. The two men engaged in a brief conversation, whereby the stranger offered to buy the horses from Dick, at a price he could not refuse; the coins duly changed hands. However, since the appearance of the man had aroused Dick's curiousity he asked the reason for him needing so many horses. The stranger invited Dick to accompany him, and he duly led the way to a knoll between the south and central peak of Eildon's three hills, known locally as the *'Lucken Hare;'* it so happens that the foot of this eminence was once used as a meeting place for local witches. Dick, being well aquainted with the Eildon hills, could not recall ever seeing the entrance into which he was being taken by the stranger. His suspicions were further aroused by the coinage received as payment for the horses, which included bonnet-pieces instead of the currency of the time. By this time, Dick's initial bravado was diminishing fast. Being aware of this, the stranger gave Dick the chance to change his mind, telling him *"You may still return."* Dick, however, not daring to be seen as a coward, bravely followed the stranger through the entrance. They travelled deep under the Eildon hill until they came to an enormous cave. By the flickering light of the flaming torches which illuminated the cave, Dick could see stalls running the entire length of one wall, in each stall stood a black horse, tacked up and ready for battle. By the side of each horse, lying on the straw was a Knight, dressed in full battle armour, with sword in hand. Yet, neither men nor beasts stirred as the horse-dealer viewed this incredible sight. At the far end of the huge hall was an antique table, upon which lay a sword and a horn. A voice boomed out and reverberated around the enormous hall *"He that shall sound that horn and draw that sword, shall, if his heart fails him not, be King over all broad Britain, so speaks the tongue that cannot lie, but all depends on your courage and which you take first."* By this time Dick was in no doubt as to the identity of the mysterious stranger, he was none other than *True Thomas* himself. Since his courage had completely deserted him by this time, Dick's first thought was to pick up the sword; however, on second thoughts, he concluded that he might incur the wrath of the mighty mountain. Hesitantly, Dick picked up the horn and blew a feeble note. Just then an almighty roar of thunder resounded round the hall, at the same time, men and mounts sprang to life. Dick dropped the horn and was about to grab the sword, when he heard the voice say "*Woe to the coward that ever he was born, who did not draw the sword before he blew the horn.*" A whirlwind blew through the long hall and ejected Dick out of the cavern. He was found by a shepherd next morning, only just managing to relate his tale before drawing his final breath.

The name of Thomas the Rhymer crops up in many tales of myth and legend. It has been said that in the later centuries, when witches and warlocks were being burned at the stake for their "*black magic,*" they would try to absolve themselves by quoting the names of previous seers - including Thomas - as having guided them.

In the late nineteeth century, the Rev. John Gregorson Campbell from Tiree wrote a book about the superstitions of the Highlands and Islands. His research was based mainly on beliefs still current in the mid-nineteeth century. Two books, the first entitled *Superstitions of the Highlands and Islands,* and the second entitled *Witchcraft and Second Sight in the Highlands and Islands,* were published posthumously in 1900, and 1902 respectively. Ronald Black, from Peebles, brought the two books together in an edition, which includes notes and introduction, called "*The Gaelic Otherworld*". The book was published in 2005, by Birlinn Ltd. of Edinburgh. The following tale, with a reference to Thomas the Rhymer, is included in the edition;

Alexander Stewart, a minister from Onich near Fort William tells of a respectable lady's reply to his question regarding water-horses. In his book called 'Twixt Ben Nevis and Glencoe,' published in 1885, he relates a

67

discussion between himself and a local lady. She told him; "The horses emerge from the water already equipped with bridles." "How," he asked, "do water horses happen to have bridles? Who could ride, or drive them, and if they can neither be driven nor ridden, why should they have bridles?" "Thomas the Rhymer," the old lady replied, "or some other magician and prophet of the olden time now detained in Fairyland, is destined yet to reappear upon earth with some companions almost as powerful as himself, then shall the water-horses be bridled and saddled by a brave company of Scottishmen from Fairyland, some Highland, some Lowland, bridled and saddled, and fearlessly mounted, a great battle will be fought, all Englishmen, and other foreigners will be driven out of the country, the crown will again revert to the rightful heirs, and Scotland once again become a free, independent and happy kingdom."

It is interesting to read this tale, which was current in the late nineteenth century; quite recent in comparison to the height of Thomas's popularity nearly two centuries previous in the seventeenth century. Such was the belief in the powers of the supernatural, that as recent as the nineteenth century, a respected and perfectly rational lady could still have such faith in those legendary powers.

Our ancestors in *Neolithic* (new Stone Age) times erected many pillars of stone. Scholars are still mystified by their purpose, and despite there being many theories, have not yet been able to reach a satisfactory conclusion. These monuments of stone can be found in abundance all over Britain; *Stonehenge,* and the *Callanish stones (Tursachan Chalanais)*, being just two examples of *Megalithic Monuments* where many stones of colossal proportions are grouped together. The *Callanish Stones,* which can be found on the Isle of Lewis in the Outer Hebrides, range from 3.5 to 15.5 feet in height. They date from approximately three to four thousand years ago. Their arrangement is such that five lines of stones radiate out from a central circle. Inside the circle is a single tall stone, which may have been used for human sacrifice in ancient ritualistic ceremonies. Archaeologists have found evidence to suggest that the site was used as a burial chamber, with signs that the deceased were cremated. The ancient *burial chambers* contain relics from the life of the deceased alongside the bodies; their status in life is reflected in the quantity and nature of these *tokens.* In *Gaelic* tradition, the stones of Callanish are called *Na Fir Bhreige* – The False Men. One suggestion for the purpose of these ancient monuments is that of an observatory for the sun, moon, and stars. The accurate alignment of the stones would substantiate this theory; however, despite much research, the true purpose of these standing stones continues to baffle the experts.

Single standing stones, or *Monolithic Monuments,* can also be found all over Britain, many being located on the Island of *Orkney* off the north coast of Scotland. These *Monoliths* can also be found on the lands near Thomas's home in the lowlands of Scotland; many of them being aligned with the Eildon Hills.

Bernera, a small Isle in the Outer Hebrides, has a stone circle with a large stone in the centre, the Gaelic name for the large stone is *Clach na Greine,* which translates as 'S*tone of the Sun.'* These ancient monuments were

69

erected many centuries before the Egyptians built the pyramids.

In pre-Christian times, stones and trees were important features in the lives of the indigenous tribal inhabitants of our island. Religious ceremonies and rituals were held at these stone circles; the forests, and the supernatural spirits who dwelled there, were held in great respect. Perhaps *primitive* man had knowledge far beyond our perception today. Our predecessors, who lived in harmony with nature, were receptive and sympathetic to the natural elements; they were empathic with *Mother Earth* - qualities which have been lost in the *evolution* and *progress* of mankind.

In the words of Professor Veitch, *"The Cymric tribes had no fear of the 'dark hill' or 'stern glen,'"* while the *Saxon* invaders had no empathy with the beauty and wonders of the natural world. The poems from the sixth, seventh and eighth centuries speak of the *"magic of nature,"* a charm which typifies *Celtic* poetry.

The allure of the *spiritual feeling* of the area apparently impressed the Romans when they occupied this land. Two Roman altars, unearthed during excavations near Newstead, one in 1783, and the other in 1830, were inscribed to the Gods; one being inscribed to the god *Sylvanus.* Another similar altar was discovered near the ruins of *Roxburgh Castle.*

The intrigue and mystery associated with *Thomas the Rhymer of Ercildune* begins with the rhyming tale of his acquisition of the gift of prophecy.

Chapter 5

The Ballad of Thomas the Rhymer
Version by Robert Jamieson

True Thomas lay o'er yonder bank,
And he beheld a ladie gay,
A ladie that was brisk and bold,
Come riding o'er the fernie brae.

Her skirt was of the grass-green silk,
Her mantle of the velvet fine,
At ilka tett of her horse's mane
Hung fifty silver bells and nine.

True Thomas he took off his hat,
And bow'd him low down to his knee:
"All hail, thou mighty Queen of Heaven!
For your like on earth I never did see".

"O no, O no, True Thomas, says she,
"That name does not belong to me;
I am but the Queen of fair Elfland
And I am come here to visit thee."

"But ye maun go wi' me now, Thomas,
True Thomas ye maun go wi' me;
For ye maun serve me seven years
Through weal and woe, as may chance be."

She turned about her milk-white steed,
And took True Thomas up behind,

And ay whene'er her bridle rang,
Her steed flew swifter than the wind.

O they rade on, and further on,
Until they came to a garden green;
"Light down, light down ye lady free,
Some o' that fruit let me pull to thee."

"O no, O no, True Thomas," she says,
"That fruit maun no be touched by thee;
For a' the plagues that are in Hell
Light on the fruit of this countrie."

"But I have a laef here in my lap,
Likewise a bottle o' clarry wine;
And now, er we go further on,
We'll rest a while, and ye may dine."

When he had eaten and drank his fill,
The Lady sayd, "ere we climb yon hill,
Lay your head upon my knee
And I will show you ferlies three."

"O see not ye yon narrow road,
So thick beset wi thorns and briers?-
That is the path of righteousness,
Tho after it but few enquires

"And see ye not that braid, braid road,
That lies across yon lillie leven?
That is the path of wickedness,
Tho some call it the road to heaven.

And see ye not that bonny road,
Which winds about the fernie brae?
That is the road to fair Elfland,
Where you and I this night maun gae.

But Thomas, ye maun hold your tounge,
Whatever ye may hear or see;
For gin ae word ye should chance to speak,
You will ne'er get back to your ain countrie."

For forty days and forty nights
He wade through red blood to the knee;
And he saw neither sun nor moon,
But heard the roaring of the sea.

He's gotten a coat o' the even cloth,
And a pair of shoes of velvet green,
And till seven years were past and gone
True Thomas on earth was never seen.

This version of the 'Ballad of Thomas the Rhymer' was edited by Robert Jamieson; being printed in his collection of popular *Ballads and Songs* in 1806. This, and the following version by Sir Walter Scott, are included in a book entitled, *'The Romance and Prophecies of Thomas the Rhymer of Erceldoune,'* edited by *Dr James Augustus Henry Murray,* and first published in 1875.

Seven verses, omitted from the Robert Jamieson version of the ballad, are included in the following version by Sir Walter Scott; this being printed in his 'Minstrelsy of the Scottish Border, printed by James Ballantyne of Kelso in

73

1802. However, three verses included in Jamieson's version are omitted from Sir Walter Scott's version. Although the two versions differ considerably, Dr Murray concluded that both Scott and Jamieson obtained their copy from the same source, namely Mrs Brown's MS.

Mrs Brown's claim, that she had never actually read the ballads, but wrote them down from her childhood memories of hearing them recited repeatedly, is quite astounding.

The Ballad of Thomas the Rhymer

version by Sir Walter Scott

True Thomas lay on Huntlie bank;
A ferlie he spied wi' his ee;
And there he saw a ladye bright,
Come riding down by the Eildon tree.

Her skirt was o' the grass-green silk,
Her mantle o' the velvet fyne;
At ilka tett of her horse's mane,
Hung fifty siller bells and nine.

True Thomas, he pull'd aff his cap,
And louted low down to the knee,
"All hail, thou mighty Queen of heaven
For thy peer on earth I never did see."

"O no, O no, Thomas", she said,
"That name does not belang to me;

I am but the queen of fair Elfland,
That am hither come to visit thee."

"Harp and carp, Thomas," she said;
"Harp and carp along wi' me;
And if ye dare to kiss my lips,
Sure of your bodie I will be."

"Betide me weal, betide me woe,
That weird shall never daunton me"
Syne he has kissed her rosy lips,
All underneath the Eildon tree.

"Now ye maun go wi' me," she said:
"True Thomas, ye maun go wi' me:
And ye maun serve me seven years,
Thro' weal or woe as may chance to be."

She's mounted on her milk-white steed;
She's ta'en True Thomas up behind:
And Aye whene'er her bridle rung,
The steed flew swifter then the wind.

O they rode on and further on:
The steed ga'ed swifter than the wind;
Until they reached a desert wide,
And living land was left behind.

"Light down, light down, now, true Thomas,
And lean your head upon my knee;
Abide and rest a little space,
And I will show you ferlies three.

75

O see ye not yon narrow road,
So thick beset with thorns and briers?
That is the path of righteousness,
Though after it but few enquires.

And see ye not that braid braid road
That winds about the fernie brae?
That is the road to fair Elfland,
Where thou and I this night maun gae.

But Thomas ye maun hold yout tongue,
Whatever ye may hear or see;
For, if you speak a word in Elfyn land,
Ye'll ne'er get back to your ain countrie."

O they rade on, and farther on,
And they waded through rivers aboon the knee,
And they saw neither sun nor moon,
But they heard the roaring of the sea.

It was mirk mirk night, and there was nae stern light,
And they waded through red blode to the knee;
For a' the blude that's shed on earth
Rins through the springs o' that countrie.

Syne they came to a garden green,
And she pu'd an apple frae a tree
"Take this for thy wages, true Thomas:
It will give thee the tongue that can never lee."

"My tongue is mine ain," true Thomas said;
"A gudely gift ye wad gie to me!

I neither dought to buy nor sell,
At fair or tryst where I may be.

I dought neither speak to prince or peer,
Nor ask of grace from fair ladye"-
"Now ask thy peace," the lady said.
"For as I say, so must it be."-

He has gotten a coat of the even cloth,
And a pair of shoes of velvet green:
And till seven years were gane and past,
True Thomas on earth was never seen.

Many versions of the ballad have been written throughout the centuries, and although the theme has remained consistent, the wording of the original ballad would be entirely different.

The earliest extant copies of the Romance and prophecies are contained in four manuscripts, with the prophecies alone being contained in a fifth; these being kept in various museum libraries in England. The wording in the manuscripts differs considerably from one to the other.

The earliest handwritten version of the *Romance* is thought to have appeared as far back as the fourteenth century. The following version is from 1652, and is included in a book entitled *"The Journey of Thomas the Rhymer."* The book, which was printed by The Old Stile Press' in the year 2000, includes wood engravings and an afterword by Angela Lemaire. Only the first Fytte is printed in the book, without the inclusion of the prophecies.

The Romance of Thomas the Rhymer

As I me went this enders day,
By west alone making my moan,
All in the morning of the may,
By Huntly banks, my self alone,
I heard the Jay, the Thristle cock,
The Mavis minding of her song,
The Woodwal with her merry note,
That all the wood about me rung;
Alone in longing as I lay,
Underneath a seemly tree,
Saw I where a Lady gay,
Came riding over a faire long ley;
If I should sit to dooms day,
With inke and paper for to write,
Certainly all her faire array,
For me it cannot be descry'd,
Her palfrey was of dapple grey,
Such a one saw I never none,
As the Sun on summer's day,
That faire Lady shined and shone,
Her saddle was of rewel bone,
Seemly was that sight to see,
And seemly set with precious stone,
Compast about right richly
With stones of orient great plenty.
Her haire about her head than hung,
She rode over the leve long leye;
Her girths of noble silk they were;
The buckles were of berrel stone,
Her stirrups were of chrystal cleer,

And all with pyrrie overgone.
Her pearls were pellus full fine.
Her crown was of orfry;
Her bridle shone of gold clean,
On either side hung bels three.
She led three grey-hounds in a leash,
Seven rachets by her side ran;
She bore a horn about her halse,
And under her belt many a flon.
Thomas lay and saw that sight
Underneath a seemly tree.
He said, yonder is *Mary* of might,
That bore the childe that died for me;
But I speak with that Lady bright,
I hope my heart wil break in three.
I wil go fast with all my might,
Her to meet at *Elden* tree.
Thomas rudely up he rose,
And he ran over the mountain high,
If it be true as the story saies,
He met with her at *Elden* tree.
He kneeled down upon his knee,
Underneath the green wood spray,
Lovely Lady rue on me,
Queen of heaven, as you wel may.
The Lady, that was mild of thought,
Said, *Thomas,* let such words be,
For Queen of Heaven I am not,
I never took such high degree.
I am of another country,
That I pearled most of price,
I ride over this livelong leye,

My rachets run at my device.
If you be pearled most of price,
And ridden here in rove folly
Of love, Lady, you bin nice,
Give me leave to lie you by.
She said, *Thomas,* that were folly:
I pray thee, *Thomas,* let me be,
For I say, *Thomas,* sikerly,
You wil fordo al my beauty,
Lovely Lady, rue on me,
And I wil ever with you dwel;
Here my troth I plight to thee,
Whether it be in heaven or hel.
Man of mold, thou wilt me mar,
But yet you shal have al your wil,
But trow thou wel thou dost the wor,
For al my beauty thou wilt spil.
Down then lights that Lady bright,
Underneath the green wood spray,
As the story tells ful right,
Seven times by her he lay.
She said, *Thomas,* you like this play;
What bird in bough may deale with thee?
Thou marst me mickle all this day.
I pray thee, *Thomas,* let me be.
Thomas looked in that sted,
Upon that Lady that was so gay;
Her haire hung about her head,
Her eyes seemed out, that were so grey.
All her clothing then was away,
That he before saw in that stead,
One leg was black, the other grey,

And al her body like to lead.
Thomas cried out, alas,
Now is this a doleful sight,
Thou art now faded in the face,
That shone before as sun so bright.
Take leaf, *Thomas,* at sun and moon,
And leaf that grows upon the tree.
This twelvemonth shalt thou with me go,
Middle earth shalt thou not see.
Then kneeled *Thomas* on his knee,
To *Mary* milde he made his moan:
Lady, but you rue on me.
All my Games away be gone.
Alas, he said, and woe is me.
I trow my deeds wil doom care,
My soul, Jesus, I teach to thee,
Where ever away my body fare.
She led him in at Elden hil,
Underneath that dearn lee,
Where it was murk and way ful ill,
And ever in water to the knee.
The mountenance of daies three;
He heard but sweyings of the flood;
Alas, said *Thomas,* woe is me,
Almost, he said, I spil for food.
She led him to a faire arbour,
Where fruit was growing great plenty,
Pears and apples, ripe they were,
The dates and damase, the figs, and the winebury,
And nightingales building their nest,
The popinjay about can flie,
The thrustle sung, and had no rest;

And the Mavis tuning notes high,
He preassed to pul fruit with his hand,
As man for food, that was almost faint.
She said, *Thomas,* let it stand,
Or else the fiend she wil thee taint.
If you it pul, the sooth to say,
Thy soul goeth to the fiend of hel,
It cometh never out ere dooms day,
But ever in pain there to dwel.
Thomas soothly I thee hite,
Come lay thy head upon my knee,
And thou shalt see the fairest sight
That ever saw man of thy Countrie.
He did then as the Lady bade,
And laid his head upon her knee,
Her to please he was full glad;
Then said that Lady faire and free,
Seest thou not yonder faire way,
That lieth over yonder mountain/
That is the way, the sooth to say,
Where sinful souls are past their pain.
Seest thou now yonder other way,
That liggeth low under the rise,
That is the way, the sooth to say,
Unto the joyes of paradise.
Seest thou now yonder third way,
That liggeth over yonder green plain,
Yonder is the way, the sooth to say,
Where sinners passé both teen and train.
Seest thou now yonder fourth way,
That liggeth over yond foule fel,
That is the way of wellaway

Unto the burning fire of hel.
Seest thou now yonder faire castle,
That standeth high on yonder hil,
Of town and tower it beareth the bel,
In earth is men like there until;
Forsooth, *Thomas,* yonder is mine own
And the kings of this country;
Me were lever be hanged and drawn,
Then he wist that thou lay by me.
And whatsoever men to thee say,
I pray thee answer none but me;
My Lord is served at every messe
With thirty bold Barons and three;
I shal say nothing at the desse,
That I have wrest thy speech from thee.
Thomas looked in that sted,
And beheld that Lady so gay,
She was again also faire and good,
And also fresh on her palfrey.
Her Grey-hounds fed on Deers blood,
And her rachets by my faye,
She blew her horn with main and mood,
And to the castle took the way;
Into the hal rightly shae went,
Thomas followed at her hand.
Ladies came both faire and gent,
With courtesie to her knee land;
Harp and fiddle there they found,
The gittern and the psaltery,
Lute and rebeck, there con gong,
And al manner of minstrelsie,
The most freely, that *Thomas* thought

83

When he stood upon the floore,
Fifty harts in were brought,
That were fat, great, and stower,
Rachets lay lapping of their blood,
Cooks standing with dressing knife,
Breaking up the deare wood;
There was revel going rife,
Knights were dauncing by three and three;
There was revel game and play,
Lovely Ladies faire and free
Sate singing in ful rich array.
Thomas dwelled in that place
Somewhat more then yeers three,
So on a day it fel a case
That lonely Lady said so free,
Busk thee, *Thomas*, and go again,
For here thou maist no longer be,
Hie thee fast with might and main,
I shall thee bring to eldern tree.
Thomas said with heavy cheer,
Lovely Lady, let me here be,
For sikerly I have been here
But the space of daies three.
Forsooth, *Thomas,* I thee tel,
Thou hast been here three years and more,
But here shal you no longer dwel;
I shal thee tel a cause wherefore;
To morn of hel a foule fiend
Among these folks shal choole his fee,
Thou art a mickle man and hinde,
I trow ful wel he wil take thee.
For all the gold that may be

84

From heaven unto the worlds end,
Thou shalt never be betrayed for me;
Therefore I rede thee with me wend.
She brought him again to eldern tree,
Underneath the green wood spray,
In *Huntley* banks merry to be,
Where fowls sing both night and day.
Farewel *Thomas*, I wend my way;
I wil go over yonder bent so brown.
And here endeth the first fit, I say,
Of Sir *Thomas* of *Astledowne*

Thomas tries to detain the lady by asking for a token of
their meeting, and to be told some *ferly*;

Farewel *Thomas*, I wend my way,
I may no longer dwel with thee.
Then give me some token, Lady gay,
That I may say I spake with thee.
To harp or carp, whether you can,
Thomas, thou shalt have soothly.
He said, harping keep I none,
For tongue is chief of minstrelsie.
If thou wilt speak, and tales tell,
Thou shalt never leasing lye;
Whether thou walk by frith or fell,
I pray thee speak none ill by me.
Farewel *Thomas*, without any guile,
I may no longer abide with thee.
Lovely Lady, abide a while,
And some far lye tell thou me.
Thomas, hearken what I shall say,

85

When a tree rotten is dead,
The leaves faden and fallen away,
Fruit it beareth none in head,
All shal fade and fal away;
No marvel then if that fruit die,
And mickle bale shal after spray,
Where that blisse was wont to be.
Farewel, *Thomas*, I wend my way,
I may no longer stand with thee.
Lovely Lady, good and gay,
Tell me yet of some far lie.
What kinde far lie, *Thomas* good,
Should I thee tell? If thy will be,
Tell me, of the gentleblood
Who shal unthrive, and who shall thee;
Who shalbe king, who shalbe none,
And who shal weild the north country;
Who shal fly, who shalbe tane,
And where the battle, done shalbe........

It is immediately apparent that the language used in this version is from an earlier period. In comparison to the versions by Sir Water Scott and Robert Jamieson two hundred years later, not only is this version lengthier and more detailed, it also takes on a different perspective. The theme in all the versions is consistent; the first verse describing a scene which could be taken from any modern poem.

The opening lines are written in the first person and describe the scene as Thomas makes his way alone, in a westerly direction on *Huntley Banks* one morning in May - the time of the *Beltane*. The sound of birdsong fills the air, the mavis, thrush, jay and the wood-lark. The wording in the earlier version of the romance implies that Thomas is enchanted with the wonders of nature as he lies down to rest on Huntly Banks. However, his repose is interrupted as he catches a glimpse of a beautiful lady riding down the gentle slope of the north Eildon hill.

In the 1652 version, when Thomas first saw the lady riding down the side of the Eildon hill, his words were *"yonder is Mary of might that bore the child that died for me."* Rising from the spot where he lay, Thomas ran to meet the lady at the *Elden Tree;* the Elden, or Eildon tree being a solitary thorn tree beside a *waterfall* at B*ogle Burn (G*oblin Brook), at the foot of the *Eildon Hills.*

The beautiful *Lady* was *"riding over a faire long ley."* She is mounted on a *white horse* (a dapple grey), leading three greyhounds on a leash, and has seven *rachets (hunting dogs)* running by her side. He addresses her as 'The Queen of Heaven,' but she tells him *"No, I am the Queen of Fair Elfland, and I have come to visit thee,"* implying that she has not found him by chance. Thomas, bewitched by her beauty, tells the lady that he desires her body and plights his troth, whether it be in heaven or hell. Still in the first person, he goes on to describe in great detail the attire of the lady, her mount, and her accompanying dogs. The story continues by giving an account of the conversation between Thomas and the Fairy Queen, the intercourse, with its bizarre consequences, followed by the subsequent journey of Thomas and the Fairy Queen to her 'Otherworld' Kingdom.

According to all the manuscripts, *"seven times by her he*

lay," after which, the Fairy Queen says to Thomas *"man the lykes thy playe,"* and pleads with Thomas, *"I pray thee Thomas let me be"* otherwise all her beauty will be undone. When Thomas looks again at the Fairy Queen, she is transformed from her regal guise into a *"dullful syghte".* Thomas now regrets his actions and is fearful of the consequences. He implores the grotesque figure not to come near him, but to return from whence she came. The lady tells Thomas that she is not the fiend of hell, he has no need to fear her, but he must now leave middle earth for twelve months and travel with her to see *"the manner of her life."* She leads him under the Eildon hill and the journey begins.

What is described from this point onwards could either be construed as a visionary journey, or one of reality, the choice is left to the reader, however the image it conjures up is quite horrific. Thomas is astride a galloping steed, seated behind a grotesque creature, who, only minutes earlier had been the most beautiful woman he had ever seen, and is being taken on a journey into the unknown, a journey from which he may never return.

The steed gallops on in pitch blackness through deep water reaching to the knee; the only sound Thomas can hear is the roaring of the sea. In the versions of the ballad by Robert Jamieson and Sir Walter Scott, the water is replaced by blood *"It was mirk mirk night, and there was nae stern light, and they waded through red blude to the knee; for a' the blude that's shed on earth runs through the springs o' that countrie."* In Jamieson's version they wade through *red blood to the knee* for forty days and forty nights, whereas in the earlier versions, they travel for three days.

After travelling without rest, Thomas is faint for food and begs to be allowed to rest and eat. The creature leads Thomas to an orchard, which is filled with all manner of delicious fruits; the sound of birdsong fills the air. Thomas is about to pluck some fruit from a tree, when he is abruptly warned to leave it be. She tells him "*let it stand or else the fiend she wil thee taint.*" Thomas is then invited to lay his head upon her lap; this being consistent with similar folk-tales, after which four paths become visible. The various paths are then described to Thomas; one is the path to paradise, another, the path to wellaway, while the remaining two are the paths used by sinners. The path which they will take however is none of these, but a fifth path leading to a castle on the hilltop, which has become visible in the distance. His companion tells Thomas that this is her own country, and while in this place he must speak only to her, otherwise he will not be allowed to return to his own country.

When Thomas looks again at his companion, her beauty and wonderful attire have been restored. The lady tells Thomas she would rather be "*hanged and drawn*" than let her husband - the king - know they had been intimate.

Thomas and the lady enter the great hall of the castle, where the Queen is greeted with reverence. All manner of music and merriment is taking place "*There was revel going rife, Knights dauncing by three and three; there was revel game and play, Lovely Ladies faire and free sate singing in ful rich array.*" Cooks stand with *dressing knives* and begin to carve deer as if they were wood,

89

while the dogs lap the blood.

Thomas dwells in this place for many years, until one day the Queen tells him that he must return to his own country. Thomas pleads with his mistress to be allowed to stay with her a while longer, since he has only been *"here but the space of days three,"* to which she replies, *"Forsooth, Thomas, I thee tel, thou hast been here three years and more, but here shal you no longer dwel; I shal thee tel a cause wherefore; to morn of hel a foule fiend among these folk shal choole his fee, thou art a mickle man and hinde, I trow ful wel he wil take thee."* This stems from an ancient superstition that the Fairies sacrifice the soul of a mortal to the Devil every seven years. The lady saves him yet again from the *"fiend of hell."* She tells Thomas *"For all the gold that there may be, from heaven unto the worlds end, thou shalt never be betrayed for me."* The Queen urges Thomas to make haste, before transporting him back to the spot at the Eildon Tree where they first met.

Once safely back at the *Elden Tree,* the lady bids Thomas farewell. *"Farewell Thomas, I wend my way, I may no longer dwell with thee."* Thomas asks the *Fairy Queen* for a token as proof of their meeting, *"Then give me some token, Lady gay, that I may say I spake with thee."* The lady replies, *"To harp or carp, whether you can, Thomas, thou shalt have soothly."* To which Thomas replies, *"harping keep I none, for tongue is chief of minstrelsie."* In other words, the lady is giving Thomas the choice of excelling in music or verse; Thomas chooses to excel in poetry.

In Scott's version, the *Fairy Queen* plucks an apple from a tree and says, *"Take this for thy wages True Thomas, it*

will give ye a tongue which can never lie." To which
Thomas replies, *"my tongue is mine ain,"* True Thomas
said, *"a gudely gift ye wad gie me, I neither dought to
buy nor sell, at fair or tryst where I may be."* Before they
part at the *Eildon Tree* Thomas asks the lady to foretell
the future of his country;

> *"Tell me of this gentill blode,*
> *wha sall thrife and wha sall thee,*
> *Wha sall be kynge, wha sall be none,*
> *and wha sall welde this northe countre"?*

In Scott and Jamieson's versions of the ballad, the
prophecies are not included; however, they are included
as an integral part of the romance in the manuscripts of
the *Thornton, Cotton, Lansdowne,* and *Cambridge*
collections. The *Sloane* manuscript contains only the
prophecies, without the inclusion of the Romance.
The lady proceeds to tell Thomas of the many
catastrophic events which will occur in the years to
come. Included in these are; the ensuing *Wars between
Scotland and England,* the battle of *Duplin* and *Eldyn
Hill,* the *Death of Black Agnes of Dunbar,* and many
other events which have *yet to come.*

A list of some of the predictions;
The ruin of the Baliols in the struggle with David Bruce
The Battle of Halidon Hill
The Battle of Falkirk
The Battle of Bannockburn
*The death of Robert Bruce and usurpation of Edward
Baliol*

The Battle of Dupplin, and seizure of Perth
The Coronation of David Bruce and his invasion of England
David Bruce taken at Nevill's Cross near Durham
David Bruce a prisoner in London
Robert Stewart, King of Scotland
The Battle of Otterburn
Douglas slain and Horspur taken prisoner
The invasion of Scotland under Henry 1V
The English go to war with France
A Battle between Seton and the Sea
A Battle at Gladsmoor
The Lords who should come to that Battle
How a Bastard should come out of the West and become leader of all Britain
The last battle should be at Sandyford
The Bastard will die in the Holy Land,
Thomas asks the fate of 'Black Agnes.'

Thomas once again tries to detain the lady, but she insists that since her greyhounds are becoming impatient she must leave at once. She takes her leave, but makes a promise that they will meet again on *Huntley Bankys.*The wording is changed in the *popular edition* in Scott's minstrelsy to, "*Gin ye wad meet wi' me again, Gang tae the bonnie banks o' Fairnalie.*" The lady blows her horn to summon her dogs, then bids Thomas farewell, before riding off "*over yon bentis browne.*"

It has been suggested that the first verse, and subsequent verses written in the first person, are the original work of Thomas himself and were in circulation as soon as thirty years after his death.

92

The tale of Thomas's encounter with the *Fairy Queen* is similar to the popular folklore tales of Celtic, Irish, and Welsh mythology. Thomas would have knowledge of the ancient Celtic lore which was in vogue in his lifetime, and for many generations previous. Did Thomas simply recreate an old tale and assume the role of the main character? This would provide him with a credible excuse for his, otherwise unexplained, absence of seven years from Ercildune. However, it would not explain his gift of prophesy on his return.

This tale of fantasy sets Thomas apart from all the other famous seers, and has, for many centuries continued to capture the readers' imagination and curiosity. Apart from this legendary tale, there is no logical explanation for Thomas's incredibly accurate gift of prophesy. We are left with two choices, either to believe the documented accounts of the early writers, which allege that Thomas did indeed return after an absence of seven years with this gift, or to disregard their accounts and treat them merely as hocus- pocus.

It is written that the alchemists of old could mix potions so potent that they could induce hallucinations of spectres and such-like. However, I doubt very much that Thomas would indulge in such potions, or that the taking of such potions would account for Thomas's fantasy.

According to the ancient tales, which were passed down verbally through hundreds of generations, when Thomas returns to his home in Ercildoune he is carrying a harp, dressed in silk clothing, and wearing green velvet shoes.

In the 1652 version of the Romance, one line spoken by the Fairy Queen reads *"I ride over this livelong leye."* The ley is also mentioned in the earlier manuscripts, the word *ley* could be a shortened version of the word *ley-line*. The wording has been changed in the more recent versions - the word *ley* being omitted. The wording of the original Romance is of great importance to the credibility of the story, much of which has been lost during the *modernisation* of the more recent ballad versions.

In Neolithic times, the intersections of the *ley-lines* were considered to be places of *psychic* or *mystical energy*. Ley-lines can be located on routes coming down from a mountain peak; many monolithic standing stones can be found along such paths. *Alfred Watkins*, an amateur archaeologist, made an astonishing discovery in the early twentieth century. In his book called *'The Old Straight Track'*, which was published in *1921*, he explains that these geometric lines, which cover the whole of Western Europe, are straight lines joining one point of geographical interest to another. His theory being, that in the densely forested lands of our ancestors, the ley-lines would act as route markers. Alfred Watkins continued to work on the development of his theory until his death in 1935. Many *standing stones* and *megalithic monuments* are situated along these *ley-lines*. They are referred to in ancient folklore as *Fairy Paths;* the *Fairy Queen,* in the original words of the Romance, according to Thomas, *"Come riding over a faire long ley."*

The following is my version of the original ballad, complete with prophecies, transcribed into modern English.

94

The Ballad of Thomas the Rhymer

2011

Part 1

As I went west this day on earth,
Nature's wonders to behold,
On a morning in the month of May,
When fairy folk are brave and bold.

The sound of birdsong filled the glade;
The Mavis, Thrush and Jay.
I paused to rest beneath a bower,
In quiet repose, there I lay.

I saw a lady, noble and fair
Come riding down a fair long ley,
Astride a mount of dapple grey
To Huntly Bank, she made her way.

If I should sit 'til eternity,
To describe her fine array,
Or illustrate that wondrous sight,
No pen or ink could e'er portray.

Her stirrups were of crystal clear,
Her saddle carved from finest bone,
With diamonds and pearls from Orient grand,
Inlaid with rubies and precious stone.

Three silver bells hung either side
On a bridle of burnished gold,
Her girths were made from purest silk,
With buckles adorned with wealth untold.

Her eyes were of the clearest grey,
Golden hair round her face did hang.
Many an arrow was under her belt,
Awhile she whistled, awhile she sang.

She led three greyhounds on a leash,
Seven bloodhounds ran by her side,
A horn was slung around her neck:
As ever closer she did ride.

As Thomas viewed this splendid sight,
These words were said by he:
"Yonder is Mary who bore the child
That suffered and died on the cross for me."

Thomas thought his heart would break,
If he did not speak with that lady fair,
He ran like the wind to Eildon tree:
So the story goes, he met her there.

Underneath that greenwood spray,
Thomas knelt down low upon his knee,
Said, "Queen of heaven you surely are,
Today I fear you will rue on me."

She answered in a gentle tone;
"That name does not belong to me,

Although I am from another world,
I never took such high degree."

"Oh give me leave to lie by you,
Fair lady from afar."
"I pray thee Thomas let me be,
Or else, this day, you will me mar."

"Of this, you must be made aware,
If you must have your will,
And if my body you must take,
You will surely do me ill."

Down from her mount the lady came,
All underneath that greenwood spray,
According to the age-old tale,
Seven times by her he lay.

She said, "Thomas you must like this play,
What bird in bough may deal with thee?
Thou marrest me this earthly day,
I pray thee Thomas, let me be."

WhenThomas beheld that lady fair,
As he stood up with fear and fright,
One leg was black, the other grey,
Thomas said, "This is indeed a dullful sight.

You have now fallen from my grace,
Your fine attire, no more you wear,
The sun has faded from your face,
And grey now hangs your golden hair."

97

On every side Thomas looked about,
But nowhere could he flee,
Her eyes were out that once were grey,
The devil himself, she must surely be.

Thomas knelt to the Lord in prayer,
His heart was filled with fear and fright,
He begged the lady to leave him be,
And go forever from his sight.

She said, "Thomas, there is no need,
For the devil I am not,
For now I am full of great disease,
Many ills, now have I got.

Take one last look at sun and moon,
And leaves of green that grow on tree,
For twelve months you must go with me,
And middle earth no more you'll see."

Thomas knelt down on his knee,
Saying, "Lady but you rue on me,
O Queen of heaven, or of hell,
Alas," he said, and, "Woe is me.

My wicked deeds have cost me dear,
My soul I place in Jesus' care,
And in his hands I put my trust,
This cross, alone, I now must bear."

She led him in at Eildon hill,
Beneath that hidden lee,

Where shone no moon, neither sun, nor star,
But raging rivers came to the knee.

For forty days and forty nights,
He heard the roaring of the sea.
And nearly faint for want of food,
"Alas," he said, and, "Woe is me."

She led him to an orchard fair,
Where damson, apples, figs and pear,
Ripely hung on every tree,
The sound of birdsong filled the air.

As Thomas reached to pluck that fare,
For want of food, he was nearly faint,
The lady said, "Thomas, let it stand,
Or else the fiend, she will thee taint.

For if you choose to have your way
Your soul will go to the fires of hell,
There it will stay until doomsday,
In pain, forever, there to dwell.

Come lay your head upon my knee,
And truly you will see,
The fairest sight that any man saw,
That came from your country.

Can you see that distant road
That winds up high over yon mountain?
That is the way, truth to say,
Where sinful souls suffer their pain.

See you now that bonnie road,
That weaves about the valley low?
That is the way, truth to say,
Where seekers of paradise wish to go.

Can you see that even road,
That stretches over yon green plain?
That is the way, truth to say,
Where sinners pass, both teen and train.

Look yonder at that fourth way,
That lies over yon dark fell?
That is the way to purgatory,
And leads to the burning fires of hell.

Can you see that castle grand,
High on the hill, that stands serene?
Of town and tower it bears the bell,
Its like on earth you have never seen.

Thomas, that is my own land,
Where you and I this night must ride."
They mounted on her milk-white steed,
Her pack of hounds ran by their side.

"Thomas," the lady said,
"My king is lord of that country.
I would rather be hanged and drawn,
Than he found out you lay by me.

No matter what men say to you,
I ask that you answer none but me.

Whene'er my lord sits down to dine,
He is served by knights of thirty and three.

My lord, he is both stern and wise,
And he is king of that country,
And very soon he would jalouse,
You had your wicked way with me.

I will answer any spier,
And be your voice while here you be,
I'll tell the reason you are mute;
I took your speech at Eildon tree."

Thomas, still as stone he stood,
And he beheld that lady gay,
So proud she sat upon her steed,
Once more attired in fine array.

Thomas said, "Now, well is me,
This is indeed a happy day,
Now you are so fair and white,
Before, you were so black and grey."

My Lady, if it pleases you,
I ask that you will say,
If it was because of me,
You were so black and grey?

For truth to say, had it been so,
Certainly, I would thee tell,
I surely would have given my soul
To the devil himself and the fires of hell."

101

Her greyhounds fed on deer's blood,
Her ratchets round their feet did play,
With a blow of her horn, they all went forth,
To the castle grand, she led the way.

As she made her way to the castle hall,
Thomas followed close at hand,
Graceful ladies curtsied low,
Sweet music filled the castle grand.

Came forty harts just newly slain,
Hounds were lapping at their blood,
Cooks stood with dressing knives,
Chopping the deer like they were wood.

There was revel, game and minstrelsy,
Knights were dancing, three by three,
Harp and fiddle played along,
Gittern, lute, and psaltery.

Lovely ladies of high degree,
Sat dressed in rich array,
And sang as sweet as any lark
On a morning in the month of May.

There Thomas dwelled for many years,
In this land of quiet solace,
One day the Queen to Thomas said;
"Tomorrow you must leave this place.

Get ready Thomas, prepare to leave,
You may no longer dwell with me,

With speed and courage you must go,
I will take you back to Eildon tree."

"I have only been here but days three."
Thomas said, with heavy heart,
"Please let me stay with you a while,
It is too soon for us to part."

"Thomas if the truth be known,
You have been here three years and more,
But here you can no longer dwell,
I will tell you the reason wherefore.

Tomorrow a foul fiend of hell,
Among these folk will choose his fee,
You are one of noble blood,
I know full well he will choose thee.

For all the gold that there may be,
From heaven to the worlds end,
You will never be betrayed by me,
I urge you now with me to wend."

She brought him back to Eildon tree,
Underneath the greenwood spray,
Where the sound of singing can be heard,
On Huntly Banks, both night and day.

"Over yon high mountain grey, Thomas,
My falcon builds a nest,
A falcon is an Earl's prey,
Therefore no place is safe to rest.

103

Farewell, Thomas, I wend my way,
Over yonder moor so brown."
And here ends the first part,
Of Thomas of Ercildune.

Part two

"Farewell, Thomas, I wend my way,
I may no longer dwell with thee."
"Then give me a token, lady fair,
So I can prove you spoke with me."

"To harp or carp, wherever you go,
Thomas, you can choose truly,"
He replied, "Harping keep I none,
For tongue is chief of minstrelsy."

The lady then to Thomas said,
"Whenever you speak and tales tell,
I vow your tongue will never lie,
Whether you go by firth or fell.

Farewell Thomas, without any guile,
I pray you speak no evil of me,
We must now forever part,
I can no longer stay with thee."

"Then tell me some ferlie," Thomas says,
"Thomas, listen to what I say,
When a tree is rotten and dead,
The leaves will fade and fall away.

Of the Baliol's blood so shall it fall,
It shall be like the rotten tree,
The Comyns and the Barclays all,
The Russels and the Frissels free.

All shall fade and wilt away,
No wonder then if that fruit shall die,
And many fires will later spread,
Where joy and bliss, before did lie.

Thomas, I must surely go,
I can no longer stand with you."
"Now lovely lady fair and good,
Please tell me more of stories true."

"What other stories Thomas good,
Should I tell you of what will be?"
"Tell me of this, O gentle blood,
Who shall perish and prosper free?

Who will be king and who will not?
Who will rule this North Country?
Who shall flee, and who shall be caught?
And where will the battles be?"

"Thomas, of a battle, I will thee tell,
It will happen soon and blood will spill.
Nobles will meet at firth and fell,
And fiercly fight at Halidon Hill.

The Bruce's blood shall lose the fight,
The Breton's blood shall win that day,

Six thousand Scots shall there be slain-
Farewell Thomas, I wend my way.

To stay with you would irk me so,
But of a battle I will say,
That shall be done at Falkirk,
And all shall fade and fall away.

Banners will stand, long and long,
Heed my words with mode and main,
The Bruce's blood shall lose the fight,
Seven thousand Scots shall there be slain.

Thomas, no longer can I tarry here,
Farewell Thomas, I beg you, cease,
My rachets are coupled in three,
And my greyhounds have broken their leash.

I must go where the deer go two by two,
And run over yonder mountain far."
"God forbid," said Thomas, "You may go,
But first tell me of another war."

"Hold my greyhounds in your hand,
And tie my rachets to a tree,
I'll let the deer escape oe'er land,
In yonder wood a herd will be.

Of a battle I shall say,
That will make many a lady mourn,
It shall be fought between water and clay,
In a field near the bannocks burn.

106

Gentle knights will stumble and fall,
Because they will take a wicked way,
The Breton's blood will lose the fight,
The Bruce's blood shall win that day.

Six thousand English, great and small,
There shall be slain in just one day,
Then shall Scotland kingless stand,
Hark, and believe in what I say.

A young falcon of the same land,
To Kinghorn shall make his way,
And take with him many lords,
Who will come from the same country.

There will be lords and nobles grand,
Who will come by land and sea,
They will destroy the North Country,
And many widows there will be.

Ladies will say, Alas, and Welaway,
That ever that Royal blode was born,
That killed our lords there on the sand,
At Duplin moor upon the morn.

Lords will stand and think for long,
Where the water runs on red clay,
Between Duplin and the dale,
Eleven thousand Scots shall die that day.

They shall take a town of great renown,
That stands near the waters of the Tay,

107

Many fathers and sons shall be struck down,
With murderous strokes, they will be slain away.

When they have taken that walled town,
And every man has taken his chance,
Then shall the English leave this land,
And go forth to make war with France.

Then shall Scotland kingless stand,
Believe Thomas in what I say,
Then shall a young king be chosen,
One who cannot lead the way.

David, with care he shall begin,
And with care he will make his way,
Lords and Ladies great and small,
Shall come all dressed in rich array.

He will be crowned at the town of Scone,
Upon a very solemn day,
Bull's blood shall be sent from Rome,
To anoint the king, in a special way.

Into England he will ride,
East and west as lies that way,
And take a town of great pride,
Many knights will be slain that day.

Between a park and an abbey,
A palace, and a parish kirk,
There shall your king be taken away,
And cause him much grief and irk.

Wounded sore and tethered,
So that he cannot flee,
His nose shall run with so much blood,
It will trickle down unto his knee.

Betrayed then by a false brood,
Who will come from his own land,
Whether it be for evil or good,
He shall stay in the raven's hand.

The raven shall the goshawk win,
Though his feathers be black as jet,
And lead him straight to London town,
The goshawk there shall find his mate.

The raven shall shake his feathers,
Young lords he will take
With him from his own land,
And the king shall him master make.

He will go north and cause mayhem,
As power he hopes to gain,
And just as he gains that power,
On a ley-land he will be slain.

Then in Scotland shall be sold,
Possesions, many a one,
To pay a king's ransom,
But no end to it will come.

Then shall Scotland kingless stand,
Heed well what I say to thee,

Three lords from that same land,
Shall strive to build and use a tree.

He who shall build and use the tree,
Has no flight to fly away,
Robert Stewart shall be king,
And shall rule Scotland for many a day.

Then shall a chieftan rise,
And bear Scotland's flower with pride,
East and west as lies the way,
Into England he will ride.

There, beside a holy church,
Religious men shall burn in the fire,
Then they shall to the castle glide,
And face them there with wrath and ire.

On a land filled with water,
Between a well and a grey stane,
There shall two chieftans meet,
The man called Douglas will be slain.

The other chieftan will be taken,
The proud Bruce's blood thereby,
They will lead him to a worthy town,
And lock him up in castle high.

Farewell Thomas, I wend my way,
I must make haste over bent so brown,"
Here endeth the second part,
Of Thomas of Erseldown.

Part three

"Now lovely lady, gentle and kind,
Tell me more of what will be,
Of all the battles, how it will end,
And what will become of this North Country?"

"This world, Thomas, truth to tell,
Is naught but sorrow, grief and woe,
Of a battle I will tell to you,
That shall be done at Spynkarde Clough.

The Breton's blood shall fade and fall,
The Bruce's blood shall walk away,
Six thousand English great and small,
There shall be slain that night and day.

The rearward shall not fight,
Or take part in that sad deed,
But they shall make a journey,
Ten days without dreid.

And of a battle I will tell,
That shall be done soon after that spill,
Ferocious barons then will meet,
And fiercely fight at Pentland hill.

Between Edinburgh and Pentland,
There stands a hill of red clay,
There, eleven thousand Scots,
Shall be slain, that night and day.

They shall take a walled town,
Father and son shall be slain away,
Knights shall win that war,
By blows from swords, for ever and aye.

Once they have taken that walled town,
And each man has taken his chance,
The Breton's blood shall force them,
To go forth to the wars in France.

There they shall stay for many a day,
Thomas, I say, three years and more,
They will beat down castles and towers strong,
Then all shall return to their home shore.

Then shall they meet both fierce and strong,
Between Seton and the sea.
The English shall lie among the rocks,
While the others, at Berwick will be.

Of each side, both great and small,
Five thousand slain there will be,
Then no baner shall be raised,
Neither side shall win the gree.

Between Seton and the sea,
Ships shall stand upon the sand,
Tossing in the waves and foam,
Three years and more they will stand.

Steeds, masterless shall ride,
Over the mountains to and fro,

112

Their saddles on their backs shall hang,
Until girths, into flesh, will go.

There, shall they fight, all the day,
Until the sun sinks in the west,
No-one shall win in that field,
No side shall be the best.

They shall make a truce, and swear,
For three years as I understand,
Neither side shall the other harm,
Whether by water, or by land.

Between two St Mary's days,
When the days wax long,
Then shall they meet and baners raise,
On Gleds more, both fierce, and strong.

Gleds more that glads us all,
This is the beginning of our glee,
Great sorrow then shall fall,
Where rest and peace were want to be.

Wounded kings will fall that day,
And Thomas, surely they will die,
A raven shall come over the moor,
And after him a crow will fly.

He shall seek the moor and take no rest,
To find a cross made out of stone,
Over hill and dale, east and west,
But truth to tell, he will find none.

113

He shall light down where the cross should be,
And hold his nose up to the sky,
And drink of gentle blood and free,
Then ladies they will wail and cry.

Then a lord shall come to that war,
Who is full of great renown,
And on his baner he shall bear,
Trust me well, a red lion.

Another then shall come to that war,
He shall fight both fair and bold,
And on his baner shall he bear,
A ship, with an anchor of gold.

Then another shall come to that war,
Who is not known, neither north nor south,
And on his baner shall he bear,
A wolf, with a naked child in his mouth.

Then the fourth lord shall come to that war,
Who shall later, great masters make,
And on his baner shall he bear,
The bear.................
(words missing from all MSS.)

They shall fight that day with sword and shield,
Until the sun sinks in the west.
But no side shall win that day,
No matter which side has the best.

A bastard shall come out of the west,
He shall win supremacy,
He shall rule east and west,
And leader of all Britain shall he be.

Then he shall to England ride,
East and west it would seem,
And hold a parliament of mock pride,
Where none before had ever been.

And false laws he shall put down,
That ever was in that country,
Then true laws he shall bring,
And leader of all Britain shall he be.

The bastard shall be strong in power,
And all his foes he shall slay.
Of all the five kings lands,
None shall a bad word say.

This is the truth I thee tell,
Believe it well, every word.
Of the last battle I will say,
Shall be done at Sandyford.

Near Sandyford there is a brae,
And near the brae there is a well,
Near the well there is a stone,
And, by the stone, truth to tell,

There grows three oak trees,
The place is called Sandyford,

There, the last battle shall be done,
Thomas, believe my every word.

Remnerds and Cliffords, bold shall be,
In Bruce's land, three years and mair,
And bring down towers and castles high,
To do outrage they shall not spare.

The bastard shall die in the Holy Land,
Jesus Christ, who is so great,
Take his soul into your hand,
When he is dead, and laid in clay."

As she told this final tale,
The tears fell from her eyes so grey.
"Lovely Lady, do not weep,
Take your leave and go on your way."

"I weep not for myself, Thomas,
But believe me when I say,
For the ladies who will wed the lads,
When their lords have passed away.

The lads will have steeds in their stable,
A hawk to bear upon their hand,
A lovely lady in their bed;
They will inherit the lord's land.

Farewell, Thomas, I wend my way,
For all this day you will me mar."
"Lovely lady, please tell to me,
The fate of Black Agnes of Dunbar.

Why has she given me the war,
And put me in her prison deep?
For I would ever dwell with her,
And keep her ploughs and her sheep."

"Of Black Agnes will come no good,
To London she will be taken,
Her great wealth and worldly goods -
All shall be forsaken.

The noble offspring of her blood,
In a ditch shall he die,
Hounds of him shall take their food,
Her kin will fade thereby."

Then Thomas, a sorry man was he,
Tears fell, and his heart was sore,
"Now lovely lady, tell to me,
Shall we part for evermore?"

"No, Thomas, when you sit at Ercildune,
To Huntly Banks, then make your way,
There by the tree I'll wait for you,
And meet you there, if indeed I may.

I shall teach you wherever you go,
To act with price of courtesy,
For tongue is great and tongue is small,
And tongue is chief of minstrelsy."

Astride her steed, she blew her horn,
As Thomas stood by the Eildon tree,

117

To Helmsdale she made her way,
Thus departed the lady and he.

Of such a woman I wish were here,
That could tell me such ferlie,
Jesus, with his crown of thorns,
Bring us to your heaven on high.

Explicit prophecia thome de Arseldonne

•••••••••••••••••••••••••••

Chapter 6

Thome Rymor de Ercildune

Since virtually no factual information exists on the life of Thomas Learmont, the myths and legends, handed down orally from one generation to the next, have undoubtedly created an image of Thomas as a mere figure of fantasy. The lack of factual information only serves to fuel the myth and mystery of this mortal/otherworld individual. Therefore, it is little wonder that very few people believe in his existence, it is much easier to believe the fantasy; there are fewer unanswered questions that way. However, this *fantasy figure* was named "The Messiah of the Gaels," he was also held in high regard by his contemporaries, and his legend has been kept alive by writers and musicians from the period beginning after his disappearance until the present day. His vision and foresight was surreal, and the words in the Romance still strike a chord today. On reading the full version of the original ballad, it is still possible to relate to the words and feelings expressed therein. It could quite easily have been composed by a present day poet with a vivid imagination, yet it was composed nearly eight hundred years ago, in a period in history when the written word was a rare gift.

Two documents, each written in Latin, are the only credible evidence from which we can establish approximately the year of Thomas's birth, and the time when he was last seen alive in Ercildune. His date of birth has been given as early as 1210, yet other sources maintain it could have been much later, fifteen years later according to Hector Boece. Similarly, we have no way of ascertaining his age when he mysteriously disappeared from Ercildoune for seven years. However, according to the Romance and general opinion, he was in his youth; the year is thought to have been c1240. The only document bearing his signature, 'The Bemersyde Charter,' is not dated, but is thought to have been signed c1260. According to the estimated date of Thomas's birth, he would be approximately forty years old at this time. This document proves beyond doubt that Thomas did exist, and also certifies his place of residence. Had it not been for this document, and the later one c1299, whereby the Rhymer's home and lands were gifted to the monks of *Soltra* by his *son and heir*, the story of Thomas the Rhymer of Ercildune would most certainly be relegated solely to the annals of myth and fantasy.

It is apparent that Thomas was held in high regard in the community when the Bemerside Charter was witnessed, since the other signatories are, *Oliver, Abbot of Dryburgh, Hugh de Peresby Shirrif of Rokysburgh, Williem de Burundum,* and *Will de Hattely,* all local men of high esteem. The signature of Thomas on the charter is thus, *Thome Rymor de Ercildune.*

The terms of the charter binds *Petrus de Haga* of Bemersyde, and his heirs, to donate half a stone of wax annually to the Abbot of the convent at Melrose for the *Chapel of St.Cuthbert at Old Melrose;* the previous gift being ten salmon per year. The charter also proves that the Chapel of St Cuthbert, destroyed by the army of Kenneth MacAlpin in the ninth century, was still in existence albeit in a lesser capacity, at *'Old Melrose'* or Mailros, at the beginning of the thirteenth century. The following transcript of the charter of Petrus de Haga is taken from the *Cartulary of Melrose* MS. Harl. No. 3960, leaf 109a. It is also printed in the *Liber de Melros* (Bannatyne Club);

Carta Petre de Haga de dimidia petra cere.

Omnibus hoc scriptum uisuris uel audituris. Petrus de Haga dominus de Bemerside,

Salutem in domino. Noueritis voiuersi. Quod cum olim conuenissem cum viris religiosis Abbate et Conuentu de Melros pro quibusdam transgressionibus eisdem per me et meos iilatis quod eisdem singulis annis ego et heredes mei decem salmons quinque videlicet recentes et quinque veteres in perpetuum soluerimus; Tandem ijdem religiosi pietate ducti perpendorunt hoc esse in exheredacionem mei et heredum meorum. Mediantibus viris bonis consenciente et concedente Johanne filio et herede meo cum dictis Abbate et Conuentu taliter conueu. Scilicet quod ego et heredes [mei] tenemur et presenti scripto in perpetuum obligamur ipsis Abbate et Conuentui soluerc singulis annis dimidiam petram Cere bone et pacabilis ad Capellam sancti Cuthberti. de veteri Melros die beati Cuthberti. in quadragesima uel triginta denarios, sub pena triginta denariorum singulis mensibus soluendorum ad luminare dicte Capelle. quibus in solucione dicte Cere aut triginta denariorum predictorum fuerit cessatum post diem et terminum memoratos. Subiciendo me et heredes meos Jurrisdiccioni et potestati domini Episcopy sancti Andree. que pro tempore fuerit ut me et heredes meos per censuram ecclesiasticam qualemcum que posit compellere ad solucionem dicte Cere. aut triganta denariorum

121

predictorum vna cum pena si committatur. Renunciando pro me et heredibus meis in hoc facto omni accioni defencioni et accepcioni. et omni legume auxillio canonici et civilis beneficio restitucionis in integrum et omnibus aliis que michi et heredibus meis prodesse potuerunt in hoc facto et dictis Abbati et Conuentui obese quo minus solucio fieri valeat dicte cere, aut triganta denariorum predictorum una cum pena si committatur. In cuius rei testimonium presenti scripto sigillum meum, vna cum sigillo domini Oliueri tunc Abbatis de Driburgh est appensum. Testibus domino Oliuero Abbate de Driburgh domino Willelmo de Burudim, milite Hugone de Perisby, tunc vicecomite de Rokysburgh Willelmo de Hattely, Thome Rymor de Ercildune et aliis.

At this period in time, the use of surnames was not common practice, which would seem to discredit the theory that Thomas's surname was Rimour or Rymor. The introduction of the feudal system saw lands and titles being given to the nobility, to which Thomas and his ancestors apparently belonged. The fact that certain families were allowed to use the titles, '*de Ercildune,*' '*de Moreville,*' '*de Peresby,*' etc, was a reflection of their status in the local community, usually signifying they owned land and property in that community. An earlier charter bore the signature of '*Cospatricio de Ercildune,*' this being the signature of C*ospatrick, Earl of Dunbar;* '*de Ercildune*' signified that he was a landowner, with property in Ercildune.

According to the accounts of the early writers, Thomas was married with more than one child. Much has been written about *his son and heir* bequeathing the tower, including all the *Rhymer's Lands,* to the *Monks of Soltra,*

122

however, it is known that one of Thomas's sons married *Janet de Dairsie;* her family owned lands at *Dairsie* in Fife. Thomas supposedly had a sister named *Beatrix*. It is documented, in the introduction to Sir Tristrem by Sir Walter Scott, that Thomas married the daughter of Sir Richard Maitland - the *Knight of Thirlestane* - otherwise known as *Auld Maitland.* A poem with regard to *Auld Maitland* is included in *Scott's "Minstrelsy of the Scottish Border."* However, a story handed down from a native of Earlston in the late nineteenth century, namely James Aikenhead, tells that Thomas and Lady Bethoc were married at Fail Monastery. The story goes on to say that they had a son who later owned the farm and lands at Huntshaw, on the outskirts of the village of Ercildune.

Thomas was in his youth when, following the death of his Father in 1248, a very young King Alexander III succeeded to the Scottish throne. King Alexander's residence was at *Roxburgh Castle,* a mere eight miles from the home of Thomas in Ercildune. According to information, this being contained in a chap-book writen by Allan Boyd in the seventeenth century, Thomas was knighted in 1248 by King Alexander III. In 1248, Alexander was only eight years old, so it would seem highly unlikely that this was the case. Another source, namely *Nisbet (the herald),* also affirmed Thomas's knighthood, and in his novel *"True Thomas",* Nigel Tranter writes that Thomas was knighted by King Alexander III at Roxburgh castle in the aftermath of the Battle of Largs in 1263. However, I have found no written evidence to corroborate the theory that Thomas was involved in the Battle of Largs, or that Thomas received a knighthood.

Although he was known by the titles of "Sir Thomas," and "Laird Learmonth," it can only be assumed that he inherited the title from his father. John Geddie wrote in his book, entitled *The Rhymour and his Rhymes,*' that he doubted if Thomas was a knight, or that he had received a Knighthood, saying *"he wielded a far greater weapon than a sword."*

Local tradition tells that Thomas was a confidante of King Alexander III, and as such was employed by him to collect rent from lands far and wide within Scotland. It is a known fact that Thomas travelled to the furthest extremities of mainland Scotland, the proof being the various prophecies relating to the families of note in the north east of Scotland, along with tales of Thomas attending horse-fairs in the Western Isles. A *'Rhymer's Stane'* once stood near Inverugie; this stone was built into St. Fergus' church in 1763. In Gaelic folklore, Thomas is known as *mac na mna mairbh,* which means *son of the dead woman.* One story tells that his mother died during childbirth and Thomas was cut out from her dead body. Another story tells that a cry was heard from the tomb after the burial of his mother, upon the tomb being reopened, Thomas was found in the coffin.

The composition of *Sir Tristrem,* which I have detailed in a later chapter, is the work of a writer with imagination, a sense of humour, and a literary capacity far ahead of his time. Sir Walter Scott suggests that the Romance of Sir Tristrem was composed by Thomas c1250. Although Thomas is credited with having composed the metrical romance of Sir Tristrem, or at least having edited the tale, the contrast between the two major literary works attributed to Thomas is immense. The romance of Sir

124

Tristrem, although serious in its content, borders on being farcical; the same cannot be said for the *Romance of Thomas the Rhymer*.

It has been suggested that Thomas may have been employed as a bard at the court of King Alexander III at Roxburgh Castle, or by the Earl of Dunbar when he entertained his guests at his castle in the Earls Toun. The prophets and bards, like the minstrels, were employed by the reigning monarch to entertain at their courts. They were also consulted by the aristocracy on everyday matters of importance. Among other things, they were regarded as the *met-office* of their time, their forecast for the impending weather was believed without question. The predictions of the prophets were frequently used in forward-planning and battle strategy, their *visions* and *forebodings* held in the highest regard. They were a world apart from the fortune-tellers of today, but similarly, their foresight stemmed from long held traditions handed down from previous generations. This was a time before scientific explanations held the answer to every question; a time when superstitions and ancient beliefs prevailed over reason. Towards the end of his life, the ambiguous ramblings of Thomas were beginning to make sense, his reliablity as a prophet was becoming ever more credible. His fame and legend continued to grow, as more of his prophecies came true, and continued to do so for many centuries.

Although the lowland area of Scotland was relatively peaceful at this time, there was continued aggression from the Norse *Vikings* on the north and west coasts of Scotland.

In 1251, King Alexander III married Margaret, daughter

of King Henry III of England. They had two sons, David and Alexander, and a daughter, also named Margaret. King Alexander III was pre-deceased by his wife and three children, all of whom died within ten years of each other. His wife died in 1275, followed by their son David in 1281, their second son Alexander died in 1284. King Alexander's daughter died in 1283, soon after giving birth to a daughter, also named Margaret. King Alexander's granddaughter, Margaret, would later become known as the *'Maid of Norway'*.

In October 1263, King Haakon 1V of Norway came with a fleet of ships to invade Scotland. Unfortunately for the Viking fleet, a severe storm was raging, with the result, five of their longships were forced to come ashore near the township of Largs, where they became stranded. King Haakon's army came ashore to rescue the grounded ships, and they were confronted by the Scots. The battle which ensued is known as the *'Battle of Largs,'* it took place on October 2nd, 1263. The Scots army, led by King Alexander III, comprised of three columns. The left wing, which was led by the *Earl of Dunbar,* consisted of knights from the *Lothians* and the *Merse,* Thomas's territory; however, the name of Thomas does not appear in any of the historical accounts of the Battle of Largs.

A storm forced both sides to retreat, rendering the result of the battle inconclusive. The Scots army retreated inland, while King Haakon and his men retreated to the safety of the main fleet. Due to the severity of the storm, his longships began to head for home. It was, however, a turning point in Scotland's history as fate intervened; King Haakon 1V died the same year. King Alexander III negotiated with Haakon's son and successor, *Magnus V,* who accepted King Alexander's offer to buy back the Western Islands and the Isle of Man. Following the *Treaty of Perth* in 1266, the Western Isles once again belonged to Scotland. Only the northernmost islands of Orkney and Shetland continued to be under Norse rule at this time.

Following the *Battle of Largs,* King Alexander III gave the title of *'Lord of the Isles'* to the Clan MacDonald. The two countries of Scotland and Norway were later united when King Alexander's daughter Margaret, married King Eric II of Norway in 1281; however, Margaret died two years later. Following the death of his wife and children, King Alexander III was left without an heir. He was pressurised into considering remarriage in order to produce an heir to the throne, which, it was hoped, would safeguard the future of Scotland.

King Alexander III second marriage was to *Yolande,* daughter of *Robert 1V, Count de Dreux* of France. The wedding ceremony was held at *Jedburgh Abbey.* In the evening, during the masked ball, the celebrations were interrupted by a ghostly figure appearing in the midst of the revellers, then disappearing as quickly as it had come; a warning perhaps of the impending disaster which would follow within six months. King Alexander III was said to be rather promiscuous during his lifetime. He (allegedly), had numerous intimate liaisons with ladies from a variety of social classes, ranging from countesses to prostitutes. He was, nevertheless, one of Scotland's great monarchs; his untimely death had a profound effect on Thomas as an individual, and on Scotland as a whole.

Alysandyr owre kyng wes dede
That Scotlande led in luve and le,

For many years after the first *War of Independence* the abbeys were desecrated on a regular basis. The abbeys were used as teaching institutions, much the same as the high schools and colleges of today. It is noted in the abbey charters that the sons of Lairds' and Barons' were educated at the cloister schools. Thomas, being the son of *Laird of Ercildune,* would undoubtedly receive his education at one of the local abbey's school; where much of the literary work of the period was kept. From the period of the reign of King Edward II in 1322, continuing for 250 years, the abbeys were under constant attacks from the English. It is possible that the literary works, which were kept within the abbeys, were taken south during these raids. The works of Thomas of Ercildune were highly acclaimed south of the border as early as thirty years after his disappearance.

....

Chapter 7

Sir Tristrem

Thomas the Rhymer is best remembered as the rather mysterious figure who returned to mortal earth with the gift of prophecy, allegedly bestowed on him by the *Fairy Queen*. However the masterpiece, which has been generally accepted as being the work of Thomas, is undoubtedly his edition of the composition of the *Metrical Romance* of *Sir Tristrem*.

Sir Tristrem is a medieval tale of *glamourie* and *chivalrie*, which focuses on the escapades of a knight from the period of the court of King Arthur. Sir Tristrem, unlike Sir Tristan, was not one of King Arthur's knights, but a warrior from the same era, renowned for his adventures. His courage and bravado sees him defeating giants and dragons, while in contrast, he is also a gifted poet and musician, Sir Tristrem is also proficient in the game of chess.

Tristrem is represented as being a native of *Cornwall;* these people being of the *Celtic* race, as were the natives of *Wales, Ireland,* and *Brittany.* The story has parallels with the story of *Sir Tristan,* who was one of King Arthur's knights. Sir Walter Scott credited Thomas with having composed the romance of Sir Tristrem c1250, based on tales handed down orally from the ancient *Cumbric* tribes of lowland Scotland. However, there are others who disagree with Sir Walter Scott's theory.

The names of the characters in 'Sir Tristrem' are of British origin; Tristrem, Ysonde or Yssylt, Morgan, Roland, Riis, Urgan, Ganhardin and Brengwain.

129

The story centres on the undying, eternal love and passion which engulfs *Sir Tristrem* and *Ysonde*. The events which lead to this situation are humorous, with a love potion being taken in error by Tristrem and Ysonde. From this moment on, despite their best intentions to do otherwise, they are incapable of staying apart. Ysonde, the daughter of an Irish King and Queen, is betrothed to King Mark of Cornwall, who also happens to be Sir Tristrem's uncle. Tristrem is sent to Ireland by his uncle to escort the Princess back to Cornwall for the wedding. The ensuing adventures, which include, a murder plot, betrayal, passion, and fantasy, invoke the reader's sympathy for the frequent betrayal of King Mark - Ysonde's long-suffering and besotted husband.

After many adventures, in which the lovers are separated, reunited and separated once more, Sir Tristrem is fatally wounded. In the throes of death, he longs to see Ysonde for the last time before his life expires. Ysonde appears at last to declare her undying love for Tristrem and dies in his arms; the lovers are now united forever.

"Out of the tomb of Tristrem sprung a fair eglantine & twisted around the tomb of Ysonde. Three times King Mark ordered it to be cut, but each time it had regrown and resumed its beauty."

The romance was originally written in *Quante Inglis* (quaint English), or Scots, this being one of the languages used in the region known as Strathclyde. At this period in time the language used in England was influenced by Norman-French. By 1385, following the reign of King Edward III, according to *Trevisa "in all the grammar scoles of England, children leveth French, and*

130

construeth and lerneth English."
The English Romances of the time were written in
French, the minstrels did not translate them into
English. In other words, at this time in history, the
English wrote in French, the Scots wrote in English. The
earliest version of the alleged composition of Sir Tristrem
by Thomas of Ercildune is thought to have been in print
around the beginning of the fourteenth century.
According to Robert Mannying, the intricate formation of
the stanzas enhances its genius; the formation is as
follows;

The 1st 3rd 5th &7th line must rhyme,
The 2nd 4th 6th 8th & 10th line must rhyme,
The 9th & 11th line must correspond.

Similar to the *Ballad of Thomas the Rhymer,* the
romance comprises of three fyttes, or cantos. The first
fytte contains one hundred and two stanzas, the second
fytte one hundred and seven, with ninety five in the
third fytte. Each stanza is made up of eleven lines; the
peculiar structure of the stanzas making recitation
difficult. *Robert Mannying de Brunne,* who was born
c1275, excused his own style of composition in
comparison to the ambitious and ornate style of
Thomas, saying that Thomas *"wrote for pride (fame) and
for nobles, and not for the ignorant hearers of his* own
audience."
In an English Chronicle, c1330, Robert Mannying
credits Thomas with being *"The author of an
incomparable romance on the story of Sir Tristrem."*

131

The first lines from an excerpt of one of Mannying's poems;

I see in song, in sedgeyng tale,
Of Ercildoun, and of Kendale.
Now thame says as thame wroght,
And in thare saying it seems nocht.
That thou may here in Sir Tristrem.

He also wrote *"If Minstrel could recite as Thomas composed."* He opined that the composition of Sir Tristrem was portrayed with such ornate language and in such intricate style, that no ordinary minstrel could do it justice during recitation.

The Auchinleck MS, in which the version of Sir Tristrem appears, is thought to date from c1330; approximately eighty years after the date of the composition attributed to Thomas. Sir Walter Scott believed that a minstrel of the period would most likely have learned the words from Thomas himself, and the compiler of the MS printed it thereafter. He also concludes that the words are mainly from the fourteenth century, but the *'turn of phrase'* is from an earlier period.

The minstrels of the period told tales with a similar theme, which would include feats of chivalry, a lion, or dragon, and the hero ultimately being rewarded with the eternal love of his mistress. They began with the *Romances* of Thomas's time, and continued until the tales of chivalry became outdated in the fifteeth century. The complicated stanzas were a characteristic of early Scottish poetry, being replaced by simple verse structure of short rhyming couplet. The narrator initially does not profess to be Thomas, but tells the tale on his behalf.

132

The first stanza;

"I was at Erpeldoune,
Wip Tomas spak y pare,
pere herd y rede in roune
Who tristrem gat & bare
Who was king wip croun
& who him fostered zare
& who was bold baroun
As psir elders ware
bi zere
Tomas telles in toun
Pis auentours as pai ware."

Thomas is discussed in this verse, and subsequent verses throughout the poem, in the third person, similar to the Ballad of Thomas the Rhymer. This is not necessarily an indication that the work is by someone else, since poets of the period commonly quoted their own name to lay claim to their works. Thomas's edition of *Sir Tristrem* is thought to be one of the earliest documented pieces of literature written in *Inglis,* as opposed to *Latin, French,* or *Gaelic,* to come from Scotland.

Prior to the Norman Conquest in 1066, the language of England was Anglo-Saxon, following this, the language was Norman/French. From this time until the period of Chaucer, who lived between 1343 and 1400, all the literary works in England were written in *French.* It is written that Chaucer believed Thomas to be the composer of Sir Tristrem, since the use of alliteration, and the composition of *Gestes,* or *Romances* were

133

peculiar traits of the northern poets of the time, another reason being, there were no French words in the Romance. Geoffrey Chaucer lived a relatively short time after Thomas; he was responsible for developing the use of *Middle English* as the language of England. Prior to this, Latin and French were the languages in common use.

The manuscript containing *Sir Tristrem* was thought to be lost, until its recovery in 1740. The MS was presented to the *Faculty* by *Alexander Boswell of Auchinleck*, a Lord of Session, who was otherwise known as Lord Auchinleck.

The entire manuscript, containing over fifty individual manuscripts of old English romances, and other works dating back to the fourteenth century, was discovered in the Advocates' Library in London by the antiquarian known as *Ritson*. It was gifted to the Library of Edinburgh, now known as the *National Library of Scotland,* in 1774. The manuscript consists of 333 leaves, and contains forty two pieces of poetry. Some are only fragmented copies, while others are of substantial length. The manuscript is written on parchment in neat handwriting and dates from the early fourteenth century.

Sir Walter Scott originally intented to include *Sir Tristrem* in his *'Minstrelsy of the Scottish Border,'* instead he edited the text of Sir Tristrem from the *Auchinleck Manuscript* and published it in a separate book in 1804.

It was later edited for *'The Scottish Text Society'* by *Mr G.P. McNeil,* and published in the volume for 1886. The version of Sir Tristrem contained in the Auchinleck manuscript is thought to be of a *southern dialect,* which has been transcribed from a *northern original.* The romance of *Sir Tristrem* can be found on the website of *The National Library of Scotland,* under the title *The Auchinleck Manuscript.*

A compilation of a prose romance by *Rusticean de Puise,* analysed by Monsieur de Tressan on the subject of *Sir Tristrem,* can in no way compare to the edition in the Auchinleck Manuscript. Although there are similarities in the content, the Auchinleck version is of a much earlier date. There was, supposedly, an Icelandic version of Sir Tristrem of a more ancient date, the *Quante Inglis* version is said to be very similar to the *Icelandic* version. The Scandinavian influence was still prevalent in lowland Scotland during the lifetime of Thomas.

Chretien de Troyes, composer of many French romances, wrote the prose *'Sir Tristan'* around 1170, he also wrote many other romances with connections to the period of King Arthur. Included in these are *Chevalier de la Charrette* (History of Lancelot) *Le Chevalier a Lion* (Ywain and Gawain) and *Le Chevalier a l' Epee* (The Knight and the Sword). Thomas of Brittany, c1220, was also considered to be the composer of a similar poem. Plagiarism was commonplace among the minstrels of the time, so the true source of its origins may never be ascertained. The story of Tristan and Yssilt formed the basis of a romance in *Armorican* poems. *Armorica, or Ermonie,* was the setting for many of the exploits of Sir Tristrem, and ultimately the place of his death. *Ar-mon* is defined as the country by the sea, *Ermonie* in Caernarvon, is the land opposite to *Mona. Monsieur de la Rue* claimed that the theme for *'Chevrefeuille,'* the eleventh lay of *Mademoiselle Marie,* stemmed from an

135

incident during an intimate relationship between *Tristan* and the wife of *King Mare*. *Mademoiselle Marie* was a prominent French writer of the mid twelfth century, drawing her material from *Armorica*. A modernised prose romance of Sir Tristrem was published in Paris in 1554 by Jean Maugin dit L' Angevin.

Trystan (the tumultuous), son of *Tallwz*, was a celebrated chieftain who flourished in the sixth century. According to *Mr Owen* (author of the Welch Dictionary), the scene was set in his native Cornwall; Trystan belonging to the *Celtic* race. After being driven from their land by the *Saxons* in the ninth century, the *Cumbric* tribes were forced to retreat and seek refuge in Cornwall and Brittany. Cornwall yielded to the *Saxons* between 927AD and 941AD. *Armorica*, in Brittany, was the place from where the *Cumbric* tribes of old had migrated to these shores, and to where they returned. It is believed that the origin of the tale was first taken to France from Britain, before finding its way back to Britain in the thirteenth century.

In their ballads, the *Druid* bards lamented on the struggles of the *Celtic Britons* against the tyranny of the invading *Saxons,* these ballads were popular in Europe in the middle ages. The poems, which embellished the Arthurian legends, most probably took root in *Armorica,* the quiet retreat for *Britons* exiled from the lowlands of Scotland, before coming full circle to their source. The legend of King Arthur was one of the earliest recorded in the history of French poetry.

Tristran mab Tullwich was a disciple of *Merlin,* a name familiar to Thomas, and a former inhabitant of the locality associated with King Arthur. *Monsieur Le*

Compte De Tressan concluded that the Norman *Trouveurs* (minstrels), who were the composers of the tales of King Arthur, wrote not for the amusement of the French, but for the Anglo-Norman monarchs of England. The abridged version of *Sir Tristrem* is the first article in his *Corps d'extracts de Romans de Chevalerie*.

Arthurian legend was popular in the French courts for many years; however, after the *Wars of Independence,* the material which was *in vogue* was of the new heroes. As a consequence of this, the Arthurian legend became unfashionable and subsequently was banished from the courts of France. The first Scottish epics, namely *The Brus,* by Barbour in 1375, and *The Wallace,* by Henry the Minstrel, c1460, were the new legends of the time, with the result the Arthurian legends were not preserved in the *Ballad Poetry* of Scotland. The *Anglo-Saxons* south of the border retained and embellished the theme of King Arthur, with stories such as *The Boy and the Mantle, Sir Lancelot Du Lake,* and *The Legend of King Arthur.*

One of the principle figures in Arthurian legend is *Sir Gawain.* There is a connection between Gawain and the lowlands of Scotland, both historically and mythologically. Gawain was the eldest son of *Loth,* King of the Lothians, and *Anna,* half sister of *King Arthur.* He was also a friend of *Merlin* (the wild); legend states that while searching for Merlin in the forest of *Brocelionde,* Gawain heard the voice of Merlin telling him to seek for him no more among living men. *Geoffrey of Monmouth* compiled the true exploits of King Arthur and his followers, as conveyed to him by *Walter*, Archdeacon of Oxford.

137

Whether Thomas actually composed the romance of Sir Tristrem, or took the idea from an earlier version and composed it in his own style, is of little consequence, it does not detract from the genius of the composer, or the composition itself. No matter the source of the tales of old, whether traditional, or transcribed from similar French tales, they embraced the culture, and history of the ancient European Celtic tribes.

....

The Inscribed Plaque on one of the remaining
two walls of The Rhymer's Tower.

The Rhymer's Tower 2011.

The "Rhymer's Stone" near the site of the
"Eidon Tree" Melrose. Erected in 1921 and re-erected
at this spot in 1970, however,
not the original stone or location.

Beware a fair lady on a grey horse

Legend tells how Thomas the Rhymer fell asleep near here, beneath a true thorn on the side of the Eildon Hills. He woke to see a shining lady on a dappled grey horse - the Queen of the Fairies. She entranced him and led him away to Fairyland. He stayed there for what seemed to be three days, but was in fact seven years. When he left she gave him the gift of speaking the truth, and told him many prophecies of great events in Scotland's history.

Thomas became famous both as a poet and as someone who knew the future. Just up the road you can check how accurate he was. He prophesied that one day 'a bridge over Tweed would be visible from the Eildon tree'. If you have sharp eyes you can see whether this has come true!

And if you sit down to rest - take care. The Fairy Queen promised Thomas she would return to the Eildon tree; perhaps this time you will fall under her spell.

The Interpretation Panel at Rhymer's Stone
Viewpoint near Melrose.
"Design by Heather Ross"

The Stone Tablet - at the Rhymer's Stone viewpoint near Melrose inscribed with the words of the prophecy relating to a bridge over the river Tweed.

Leaderfoot Viaduct
One of the three bridges mentioned in Thomas's prophecy

Scott's View

The grassy mound in the forefront of the picture is the site of the former monastery of Mailros, still known today as "Old Melrose"

The Rhymer's Tower c1910

Chapter 8

The Prophecies of Thomas the Rhymer

Following his encounter with *The Queen of Fair Elfland,* or his otherwise unexplained absence of seven years, Thomas returned to his home in Ercildoune. Apparently he could offer no rational explanation for his long absence, but his strange apparel must have caused a fair amount of gossip among the villagers. He resumed his life in the village as if he had been gone only a few days, however, according to all accounts, he began to utter his rhyming prophecies almost immediately. Since his words made little sense at the time, his ramblings would be largely ignored. According to the *Romance,* before they parted at the *Eildon Tree,* Thomas asked the *Fairy Queen* to tell him what the future held for his beloved country. She told him in great detail of the ensuing wars, which country would win the battles, who would be slain, and which country would eventually "*win the gree.*"

Thomas then began to relate these prophecies, exactly as he heard them spoken by the Fairy Queen. From these early words, first spoken by Thomas in the mid thirteenth century, the prophecies have come down to us in various forms over a period of eight hundred years. Some have retained the original words from the ancient *Quante Inglis* text, while others have been translated into a more modern form of the current English language. The earliest hand-written prophecies are contained in the following manuscripts, the *Sloan 2578,* and the *Lansdowne 792;* some can also be found in the

Rawlinson C. 258.
Over the centuries, many writers have copied the prophecies from one publication to another, corrupting them in the process. The original prophecies do not relate to people by name, but by their crests, and coat of arms;

> *That three ships and a shield*
> *That day shall keep the field;*
> *And be the antelope's beild.*

The *three ships and a field* are incorporated into the arms of the *Duke of Argyll*. Many of the words would not be understood by the English transcribers of the early fourteenth century, and therefore have been wrongly interpreted. For example, *beild* (meaning shelter), is a word used mainly in the old Scots language. One edition, believed to be written in the early fifteenth century, has certainly been altered and interpolated, since the prophecies are not in the correct chronological order. Dr. Murray concluded that the prophecies listed in this manuscript are a *"melange of early traditional prophecies."*

In some of the manuscripts, the names of people and the results of battles have been wrongly interpreted by the scribes, or have been altered and corrupted by the transcriber.

The first of the prophecies undoubtedly attributed to Thomas occurred in his lifetime. The account of this prophecy was contained in the *Scotichronicon* of Walter Bower, who wrote c1430. The Scotichronicon of Walter Bower is a continuation of the earlier chronicles written

140

by historian John of Fordun, who lived in the mid fourteenth century.

The prophecy centres on two of the people with whom Thomas had a close affinity, namely King Alexander III and Patrick III (7th Earl of Dunbar), the year was 1286.

According to the account, the prophecy was uttered one night as Thomas and Patrick were feasting at the castle of the Earl in Ercildune (the Earl's Toun), the date was 19th March 1286. A fierce storm was raging that night when Patrick asked Thomas, with a note of derision, what the following day would bring. He replied:

"Alas, for tomorrow, a day of calamity and misery! Before the twelfth hour, shall be heard a blast so vehement that it shall exceed all those that have that have yet been heard in Scotland: a blast which shall strike the nations with amazement. Shall confound those who hear it, shall humble what is lofty, and what is unbending shall level to the ground."

An account by *Bellenden* is written in an older style *"It is said ye day afore ye kingis deith, the Erle of Merche demandit anw propheir namit Thomas Rimour, otherwayis namit Ersiltoun, quhat weddirsuld be on ye morrow. To quhome answerit this Thomas, that on the morrow afore noon, sall blaw the greatest wynd that euir was herd afore in Scotland. On ye morrow, quhen it was neir noun, ye lift appering loune but only din or tempest, yr Erle sent for this propheit and repreuit hym that he pronosticat sie wynd to be and na appperance yairof. Yis Thomas maid litel answer, bot said, noun is not zit gane. And incontinent ane man come to the zet schawing yt the king was slain. Yan said ye propheit, Zone is the wynd yat sall blaw to ye gretcalamite and trouble of all*

141

Scotland. Yis Thomas was ane man of gret admiration to the people and schew sindry thingis as they fell. Howbeit yai wer ay hyd vnder obscure wordis"?
Another version of the same prophecy;

"Woe to the morrow,
A day of dule and sorrow,
On the morrow, afore noun,
Sall blow the gretest wynd
that ever was hard before in Scotland."

The following day broke calm and clear, so the Earl of Dunbar summoned Thomas to the castle to chastise him for falsely predicting a great wind, to which Thomas allegedly replied *"noun is not yet gane."* At that very moment a messenger arrived at the castle gates to break the terrible news that the *"King was slain."* Thomas was then reported to say *"yon is the wynd that sall blaw to the gret calamity and trouble of Scotland."* The *Royal Herald,* who came to announce the news of the king's death, was said to have announced his arrival by sounding his bugle at the *'Corse-hill,"* which is on the road between Huntshaw and Earlston. Huntshaw is a farm just one mile to the north of Earlston; the spot where the herald allegedly sounded his bugle-blast was known for many years as the *Bugle Knowe.*
On the same evening that Thomas, Earl Patrick and their friends had been merry-making, so too had King Alexander III, at Edinburgh Castle. According to accounts, King Alexander had planned to spend the night at the castle; however, he changed his mind, and against the advice of his aides, and despite the ferocity

142

of the storm, decided to ride back to his castle in Fife to be with his young wife *Queen Yolande*. The young Queen was supposedly pregnant with their first child; the heir to the Scottish throne. Despite the concerns of his escorts, and the refusal of the ferryman to row them across the river Forth, the King eventually got his way. After a hazardous crossing of the *Firth of Forth*, the cavalcade rode into the *Kingdom of Fife*, however, just as they were nearing King Alexander's castle, disaster struck. The escorts became separated from the King, and as he negotiated a rocky cliff path on the outskirts of Kinghorn, King Alexander's horse stumbled and he was thrown from his mount. King Alexander's neck was broken in the fall; it was not until the next morning at daybreak that his body was found at the bottom of the cliff path.

As the catastrophic news of the King's death slowly filtered around the country, the realisation of the dreadful consequences slowly dawned on the Scottish population; the King's death left Scotland without a monarch. The residents of the small hamlet of Ercildune would be equally astounded by the fact that *Thomas of Ercildune* predicted the event.

From that day forth, *Thomas of Ercildune* was established as a credible prophet, however, the future for Thomas, his fellow countrymen, and the nation of Scotland, looked bleak. Since there was no rightful heir to the Scottish throne, Scotland's monarchy effectively ceased to exist; the consequences of this ultimately led to the beginning of the first Scottish *War of Independence*.

Within ten years of King Alexander's death, in the year

143

1296, King Edward I of England and his army were rampaging through the border towns, slaughtering man, woman and child. William Wallace first took arms against the invading army of King Edward 1 that same year.

It is apparent, from documented quotes by *Blind Harry*, that Thomas was still alive in 1297. The young *William Wallace* (Uilleam Uallas) was making a name for himself as a rebel and patriot and came to the attention of Thomas of Ercildoune. The following is an account by the biographer of William Wallace, namely, Henry the Minstrel, otherwise known as *Blind Harry*.

After many skirmishes with English soldiers, William Wallace killed the English Sheriff of Lanark in 1297. The reason for this is unclear, it has been suggested that it was in retaliation for the murder of William's wife by English soldiers, but this has not been proven. Whatever the reason, it was regarded as a crime against the King of England, a crime punishable by death. Since William Wallace was fast gaining a reputation for instigating a rebellion against the invading English soldiers, King Edward I gave orders for him to be captured on sight. After slaying Lord Percie's Steward, William was captured by the English soldiers and imprisoned at Ayr. After suffering much torture at the hands of his captors, William developed dysentery and succumbed to a fever. His jailor found William comatose and assumed, or hoped, that he had died. Orders were given for William's body to be removed from the jail, and his lifeless body was callously discarded onto a *midden* (dung-heap.)

An old woman, said to be a former nursemaid of William, was told of his death and where his body lay.

Being distraught at the thought of a midden being William's final resting place, she persuaded the English soldiers to remove his body, and they granted her permission to take it away to carry out a "decent burial." On returning home with the body of William, she detected a faint hearbeat; his life had not expired. Thomas of Ercildune was visiting the nearby monastery of Fail, when news of William Wallace's death was relayed to the Minister by his servant. On overhearing the news that William Wallace was dead, Thomas of Ercildoune is reported to have said:

"Thir tythingis are nouct gud, and that be suth myself sall never eit breid."

(This is not good news, and if this is true, I shall never again eat bread.)

The servant assured Thomas that it was indeed true, telling him further, that an old woman had taken his body for burial, to which Thomas replied;

"Than sall I leiff na mar gif that be trow, be God, that all has wroucht."

(Then I will never believe anything again if this is true, by God who all has made.)

Thomas, still in disbelief, sends the servant to the home of the old woman to see the body and verify his death. On his arrival at the old lady's home, the servant tells the old woman that he has been dispatched by a friend

145

of William Wallace; none other than the *Seer of Ercildune* himself. The old woman compels the servant to take a vow of secrecy, before revealing that the *Knight of Ellerslie* is indeed alive.

In the words of *Blind Harry;*

Scho had hym up to Wallace by the dess,
He spake with hym, syne fast agayne can press,
With glad bodword, thair myrthes till amend;
He tald to them the first tythingis was less.

Than Thomas said,"Forsuth, or he decess,
Mony thousand on field mak thar end;
Off this regioune he sall the Southern send.
And Scotland thriss he sall bring to the pess,
So gud of hand agayne sall neuer be kend.
(Wallace, B.H. ch.3)

William was nursed back to full health by his former nursemaid; some stories tell that William was fed breast milk, supplied by a young woman who had recently given birth, to aid his recovery. Following his near-death experience, and inspired by the words of the reputable *Thomas the Rhymer,* who could only speak the truth, it is written that William Wallace regarded it his destiny to lead Scotland to freedom from English oppression.

Thomas's fame continued to grow as yet another of his prophecies came to fruition within a few years of his disappearance. He predicted that the *Bannock Burn* would be *"dunged wi' deid men,"* or *"The Burn of Bread shall run full red."*

The *Battle of Bannockburn,* an incredible victory against

all the odds for the Scots, took place in 1314. Prior to the battle, the army of King Edward II had been tactically lured by Robert Bruce to a narrow strip of marshy ground near the burn of Bannock. As the two armies were about to engage, the Abbot of Inchaffray stood before the Scots with a crucifix in his hand, whereupon the Scots lay down their arms and fell to their knees. Faced with the mighty power force of the assembled English army, the enemy presumed this to be an act of fearful submission. However, they must have been more than a little bemused when the Scots rose to their feet, picked up their weapons, and readily awaited the battle-charge.

The Scots foot-soldiers were outnumbered by four to one, coupled with the added disadvantage of two thousand heavy cavalry of the English army, compared to the five hundred light cavalry of their own small army. Before battle commenced, the servants and attendants of the Scottish army were given orders to retreat behind *Murray's Craig*, a nearby hill. There they awaited a signal, before charging down the hill at top speed. The English soldiers, on witnessing the extraordinary sight of this motley mob descending down the hillside, emitting blood-curdling cries, and waving long poles with white sheets attached, were thrown into a state of confusion. Percieving them to be reinforcements, the English army tried to flee in panic; however, they were in the unfortunate position of having no means of escape, making a hasty retreat impossible.

Robert Bruce employed cunning battle tactics, having dug pits concealed with turf prior to the battle commencing. In the ensuing confusion, as they fled on

147

the uneven ground, mounts and men stumbled into the pits; those who escaped tried to cross the Bannock Burn and were cut down en mass. As predicted by Thomas, the burn was *"dunged wi' deid men"* and indeed *"ran full red with blood."* Sir James Douglas accompanied by a cavalcade of Scots soldiers, pursued King Edward as he fled the catastrophic scene on horse-back. King Edward was on the point of capture just as he reached the safety of Dunbar castle, where he was rescued by the Earl of March and Dunbar. With the assistance of the Earl, King Edward was later conveyed to England by boat; the Earls of March and Dunbar had switched their allegiance to the English side by this time.The Scots lost *four thousand* men in the battle of Bannockburn, the English lost *thirty thousand.* Although this battle was an astounding victory, and the result a much needed morale boost for Scotland, the *ScottishWars of Independence* continued for many years. However, the *Battle of Bannockburn* was a major turning point for Scotland during the years of English persecution.

Many of the prophecies regarding forthcoming battles spoke of a "stob," which is a wooden cross, and a man, thought to be dead, rising from the corpses on the battlefield. They also spoke of a final terrific battle which would decide the ultimate fate of Scotland. *John Geddie,* in his book entitled *The Rhymour and his Rhymes,* suggests that the *Battle of Flodden* fits the description of the prophecy which tells of a battle at Sandyford.

The ford on the river *Till,* which goes by the name of *Sandyford,* played a significant part in the outcome of the Battle of Flodden. Surrey's rearguard crossed the stream at the ford, before launching their attack on King

James IV and his army on *Branxton Hill*. The legend which arose from the *Battle of Flodden* told of a wooden cross buried under the bodies of the slain, and of a *dead man* rising from the carnage.

> *"The sternes (stars) three that day shall die*
> *That bears the harte in silver sheen".*

George Douglas, heir apparent of Angus, died on the battlefield at *Flodden*. The Douglas family arms are the heart and three stars.

This rhyme is quoted in a book called '*Bede, Merlin and Gildas, and other Soothsayers in one Volume,*' by *Andro Hart*, published in 1615, and is attributed to Thomas the Rhymer, with regard to the Battle of Flodden.

> *Our Scottish King sal come full keene,*
> *The Red Lyon beareth he;*
> *A feddered arrow sharp,I weene,*
> *Shall make him winke and warre to see.*
> *Out of the field he shall be led*
> *When he is bludie and woe for blood;*
> *Yet to his men shall he say,*
> *"For God's love turn you again,*
> *And give yon Southern folk a frey;*
> *Why should I lose the right is mine?*
> *My doom is not to die this day"-*

The death of King James 1V at the *Battle of Flodden,* as noted in the history books, has often been questioned. The names of *"Gladsmuir," "Sandyford,"* and *"Gouan,"*

149

are mentioned many times in the prophecies. "*Betwixt Temptallon and the Bass*" there was to be seen "*a right fair sight*":

> "*At Aberlady he shall light*
> *With hempen halters and hors of tree;*
> *On Gosford Green it shall be seene,*
> *On Gladsmoor shall the battle be.*"

One prophecy spoke of a battle between the villages of *Goysford Green* and *Seton*, which is taken to refer to the *Battle of Prestonpans*

> "*Between Seton and the sea*
> *Many a man that day shall dee,*"

The words "*there the Lyon shall be hurt that day,*" have also been quoted in the prophecies. This prophecy is thought to refer to the *Power of Superiority* being taken away from the Highland Clans.

The following rhyme attributed to Thomas was in circulation many years before the *Battle of Pinkie;*

> "*At Pinkin (Pinkie) Cleuch there shall be spilt*
> *Much gentle blood that day.*"

Thomas also spoke of a great battle in Fife, and also on the four great rivers of Scotland, namely the Tweed, the Tay, the Forth and the Clyde. There would be a mass slaughter at the walls of *Barwick* (Berwick), all of which have come to fruition.

In the *Romance and Prophecies* by J. A. H. Murray, the

names of Comyn, Barclay, Ross, and Fressell (Fraser), are mentioned often. In the words of the prophecy, as told by the Fairy Queen, the Baliol *stem* and its *branches* are compared to a rotten tree;

"The Comyns and the Barclays a',
The Rosses and the Fressels free,
All shall fade and dwine awa';
Nae ferlie then if that fruit dee."

The curse Thomas put on *Cowdenknowes House* is written thus:

Vengeance! Vengeance! When and where
On the house of Coldingknow, Now and evermair.

The Lindsays inhabited the house of *Coldingknowes (Choille-dun)*, now known as *Cowdenknowes*, in the thirteenth century; the influential family of the Lindsays also owned a large amount of land in the vicinity. In later years Cowdenknowes was home to the family of *Douglas*, thereafter it was inhabited by the *Homes*. Thomas is said to have cursed the house because of a *"persecuting family"* who would inhabit the *House of Coldingknowes*, not necessarily in Thomas's time, but in years to come. The inhabited part of the present house is a sixteenth century Baronial mansion house of the Elizabethan period. Carved on the lintel of the former principle entrance are the letters S.J.H. V. K.H. and the date 1574. These are thought to be the initials of a former owner, Sir James Home, and his wife, Katherine Home.

151

A square tower near the house is inscribed with the date of its erection, 1555, and abutting on the riverside are the remains of a much older structure. The entrance to the dungeons, which are contained in this older building, can still be seen from the river bank. It is from these dungeons that a tunnel is said to link with the vaults underneath the castle of the Rhymer in Ercildoune.

A tale of old, handed down through the generations, told of the harsh treatment of wrong-doers by one of the Barons of Cowdenknowes. After being imprisoned and tortured in the dungeons, the prisoners would be hung from a nearby tree. This particular Baron, thought to be the persecutor referred to in Thomas's prophecy, went even further with his brutality. In scenes reminiscent of the old 'Jethart Justice,' where the victims were hung before the trial, the perpetrators of crimes at Cowdeknowes received a harsh trial. The 'criminals' were sealed inside spiked barrels - the spikes being on the inside – the barrel was then rolled from the summit of the 'Black Hill,' 1003 ft from the ground, to bounce down the rocky slope. In the unlikely event that the occupant of the barrel was still alive when it reached the bottom, they were considered to be innocent and subsequently released - which rarely ever happened.

Regarding the estate and mansion house of *Bemersyde*, Thomas predicted;

Tyde what may, whate'er betyde,
Haig will be Haig of Bemersyde.

(The Haig's family motto is *'Tyde What May.'*)

152

From the time *Petrus de Haga* first occupied *Bemersyde* in the 12th century, the direct line was unbroken for twenty nine generations. In 1802, the grandfather of the proprietor of Bemersyde had twelve daughters before a male heir was eventually born. In 1854, although the direct line had died out, the house was still occupied by another line of the Haig family. When the house was put on the market, in the early twentieth century, it was feared that the prophecy, which Thomas wrote nearly 700 years previous, would finally cease to be true. However, in 1921, the public raised enough money to purchase the estate and gifted it to Field Marshal Sir Douglas Haig (1st Earl Haig) of World War 1 fame, thus continuing the Haig connection.

Another of Thomas's prophecies connected to his home town of Ercildune is the following;

"This thorn tree, as long as it stands,
Ercildune shall possess a' her lands."

The story of the *Earlstoun Thorn Tree* dates back to the early nineteenth century; this particular tree flourished in Thomas's time, and has been described thus:

"It was a big tree wi'a trunk as thick as a man's waist
Its branches a perfect circle, an' round i' the tap.
I' the spring, a solid sheet o' white, flourishin',
Scentin' the hale toun end;
An' its haws, there wis na the like o' them in a' Scotland."

The above description of the tree is a quotation by a native of Earlston, namely John Sheil, who was twelve

153

years old when the tree was blown down. Aged seventy three in the late nineteenth century, he could still remember its grandeur, and described it as *"the grandest tree I ever saw."*

The thorn tree flourished before and during Thomas's lifetime and continued to do so for many centuries after. The locals tended the tree carefully and looked upon it with the utmost devotion. Locals and visitors alike were enthralled by its beauty. Such was its reputation that people came from far and near to view the *Rhymer's Thorn;* similar to the *Fortingall Yew* today, but with a prophecy by 'True Thomas' attached.

The tree had stood for centuries in the current rear courtyard of the *Black Bull Inn.* It stood the test of time until the year 1814, when the premises of the Black Bull Inn were owned by a man by the name of *Thin.* Mr Thin was of the opinion that the size of the tree was curtailing the growth of everything and anything in the vicinity; a little *pruning* would do it no harm. He delegated his son to cut the tree back slightly, which he duly did. However, fate intervened; a severe westerly gale blew through the village that night, resulting in the tree being uprooted by the storm's ferocity. The villagers were distraught, the tree was immediately replanted, and cart-loads of manure were brought and carefully spread around the roots. Such was the consternation over its demise, it is alleged the villagers even poured *whisky* on the roots, but to no avail. The tree, which had stood for almost one thousand years, never again took root. Was it just coincidence that the same year, all the Merchants in Earlston went out of business? A short time later, all the common lands were repossessed. In 1830, the ground on which the tree once stood came into the possession of a writer from the village, namely *John Spence*. He built a high wall round the garden, leaving a square opening at the top to mark the site of the *Rhymer's Thorn*. Many streets and houses in the vicinity of the site of the old thorn tree in Earlston are named after the famous thorn tree.

The mansion house of *Carolside-on-Leader* may not have existed during Thomas's lifetime; however the braes of Carolside were, and still are, within a mile from the home of Thomas in Ercildoune. A prediction regarding Carolside brae goes thus:

> *"A horse sall gang on Carollside brae*
> *Till the girth gaw his side in twae".*

The wording is similar to the prophecy, as told to Thomas by the Fairy Queen in the *Romance and Prophecies*, and quoted in a later chapter:

> *"steades maisterles shall flynge,*
> *To the mountains to & fro;*
> *per sadels on per backes hinge,*
> *till per girths be rotten in to.*

The words in this case relate to the prediction of a great battle between *Seton and the sea*.

Another prophecy, with reference to the border lands, tells that when the river Tweed flows into Merlin's grave, Scotland and England shall be ruled by one monarch. This happened in 1603, when KingJames V1 of Scotland became King James 1 of England. At the same time, an

155

extraordinary flood caused the river *Tweed* to burst its banks and overflow into the small burn of *Powsail* near *Drumelzier* in Peeblesshire; the site of Merlin's grave. This had never happened before, nor has it since;

> *When Tweed and Powsail meet at Merlin's grave,*
> *Scotland and England shall one Monarch have."*

Another ambiguous prediction for the future of his locality was:

> *There sall a stane doun Leader come*
> *Will mak a rich father but a poor son.*

Many of Thomas's predictions were *obscure*, or, as quoted regarding the prophecies of Merlin, "*spoken in figure*", so the wording of the prophecies would puzzle people for many years. However, as with most of Thomas's predictions, the meaning would become clear sooner or later. The *stane* in this instance was limestone, which was a boon in agriculture for a generation in the early nineteenth century. Crushed lime from the quarries in the *Lothians* was *carted* down by Leaderside to be used on the fields to encourage crop yields. Its benefits were short-lived however, and the next generation suffered hardship as a result.

In days of old, when famine and hardship were rife, the *dream-come-true* for the poverty-stricken people of Scotland would be to find buried treasure. This is not as improbable as it may initially seem, recalling that the Romans had wealth beyond the dreams of the indigenous tribes, the Druids buried metal as sacrifices to the Gods, and the more affluent in society, during the medieval period, had no banks in which to deposit their wealth.

Thomas foretold:

*"Atween the weet ground and the dry
Tamleuchar's gowden hoard doth lie."*

Tom Luachair; the name being Gaelic, translates as *Hill of Rushes,* Tamleuchar is in *Selkirkshire,* not far from the home of Thomas at Ercildoune.

The exact spot, as yet, has not been located; therefore the prophecy, for the time being, remains unfulfilled.

Another prophecy involving hidden treasure names the Auld kirk of Cowie near Findon in Kincardineshire:

*"Atween the kirk and the kirk-ford-
There lies St Nauchlan's hoard."*

St. Nathalan, or *Neachdan,* was the Gaelic patron of the *Auld Kirk of Cowie.*

Somewhere in the Ochil Hills is another treasure worth discovering, if only the key could be found:

*"In the Dryburn Well, beneath a stane,
You'll find the key o' Cairn-a-vain,
That'll mak' a' Scotland rich, ane by ane."*

The chances of finding buried treasure, even in the twenty first century, are high. Many valuable artefacts are being found with the help of metal detectors,

157

archaeologists also continue to find buried *treasure* from a bygone era.

This prophecy relates to the hills of Bennachie in the highlands:

> *"A mither's ae son, wi' ae e'e,*
> *Sall find the Keys o' Bennachie,*
> *Aneath a rash buss,*
> *I' the backward o' Tollus."*

A translation of the above is as follows:

"A Mother's one son, with one eye, shall find the keys of Bennachie, beneath a rash bush (reeds), behind Tollus."

The *key* could be metaphoric, and simply mean the ability to *visualise* and *perceive*, as Thomas did, that there is an *inhabited otherworld*. The belief that Thomas is asleep under the hills is as popular in the highlands as in the lowlands. Bennachie is in Aberdeenshire, one of the many destinations of Thomas's travels, the hill range of Bennachie is not too dissimilar to the Eildon Hills, with more than one peak rising from relatively flat ground.

Ardoch Camp was once a Roman fort; these words are also attributed to Thomas:

> *"From the Fort of Ardoch to the Grinan Well o' Keir*
> *Are nine king's rent for nine hundred year."*

The prophecies regarding buried treasure are as yet unfulfilled, however the following words spoken *"in figure"* by Thomas came true in 1839.

158

Of his home in Ercildoune he spoke these words:

"The hare shall kittle on my hearthstane,
And there will never be a Laird Learmont again."

In 1839, the fireplace, complete with corbels and lintels, was still intact, and could be seen in the ruins of the tower in Earlston. In 1839, word spread round the village that another of Thomas's predictions had come true. According to Mr Currie, a native of Earlston, he ran along with other villagers to see for himself, a hare with her young nestled among the nettles in the hearth. The last male Earlston resident with the surname of Learmont, claiming to be a direct descendant of Thomas, was a batchelor named Robert. He was a weaver to trade and died around 1840, shortly after the hare had *"kittled on the hearth-stane"*.

Many of the predictions of Thomas spoke of doom and disaster. One such prophecy is as follows:

"At Threeburn Grange, in an after day,
There shall be a lang and bloody fray;
Where a three thumbed wight by the reins shall hald
Three king's horse, baith stout and bauld,
And the Three Burns three days will rin
Wi' the blude o' the slain that fa' therein."

'*Threeburn Grange*' is in Berwickshire, where three small *burns* (streams) meet to form the river Ale. During the period of the *French Revolution,* a person by the name of *Douglas* was born in the parish of Coldingham with a

159

third thumb. At the time, it was assumed he would be the *"three-thumbed wight"* referred to in the prophecy, and the people awaited its fulfilment with bated breath. A *wight,* or *wicht,* is the old Scots word for a male person.

Thomas predicted another disaster which came to fruition when the river *Dryffe* - a tributary of the *Annan* - was in spate:

> *"Let spade and school do what they may,*
> *Dryffe will take Drysdale Kirk away."*

This prophecy was fulfilled in 1670, when the old Kirk and part of the kirkyard were swept away by the flood. Thomas also predicted the fall of the *House of Renton* in the *Merse,* because of their evil-doing:

> *"Renton is its name,*
> *And rent it shall be;*
> *The auld Laird of Renton,*
> *Shall rot by the tree."*

The *House of Renton,* which was in the possession of Alexander Home of Renton, did eventually fall in the seventeenth century.

> *A Chieftan unchosen*
> *Shall chose forth himself*
> *And rule the realm as his own.*

The above prediction is thought to refer to Prince Charles (Bonnie Prince Charlie).

160

Below is another prediction of a disaster in Thomas's locality:

"Of Kelso Kirk true is't;
It will fa' when it is fu'est."

The old Kirk in Kelso stood in the shadow of the ruins of Kelso abbey. During a crowded sermon in 1770, a piece of lime fell from the roof of the old Kirk. The congregation made a hasty exit as the words of Thomas the Rhymer came to mind. Such was the belief in the credibility of Thomas's predictions, that the Kirk was subsequently deserted from that day onwards, thus denying it the opportunity to be fulfilled.

The predictions and influence of Thomas of Ercildoune are known and felt throughout Scotland. *Foveran castle* in Aberdeenshire was the ancestral home of the family of Turing, and Thomas wrote this rhyme regarding the fall of this family home:

"When Turing's tower fall to the land,
Gladsmuir then is near at hand;
When Turing's tower falls to the sea,
Gladsmuir the next year shall be."

The Turing's house in Edinburgh was *Turing's*, now *'Trunks Close'* in the lower *High Street*, adjoining *Moubray* and *John Knox's House.*

The *Pentland Hills*, and a battle to be fought on their *red clay*, are mentioned in the prophecies. However, this prophecy predicts disaster for the finder of a *hoard*. It has been translated from a document written in Latin

161

and dated 1568, part thirteen, *Hatfield House Calendar* (Historical MSS Collection):

> *"A hoard shall be in Pentland found*
> *On an auld house's eastern bound.*
> *Beside the water of Newgirthburn,*
> *And the finder shall come to speedy harm."*

A prediction relating to *Inverugie* north of Peterhead in Aberdeenshire:

> *"Inverugie by the sea,*
> *Lordless shall thy lands be,*
> *And underneath thy hearthstane*
> *The tod (fox) shall bring her bairns hame."*

The Rev. James Anderson affirmed the tradition that the above prediction was delivered by Thomas while standing on a stone, known in the locality as the *"Rhymer's Stane."* The stone was built into St Fergus Parish church in 1763, but the field in which the stone stood is apparently still known as *"Tammas's Stane."* This prediction is thought to refer to the Marischal family, their seat at one time being at Inverugie. The Earl of Marischal was banished, and his estate forfeited, due to his part in the rebellion of 1715.

> *"When the Gows o' Gowrie come to land,*
> *The judgement day is near at hand."*

The above lines refer to the two boulders, *the gows,* which are situated beyond high-water level opposite the

162

old Royal seat of *Invergowrie*. Local tradition confirms that they move at the rate of an inch per year.

"At two full times, and three half times,
Or three score years and ten,
The ravens shall sit on the Stanes o' St Brandon,
And drink o' the blood o' the slain."

The *stanes* –or stones - of St Brandon were still erect in a field near Banff several years ago, near to the *Brandon How*. The field was the site of a battle between the Scots and the Danes in earlier times. Archaeological digs at the site have uncovered fragments of bone and weapons.

"While there's an eagle in Pennan
There will be a Baird in Auchmeddan."

The above is another of Thomas's *fulfilled* prophecies. *The New Statistical Account* of the *Parish of Aberdour* tells of a pair of eagles regularly nesting and raising their young on the rocks of *Pennan*. However, when the late *Earl of Aberdeen* bought the estate from the *Bairds*, and for the duration of his occupancy, the eagles never returned. However, uncannily, when the eldest son of the third Earl of Aberdeen, *Lord Haddo*, married *Miss Christine Baird*, the eagles returned to the rocks, remaining there until the estate passed once more into other hands.

A story, as related in the *View of the Diocese of Aberdeen*, tells that John Comyn, the *Earl of Buchan*, called Thomas the Rhymer *"Thomas the Liar"* as a slight against his credibility as a prophet.

163

The famous prophet wrote the words of the Earl's impending fate in the following prophecy:

"Tho' Thomas the Lyar thou callest me,
A sooth tale I shall tell to thee;
By Aikey side thy horse shall ride;
He shall tumble and thou shalt fa';
And thy neckbane shall brak in twa',
And dogs shall thy banes gnaw;
And, maugre all thy kin and thee,
Thy ain belt thy bier shall be."

The death of the Earl of Buchan occurred the same year, at the rocks called *"Comyn's Craig"* on *Aikey Braes.* Although Thomas lived nearly eight hundred years ago, it is uncanny that his words should still be relevant in the twentieth century.

In *Moray,* this saying is attributed to the *"worthy old orthodox Seer and Rhymer";*

"The order Pot and Lossie grey
Will sweep the Chanry Kirk away,"

The *Order Pot* was reputed to be the scene of the *'ordeal by water'* of locals accused of *witchcraft. Elgin Cathedral* was known locally as *'The Chanonry Kirk,'* the river, which runs beneath the ruins, was supposedly connected to the *"bottomless pot."* When the river *Lossie* was in spate, the water level rose in the pot. During the great flood of September 1915, the water in *The Pot* overflowed once again, despite having been filled in. Each of Thomas's rhymes was like a conundrum; it

164

wasn't always easy to figure out which particular event it referred to. The following rhyme was taken to mean the *Battle of Gladsmuir*, better known as the *Battle of Prestonpans*, which resulted in a victory for the *Highlanders* over the *Hanovarians* during the *Jacobite rebellions*.The *Battle of Gladsmuir* or Gleds Moor is mentioned in the prophecies by the Fairy Queen. However, the name of Gleds Moor, or Gladsmuir, is mentioned in other Scottish prophecies, and predicts a decisive battle in Scotland's history.

"It shall not be Gladsmuir by the sea;
It shall be Gladsmuir wherever it be,
And the little lowne that shall be
Is between the Lowmond and the sea."

In the older versions of the prophecies, the word *Gladsmuir* is written as Gleds More. Gled is the old Scots word for a hawk, *hawking* was a common hunting method in medieval times and many old placenames use the words *Gled* or *Hawk*.The names of *Hawk Kaim* and *Gledswood*, which are in Earlston, and just a few miles from Earlston respectively, being two examples.

The following rhyme may refer to the influence of new families in the northeast under the regime of *Bruce*, just as the same period saw the change in ownership of houses in Ayr and Galloway:

"Sundrum shall sink, Auchencruive shall fa'
Ere the name o' Cathcart shall wear aw'."

According to the writer *Barbour*, the marriage between

165

Auchencruive and the heiress of the *Wallaces of Sundrum* saw these properties conveyed to a knight, a companion of *Robert the Bruce,* who was:

"Worthy and wicht, stalwart and stout,
Courteous and fair, and of good fame,
Sir Alan Cathcart was his name."

A member of the Cathcart family still owned Carleton in Carrick in the nineteenth century, although the ownership of the other two estates had changed hands by then.
The *Kennedies* were another influencial family in the region where Bruce *"shook his Carrick spear."*

"'Twixt Wigtoun and the Toun o' Ayr,
An' laigh doun by the Cruives o' Cree,
Let nae man think to harbour there
Unless he court a Kennedy."

A rhyme concerning the family of the "Gentle *Johnstones*" was attributed to Thomas and received partial fulfilment:

"Within the bounds of Annandale
The gentle Johnstones ride;
The've held their ain a thousand years,
A thousand, mair they'll bide."

However, their land was eventually taken from them, just as they had taken the land which belonged to the *Hallidays of Corehead.* During the reign of King

Edward1, it was said that the Hallidays could ride for forty miles from the *Devil's Beef Tub* in any direction on their own lands. The Devil's Beef Tub is a large, 500ft deep, hollow surrounded by four hills, just north of the town of Moffat in the county of Dumfries and Galloway. During the time of the 'Border Reivers' it was used to hide stolen cattle.

> *"Frae Annanfit to Errick stane*
> *Man and horse langsyne hae gane,*
> *'Neath the greenwood a' the way,*
> *on the lands o' Halliday."*

The Rev. W.W. Skeat found an original of *Leyland's* extracts in a MS in the library of *Corpus Christi College*. *Leyland* quoted the following from the *Scalacronica*, which was written in 1355 by *Sir Thomas Grey "William Banestre, and Thomas Erceldoune whose words were spoken in figure, as were the prophecies of Merlin."* This rendered the prophecies obscure, and their true meaning almost impossible to interpret.

The prophecies of Thomas were quoted often in the early years of the first *Scottish War of Independence*.

The following rhyme is written in a book by John Barbour, born c1320. The book is called *'The Bruce'* and the rhyme relates to the slaying of the *Red Cumyn* by Bruce, in Grey Friars Church Dumfries, in 1306. News of the event eventually reached the patriotic Bishop of St Andrews;

> *The lettir tauld hym all the deid,*
> *And he till his men gert it reid,*

167

And sythyn said thaim;
"Sekerly I hop Thomas prophecy
of hersildoune sall weryfyd be
In him; for, swa our Lord help me!
I haiff gret hop he sall be King,
And haif this land all in leding."

With a reference to Thomas, *Andro of Wyntoun*, in his *Orygynale Chronikyl* (book VIII chap. 32), wrote the following rhyme regarding the *Battle of Kilblane* (Culbean), where Sir Andrew Moray and his followers fought against the Baliol and Comyn factions on November 30th 1335. David Comyn, one of Baliol's leaders, was slain in the forest of Kilblane by Sir Andrew Moray.

"Of this fycht quhlum spak Thomas
Of Ersyldoune, that sayd in derne,
There suid mete stalwart, stark and sterne.
He sayd it in his prophecy,
But how he wist it was ferly."

It is not known for certain to whom Thomas was referring by his description of *"Stalwart, Stark and Sterne,"* but all three adjectives describe David, Earl of Athol and Lord of Strathbogie, who raised the standard of rebellion at *Kildrummie.*

A sixteenth century witch-trial linked the names of *Thomas the Rhymer* and *King James 1V of Scotland*. *Andro Mann* stood accused of gaining his power to *"cure all sorts of sickness except stane deid"* from the *Queen of Elfland* in his youth. He was warned that like *The*

168

Rhymer he would *"seik his meit, afore he deit."* During his trial, he affirmed that among the folk he met in *'Fairyland'* were *"The King that deit at Flowden, and Thomas the Rhymer."*

The Peterloo riots (1819), and the death of King George III (1820), were said to be linked to another prophecy of Thomas:

> *"A windy winter and a wet spring,*
> *Brings a bloody summer and a dead King."*

A catastrophe, known as *The Peterloo Massacre,* occurred in August 1819, after a windy winter and a wet spring. The rally in Manchester had started peacefully; however, the participants of the rally were later attacked by soldiers. This resulted in eleven deaths and four hundred men and women being injured. The *'mad'* King George III was on the throne at the time, so in keeping with the prophecy, the king was expected to die the same year. However, not many days of the New Year had passed when, on January 20th 1820, he passed away, fulfilling yet another prophecy.

> *"When Dee and Don run in one,*
> *And Tweed shall run in Tay,*
> *The bonnie water o' Urie*
> *Shall bear the Bass away.*

According to Chambers, *"the Bass is a conical mound rising from the bank of the river Urie in Aberdeenshire."* According to this prophecy, the Bass will remain intact beside the river, until such times as the river of Dee shall merge with the Don, and the rivers Tweed and Tay

169

shall run as one.

The rivers Dee, Don, Tweed, and Tay, have one thing in common, in that they all eventually flow into the North Sea. The rivers Dee, Don, and Tay are in the north of Scotland, whereas the river Tweed is in the lowlands of Scotland, therefore the likelihood of this happening in the past would be considered quite impossible. It is to be hoped that the *"bonnie water o' Urie never bears the bass away,* and that *"Tweed never runs in Tay,"* otherwise the part of Scotland from the lowlands to the north would be under water. However, with climate change affecting the polar ice caps, sea levels rising, and the prediction of more prolonged periods of heavy rainfall, who knows, another of Thomas's predictions may yet come to fruition.

The words *"The south sea will come upon the north sea,"* would seem to make no sense away back in the thirteeth century. However, when the *Caledonian Canal* was completed in 1847, the Gaelic equivalent, *"Thig a' mhuir deas air a' mhuir tuath,"* came to fruition.

A prophecy, with which I was unfamiliar until recently, concerns one of the northernmost extremities of Thomas's travels, and relates to the old castle of *Cromarty.* In a book entitled, *"Scenes and Legends of the North of Scotland",* Hugh Miller tells of a prophecy made by Thomas which focuses on a castle built in 1264. Thomas was alive at this time and no doubt had connections with the castle and its owner. The castle was built by a Norman by the name of *William de Monte Alto.* Thomas predicted that *"Cromarty shall twice be destroyed by the sea",* and *"fish shall be caught in abundance on the castle-hill"* – a rounded projection of the escarpment which rises behind the houses, forming part of the ancient coastline.

Says Miller, *"It is not much more than twenty years ago, since a series of violent storms from the hostile north east, which came on at almost regular intervals for five successive winters [c.1810-11] seemed to threaten the modern town of Cromarty with the fate of the ancient. The tide rose higher than tides had ever been known to rise before, and as the soil exposed to the action of the waves was gradually disappearing, instead of the gentle slope with which the land formerly merged into the beach; its boundaries were marked out by a dark abrupt line resembling a turf wall."* The people, whose houses bordered the sea, thought the prophecy of Thomas the Rhymer was about to come to fruition.

The reputation of Thomas as a credible seer was widespread throughout Scotland and the western Isles, both during his lifetime, and almost immediately after his death. *Chambers* affirmed that his name was *"as well known among the common people of the Highlands, nay even in the remotest of the Western Isles, as it is in Berwickshire."* He told of a tradition in Aberdeenshire where the gates of *Fyvie Castle* stood for seven years and a day *"wall-wide,"* waiting for the arrival of Thomas. Thomas suddenly appeared in the midst of a howling gale and torrential rain, the force of which blew the castle gates shut with an almighty crash, *"though not a blade of grass moved around Thomas, nor a hair of his beard."*

It is said he vented his wrath in the following words:

"Fyvie, Fyvie, thou's never thrive

171

As lang's there's in thee stanes five;
There's twa intil the highest tower,
There's twa intil the Lady's bower,
There's ane aneath the water yett (gate)
An' a thir stanes ye's never get."

The stone below the water–gate leading to the Ythan river has, as yet, baffled research. Fyvie has continued to thrive, despite its visit by the ghost of Thomas, and his obscure prediction. However, according to the papers of a local man on *Old Buchan Castles,* in the *Transactions* of the Buchan Field Club, "*the Rymour's malediction still hangs over the lordly pile."*
This prophetic rhyme came to fruition when sheep-rearing replaced the arable lands of the croft:

"The teeth of the sheep shall lay the plough on the shelf."

In the Gaelic-speaking north of Scotland many legends are associated with *Thomas of Ercildune.* One of these being the legend of a hill near Inverness (*Inbhir Nis*), known as *cemetery hill,* or "*hill of the yew-wood,*" well known in Gaelic tradition as *Tom-na-h-Iubhraich:*

"Dar thigeadh sluagh Tom-na-h-Iubhraich
Co dh'eireadh air tus ach Tomas?"

English translation:

"When come the hosts of Tom-na-hurich,
Who will arise but Thomas."

He is allegedly asleep in the *"Tom"* or *"Hill of the Fairies,*

172

or according to another *Gaelic* tradition on *Dunbuch Hill*, near Dumbarton.

Nuair thig Tomas le Chuid each bi latha nan creach air cluaidh;
Millear naoi mile fear maith 'S theid rig hog air a 'chrun.

English translation:

"Now when Thomas will arrive with his horses,
To the Clyde will come the day of plunder;
For there will be slain nine thousand good men,
And a young King will sit on the throne."

According to the prophecy, the ferocity of the battle and its carnage would allow men to cross the Clyde on the bodies of the dead, without their feet getting wet. The miller of Partick Mill, - *Muileann Phearaig* – who had seven fingers, would grind the corn for two hours with blood, instead of water.

The aftermath of the battle would see such a dearth of males that sixteen ladies would pursue one lame tailor:

"bidh sia baintighearan diag as deidh a-haon tailleir chrubaicc."

Another example of an obscure prophecy was the following:

"The waters sall wax, the woods sall wane,
Hill and moss sall be a' torn in,
But the banno' 'ill be na the braider."

173

In other words, Thomas could foresee extensive land cultivation and deforestation, this was already happening, on a lesser scale, prior to and during his lifetime. The great forests were gradually disappearing and the bottomless peatbogs were being drained for crop growing. However, his prediction warns, that although progress would be made, and the rich would get richer, the poor would still go hungry. (The banno' refers to the bannock, or bread.)

> "Atween Craik-cross and Eildon tree,
> Is a' the safety there sall be."

Craik Cross is near Roberton in the Scottish Borders, where an old Roman road ran across Craik Moor, through Craik Cross and continued in a north easterly direction; possibly connecting with Dere Street. The road is thought to be the *Royal Road* – which linked the valley of Annan with Roxburgh – mentioned in a Charter of the thirteenth century. The true meaning of the words, as with several of the prophecies, is unclear, but they may refer to the period of the wars of the French Revolution. Both Annandale and Roxburgh are places which have strong connections with the life of Thomas.

> "It isna here, it isna here,
> That ye maun bigg the Kirk o' Deer.
> But on the tap o' Tillerie,
> Where mony a corp must after lie."

The '*Book o' Deer*' was written in the tenth century by the monks at the *Abbey of Deer* in Buchan. It consists of

174

the foundation legends of their abbey (or kirk). Although the text is written in Latin, it is the oldest surviving manuscript, containing notes written in *Scottish Gaelic* text, to come from the former land of the Picts.

The *Gordon* family were residents of the neighbouring parish to Ercildoune in Thomas's lifetime. The head of the family, *Sir Adam de Gordon*, was *Warden of* the *Marches* and self-proclaimed *"Baron of the Merse."* He and his family saw *"justice done"* at the *'Hanging Tree'*, near the hamlet of *Gordon* in Berwickshire. The *Gordons* moved north; descendants from this line going on to be the influential family - the *"Gordons of the North"* - settling first in *Strathbogie* after the fall of the *Comyns* and the *Cheynes*. The Cheyne family and their predecessors were supporters of the *Baliol* party; which did not endear them to Thomas. Sir Reginald Cheyne was hereditary High Constable of Scotland.

The influence of Thomas the Rhymer was, and still is, strongly felt in the northeast of Scotland, especially in the counties of *Aberdeen* and *Banff.*

"The Gool, the Gordon, and the Hoodie Craw
Are the three warst foes that Moray ever saw."

A rhyme equating the *"Gouks o' Gordon"* in the Merse with the *"Wise Men of Gotham,"* is suspected to be the work of Thomas;

"Huntly-wood is a' doun,
Bassendean and Barrastoun,
Hexpeth wi' the yellow hair,
Gordon Gouks for evermair."

175

Huntly-wood is the name of an estate, once having extensive lands, situated equidistant from Earlston and Gordon. Huntly-wood has no known association with *Huntly Bankes* (which is near the *Eildons)* mentioned in the Ballad of Thomas the Rhymer, however, *Huntly-wood* is nearer to the *Ercildoune* home of Thomas than *Huntly Bankes.*

As mentioned earlier, the *Gordons* from the *Merse* moved north into the lands of Aberdeen and Banff. The *Duke of Gordon* was known as the *"Cock of the North,"* referred to in the prophecy by the Fairy Queen.

Two further prophecies of Thomas refer to the demise of the *Gordons of Gight:*

"When the heron leaves the tree
The Laird o' Gight shall landless be."

In the late eighteenth century, many herons nested in the woods on the *Bog of Gight.* For some unexplained reason the birds deserted this spot in favour of land on the neighbouring estate of *Haddo.* According to local legend, when *Lord Haddo* was told of this, he replied *"Let the birds come and do them no harm, for the lands will soon follow."* The estate of the *'Gordons of Gight'* was sold around 1780.

Following on from this, another of Thomas' prophecies warned:

"At Gight three men a violent death shall dee,
And after that the lands shall lie in the lea."

In 1791, *Lord Haddo* was killed on the *Green of Gight*

176

after a fall from his horse. Thereafter, a servant from the farm on his estate met the same fate. A labourer, dismantling walls on the estate to allow the lands to be turned into pasture (lea), remarked *"Thomas the Rhymour made a mistak' for aince,"* whereupon the wall collapsed, crushing him to death.

George Gordon, (Lord Byron the poet), lived from 1788 until 1824. He was the only son of the last remaining direct link to the *'Gordons of Gight'*. As quoted from the book entitled "The Rymour and his Rhymes" by John Geddie, "Lord Byron himself, as the only son of the last heiress of the *Gordons of Gight,* paused before he crossed the *Brig of Don at Balgownie* near the *Auld Toun of Aberdeen,* with its one arch, and its salmon-pool below, remembering the *'awful prediction,'* perhaps the most frequently quoted of the Rhymer's rhymes in these parts:"

> *"Brig o' Balgownie, black's your wa',*
> *Wi' a wife's ae son and a mare's ae foal,*
> *Doun ye shall fa'."*

Another of the few *unfulfilled* prophecies refers to Drumlanrig Castle in Dumfriesshire:

> *"When the park burn rins,*
> *Where never men saw,*
> *The house o' the Hassock,*
> *Is near a fa'."*

Such was the profound belief in his predictions, one popular rhyme in the northeast of Scotland regarding Thomas states:

177

"When the saut goes abune the meal,
Believe nae mair o' Tammy's tale."

Translated, and still relevant today, it could be construed that when the amount of salt needed for a meal is larger than the meal itself, only then will the words of Thomas cease to be true. Or, in the days of old, when the price of oatmeal was high and salt was relatively cheap in comparison; the likelihood of the price of salt exceeding the price of meal was inconceivable. Either way, it is never going to happen.
According to folklore, Thomas returns to earth from time to time, as only the inhabitants of the otherworld can. Stories telling of Thomas and his cavalry of horses; his soldiers adorned with breastplates and helmets made of gold, are common throughout the legendary tales of Thomas.

The Prophecie of Thomas Rymour

From *"The Whole Prophesie of Scotland,"* etc, printed by *Robert Waldegrave, printer to the King's most excellent majesty, Edinburgh Anno1603.*
Collated with *Andro Hart's Edition, 1615*

Still on my waies as I went,
Out through a land, beside a lie,
I met a beirne vpon the way.
Me thought him seemlie for to see,
I asked him holly his intent,
Good Sir, if your wil be,
Sen that ye byde vpon the bent
Some vncouth tydinges tell you me,

178

When shal al these warres be gone,
That leile men may leue in lee,
Or when shall falsehood goe from home
And laughtie blow his horne on hie.
I looked from me not a mile,
And saw two Knights vpon a lie,
they were armed seemly new,
two Croces on there brestes they bare,
and they were cled in diuers hew,
Of sindrie countries as they were,
the one was red as any blood,
Set in his Shield a Dragone Keene,
He steird his Steed as he were mad,
With crabbit words sharpe and keene
Right to the other beirne him by.
His Horse was al of siluer sheene
His shield was shaped right seemlie,
In it a Ramping Lyon keene.
Seemly into golde was set,
His bordour was of Asure sheene,
With silke and Sabil well was plet,
I looked from me ouer a greene,
And saw a Ladie on a lie,
That such a one had I neuer seene.
The light of her shined so hie,
Attour the moore where at she fure,
The fields me thought faire and greene
She rode vpon a Steid ful sture,
That such a one had I seldome seene:
Her Steid was white as any milke,
His top his taile war both full blae
A side sadyle sewed with silk,

179

As al were golde it glittered so,
His harnessing was of sylke of ynde,
Set with precious stones free,
He ambled ona noble kinde:
Vpon her head stoode Crownes three:
Her garment was of Gowles gay,
But other colour saw I none,
A flying fowle then I saw,
Light beside her on a stone
A stoope into her hand she baere ,
and holy water she had readie,
She sprinkled the field both here & there
Said here shal many dead corpses lie.
At yon bridge vpon yon burne,
Where the water runnes bright and sheene,
There shal many steides spurne,
And Knightes die throw battles keene
To the two Knightes did she say,
Let be your strife my Knightes free,
Ye take your Horse and ride your way
As God hath ordained so must it be,
Saint Andrew thou hast the hight,
Saint George thou art my owne Knight,
they wrongous aires shall worke thee woe,
Now are they one there waies gone,
The Ladie and the Knightes two,
to that beirne then can I ment,
and asked tythings be my fey.
What kinde of sight was that I said?
Thou shewed to me upon yon lie,
Or wherefrom came thou Knightes
They seemed of a farre countrie,

That Ladie that I let thee see,
that is the Queene of heaven so bright
the fowle that flew by her knee,
that is Saint Michael much of might
that knightes two the field to ta
Where manie men in field shall fight
know you well it shal be so,
that die shal many a gentle knight.
With death shall many doughtie daile
The Lordes shal be then away,
there is no Harret that can tell
who shal win the field that day,
A crowned King in armes three
Vnder the Baner shal be set,
two false and feyned shal be,
the third shal light and make great let
Baners fiue againe shal striue,
and come in on the other side,
the white Lyon shall beate them downe,
and worke them woe with woundes wide,
The Bares heade with the read Lyon,
So seemly into read golde set,
That day shal slay the King with Crowne,
Though many Lordes make great let,
there shal attour the water of Forth
Set in golde the read Lyon.
And many Lords out of the North
to that battell shal make them boun,
there shal Crescentes come ful keene,
that weares the Croce as read as blood
On cuerie side shal be sorrow seene,
Defouled is many doughtie foode,

181

Beside a Lough, vpon a lie,
they shal assemble vpon a day,
And many doughtie men shal die
Few in quiet shal be found away,
Our Scottish King shal come full keene,
The read Lyon beareth he,
A feddered arrow sharpe I weene
Shal make him winke and warre to see,
Out of the filde he shal be led
When he is bloody and woe for blood,
Yet to his men shall he say
For Gods loue you turne againe
And giue those Sutherne folke a fray,
Why should I lose, the right is mine,
My date is not to die this day.
Yonder is falsehoode fled away,
and laughtie blowes his horse on hie,
Our bloodie King that wears the Crowne,
Ful boldlie shal he battell byde
His Baner shal be beaten downe
And hath no hole his head to hide,
the Sternes three that day shall die,
That bears the Harte in siluer sheene:
there is no riches golde nor fee,
May lengthen his life an howre I weene,
Thus through the field that Knight shal ride
And twise reskew the King with Crowne,
He will make many a Banner yield,
The Knight that beares the toddes three,
He will by force the field to ta,
But when he sees the Lyon die,
Thinke ye wel he wil be wae,

182

Beside him lightes beirnes three,
Two is white the third is blae,
the toddes three shall slay the two,
The third of them shall make him die,
Out of the field shall go no more
But one Knight and knaues three
There comes a Banner red as blud
In a Ship of siluer sheene,
With him comes many ferlie fude,
to worke the Scottes much hurte and woe,
There comes a Ghost out of the west,
Is of another language then he,
To the battle bownes him best,
As soone as he the Senyour can see,
the ratches workes them great wanrest,
Where they are rayed on a lie,
I cannot tell who hath the best
Each of them makes other die
A white Swan set into blae,
Shal semble from the South sey,
To worke the Northern folk great wae,
For know you well thus shal it be,
the staikes aucht with siluer set,
Shal semble from the other side,
Till he and the Swan be met,
They shal worke woe and woundes wide,
throw woundes wide, there weeds hath wet,
So boldlie will their beirnes byde,
It is no rek who gets the best,
They shal both die in that same tide.
There comes a Lord out of the North,
Riding vpon a horse of tree,

that broad landes hath beyond the Forth,
The white Hinde beareth he,
And two Ratchets that are blew,
Set into golde that is so free,
that day the Egill shal him slay,
and then put up his Banner hie:
The Lord that beares the Losanes three,
Set into gold with Gowles two,
Before him shal a battle be,
He weares a banner that is blew,
Set with Pecok tailes three:
and lustie Ladies heads two,
Vnfane of one, each other shal be,
all through griefe to gether they goe
I cannot tel who wins the gree,
Each of them shal other slay,
the Egill gray set into greene,
that weares the hartes heades three,
Out of the South he shal be seene,
to light and ray him on a lie,
With 55 Knights that are keene,
And Earles either two or three,
From Carlel shal come bedene,
Againe shal they it neuer see,
at Pinkin Cleuch their shal be spilt,
Much gentle blood that day,
Their shal the Baire lose the gylt,
And the Eagle beare it away,
Before the water man calles Tyne,
And there ouer lyes a brig of stone,
the Baires three, looses the gree.
there shal the Eagle win his name,

There comes a beast out of the west
With him shal come a faire manie,
His Baner hes beene seldom seene,
A bastard trowe I best he be,
Gotten with a Ladie sheene,
With a Knight in priuitie
His armes are full eath to knowe,
the read Lyon bears he,
that Lyon shall forsaken be,
and he right glad to flee away
Into an Orchyard on a lie,
With hearbs greene and allayes gray,
there will he inlaiked be,
His men sayes harmesay,
the Eagle puts his Baner on hie
and sayes the field he woone that day,
their shal the Lyon lye full still,
Into a vallie faire and bright,
A Ladie shoutes with words shrile,
and sayes woe worth the coward knight
Thy men are slaine vpon yon hil,
To dead are many doughtie dight,
Thereat the Lyon likes ill,
And raises his baner hie on hight
Vpon the moore that is so gray,
Beside a headless Croce of stone,
There shal the Eagle die that day,
And the read Lyon win the name
The Eagle three shal lose the gree,
that they haue had this manie day,
the read Lyon shal win renowne,
Win all the field and beare away,

185

One Crowe shal come, another shal goe,
And drink the gentle blood so free.
When all these ferlies was away
then saw I non, but I and he
then to the birne couth I say
Where dwels thou or in what countrie:
Or who shal rule the Ile of Bretaine
From the North to the South sey:
a French wife shal beare the Son,
Shall rule all Bretaine to the sey,
that of Bruces blood shall come,
As neere as the nint degree.
I franed fast what was his name,
Where that he came from what countrie?
In Erslingtoun, I dwell at hame
Thomas Rymour men calles me.

According to J.A.H. Murray, the original structure of this prophetic poem would be in four line stanzas. However, it breaks down in twelve places in this imperfect copy. Dr Murray in his edition, decided to print it as he found it. I have done likewise, except that it was originally written in double columns per page, with a dividing black line, in the MS from which it was taken.

The author states, that while walking "*upon a land beside a lie*" he saw visions, these being explained by a person he met. When the visions had disappeared, he was left alone with the interpreter.

••••••••••••••••••

Chapter 9

The Manuscripts

This chapter incorporates five of the manuscripts which contain the work of Thomas of Ercildoune; these being stored in various libraries in England. The Manuscripts are named, the *Cambridge*, the *Cotton*, the *Thornton*, the *Lansdowne* and the *Sloane*. The three fyttes of *The Romance and Prophecies of Thomas of Ercildoune* are preserved in four MSS, the prophecies alone are recorded in the *Sloane* 2578 MS. The *Thornton* MS is kept in the library of *Lincoln Cathedral;* while the *Cambridge* MS is kept in the *University Library Cambridge,* the *Cotton MS Vitellius Ex* and the *Lansdowne MS 762* are stored in the *British Museum.* The fifth manuscript, namely the *Sloane 2578,* which contains the prophecies without the introductory fytte, can also be found in the British Museum.

The following information is an abbreviated version of the manuscripts' analysis, as edited by J.A.H.Murray in his book entitled *The Romance and Prophecies of Thomas of Erceldoune.* The book was originally published for the *Early English Text Society,* by Trubner & Co. London, in 1875. A facsimile reprint was produced by Llanerch Publishers, Felinfach, in 1991. Dr Murray visited the various libraries on numerous occasions during the year of 1874, which enabled him to produce an accurate and detailed account of the existing manuscripts.

The manuscripts have suffered greatly with the passage of time, damaged either by fire or water, not to mention being deliberately altered by human intervention. None of the manuscripts is complete, with some of the text in all five being either missing or illegible; however, by combining the text from each, later transcribers have produced complete editions from the fragmented contents of the existing copies. The extant manuscripts reflect the various interpretations of the available text, arrived at by the individual transcribers; the consequences of this being, each manuscript is quite different, and often contradictory. The various versions of the ballad, combined with variations in the wording of the prophecies, serve only to provide us with an inkling of the original words spoken by Thomas.

The existing early copies of the *Romance* and *Prophecies* are the work of English transcribers. Dr Murray concluded that the conversion to southern dialect had corrupted the original lines of the poem. One example of this being a line in the *Thornton* MS which reads, "*it was derk as mydnyght myrke,*" this also being the original wording in the *Cambridge* MS, however, at some point, the Cambridge MS was amended to read "*wher hit was derk as any hell.*" One line, referring to the Fairy Queen *riding off to Helmsdale,* is not included in the more recent versions of the ballad; *Helmsdale* is a village in Sutherland in the north east of Scotland, a place, in the traditions of ancient folklore, where *Fairies* and *Witches* were believed to originate.

Many of the rhymes of Thomas were written down after his disappearance. In later years, as the various transcribers edited them, the original words were misconstrued; consequently the words were altered, rendering them barely recognisable. The more recent

188

ballad versions of the *Romance of Thomas the Rhymer* do not include the prophecies, whereas in the following manuscripts, except for the *Sloan MS,* the ballad and prophecies are integral to each other. The following is a brief description of each MS, followed by the Romance, including the prophecies, collated from the manuscripts.

The Cambridge MS

This is a paper manuscript in handwriting of the mid fifteenth century. It contains one hundred and forty leaves and consists of five parts and four articles. Number twenty six in the MS (2nd article) is *Thomas of Erseldoun.* It begins without any title and occupies ten leaves written in single columns, ending with the word; *Explicit.* The writing is indistinct and greatly effaced, which adds to its obscurity. Robert Jamieson printed this version of the poem in his edition of *'Ballads and Songs from Traditional Manuscripts And Scarce Editions'* in the eighteenth century. However, due to his inability to decipher parts of the text, Jamieson's version contains inclusions from the *Cotton* MS and the *Lincoln MS.* Jamieson's version contains many misquotes, and alterations to the original text. J.O. Halliwell Esq. used the text from the Cambridge MS in 1845 when he composed *"Illustrations of the Fairy Mythology of A Midsummer's Nights Dream"* for the *Shakespeare Society.* Mr Halliwell referred to the Cambridge as *"The earliest and best"* and dated it from the early fifteenth century. Mr Wright disagreed with this date however, and dated it from a much earlier period, during the reign of King Edward II, in the fourteenth century.

Dr Murray disagreed with both these dates, but was of the opinion that the inclusion of the work of Thomas the Rhymer in the *Cambridge MS* was a valuable asset, if only to fill in the blanks from the *Thornton* and *Cotton MSS.*

The *Cambridge MS* was damaged by rainwater, further damaged by the intentional crossing out of some parts of the text, and by substitutions from an unknown source. This resulted in the presentation of many deviations from the original text.

Dr Murray, with the expert assistance of Mr Bradshaw from the University Library Cambridge, was able to reproduce parts of the text which had been further damaged by Mr Jamieson's attempts at restoration; however some parts of the text in the Cambridge MS remain completely illegible.

The Cotton Vitellius E.x. MS.

This collection was compiled by Sir Robert Bruce Cotton. He lived from 1571 to 1631, his home being in Denton, Huntingdonshire in the south of England. This is a paper volume comprising of two hundred and forty leaves. The individual contents of this manuscript have been badly damaged by fire, and overall it is in a very poor condition. Many of the leaves are merely charred fragments; the original charred leaves having been inlaid and rebound. The fire damage occurred in the mid-eighteenth century, the result of a house-fire which broke out while the manuscripts were being temporarily stored at the premises.

Many volumes were completely destroyed, while others

190

were saved, but remain severely damaged and fragile. It is a folio written on paper comprising of two hundred and forty two leaves. The character of the handwriting is varied; the MS includes twenty six articles and is thought to date from the fifteenth century.

The MS contains articles on sermons preached c1483, and also during the reign of King Edward V or King Richard III, many ancient charters are also contained in the manuscript.

The article on *Thomas of Erseldown* is written in clumsy handwriting, it begins on the middle of leaf 240*b* with the title *Incipit prophecia Thome Arseldon.* The text is written in double lines across the page, with approximately one hundred lines per page. A central red line divides pages 241*b*, and 242*a*, part of page 242*b* has a red paragraph line.

The poem is written from start to finish without a break. Line 309/10 follows line 301/2, is written in red ink, and repeated after a blank space of one line, resulting in the last three lines being omitted. Although much of the text has been burned away, the legible text is consistent with that of the *Thornton MS*, however stanzas are often omitted. As in the other MSS, with the exception of the *Thornton,* there are omissions in this version; this manuscript alone, having additions. The poem ends at the foot of leaf 243 with the rubic *hecia thome de Arseldoune*

The Thornton MS (Lincoln A. 1. 17.)

This manuscript is mostly, but not entirely, the work of *Robert Thornton* from North Yorkshire and is thought to

191

have been compiled c1430. Robert Thornton lived from 1418 to 1456. Contained in this manuscript are romances and other relevant articles, all written in the northern dialect. This is a paper volume of approximately 314 leaves, many of which are missing or torn, the manuscript is also damaged at the beginning and end. It concludes with the words *Explicit Thomas OF Erseledowne*. The handwriting is in small letters, the piece entitled '*A Life of Alexander the Great*', is written in an older style, which suggests that this inclusion has been taken from a separate manuscript; the romance of *Syr Perecyuelle of Galles* is also written in a different style. Both *Professor F.J. Child* of *Harvard University U.S.A.*, and *Dr Laing*, regard the *Thornton* MS as the earliest and most accurate manuscript. Despite this commendation, it is apparent that this version of the *Romance and Prophecies* is not the original, since the text has been misconstrued and altered. The rhyming tale existed in its original format prior to this date, unfortunately, as yet, its location remains unknown.

The introduction to the tale of Thomas and the Fairy Queen, which appears in the Thornton MS alone, would appear to be the script of a minstrel or narrator. The dialect is northern and the term *Ynglyshmen*, as opposed to *Scottishmen*, suggests it was written for the benefit of an *English* audience. The text is written in double columns, with 36 to 40 lines per column, unfortunately, as with all the manuscripts, many of the pages are badly damaged, in this case by tearing. One part of the poem, which existed in the Thornton alone, has been entirely lost; however, this MS has managed to retain most of the original *Northern* form of the

192

language, as opposed to the *Southernised* version found in the others. Much of the text is authentic and does not contain the alterations and corruptions of the Cotton and Cambridge MSS.

Professor *F.J. Child* of *Harvard University U.S.A.*, in the first volume of his *English and Scottish Ballads* printed in London in 1861, reprinted the first fytte of the *Thornton* text from *Dr Laing's* 1822 edition, with corrections. Dr Murray credited Robert Thornton with transcribing a careful and almost accurate text.

The Lansdowne 792 MS

The Lansdowne is a smaller manuscript than the others, containing only ninety nine leaves combining parchment and paper. The date of its compilation is thought to be around 1524/30. In the main it contains predictions; however, it also contains a memorandum of the orders of Friars in London and their quarters, as they existed at the time. Also included is *"the writing of Valeraunce upon the xxi conjunccion of planets in the month of February, the yere of our Lord 1524."*

This MS includes prophecies already fulfilled and those yet to happen; the content of the second half is entirely prophetic literature. The writing is neat and legible, although many lines are omitted. The text is written in single columns, with thirty-two lines per page. There are no breaks from start to finish and no change in the size of letters at the fyttes.

The section relating to *Thomas of Arsildoun* starts without a title in the middle of leaf twenty-four, breaking off on page thirty-one. Leaves twenty- four to twenty-

eight are paper, while leaves twenty- nine to thirty-one are parchment. On leaf forty-nine, with the title, *'Thomas of Erceldoune'*, is the following, *Thomas of Asheldon sayeth "The faderis of the modern church/ shall cause the Roes bothe to dye in his Avne fontether/he was christened.* On leaf fifty; *Thomas of Asheldon sayeth; "the egle of the/trew brute shall see all Ingland in peas & rest/ both spirituall and temporall; and every estate of/in thair degree and the maydens of Englande/bylde you howses of lyme and stone."*
Similar to the other manuscripts, much of the text is missing, there is inconsistency in the dialect and the final part of the poem is abruptly omitted, with the remainder of the page blank. The Lansdowne MS has three additions which are not found in any of the other manuscripts.

The Sloane 2578 MS

This collection of manuscripts and artefacts originally formed part of a private collection belonging to Sir Hans Sloane. He lived between 1660 and 1753 and was born in County Down, Northern Ireland. His career was that of a Physician and Scientist. Sir Hans Sloane accumulated a vast collection of plants, coins, and artefacts during his lifetime, manuscripts making up only a small part of his memorabilia. Following his death, his entire collection was purchased for the nation and subsequently formed the basis of the British Museum. The Sloane MS, which is thought to date from around 1547, includes the prophecies of Thomas of Ercildoune; it also contains the prophecies of *Wizards.*

The MS consists of one hundred and seventeen leaves and contains unfulfilled predictions from the years 1550, 1553, and 1556.
The prophecies of *Erceldoun* begin at the top of leaf six, with the heading;

> *Heare begynethe pe ij fytt I say*
> *Of Sir Thomas of Arseldon.*

Included are the prophecies of *Merlin* and the *Prophetic Rhymes of Thomas of Ercildon.* It is laid out in single columns of twenty-eight lines, without a break, ending at the foot of leaf eleven with the word *Finis.* In many respects, this MS is similar to the *Thornton* MS; however the first line of each stanza is often missing, with the peculiar feature of an extra line being inserted at the end. The Sloane MS contains only the prophecies of Thomas the Rhymer, without the inclusion of the *"Romance of Thomas of Ercildoune."*

The Fyttes

The spelling of the word *Fytte* varies from one manuscript to the next, it is also inconsistent within each manuscript. For example, in the *Lansdowne* MS, the first and second are spelt *foott,* while the third is spelt *Fote.* In the *Thornton* MS, the first is spelt *Fytte,* the second and third are spelt *Fytt.* The *Sloan* has no first fytte, but the second is spelt *Fytt* and the third is spelt *Fytte.*The *Cotton,* as previously mentioned, has no Fytte heading in the first part and begins with the words *'Incipit prophecia Thome Arseldon',* the second and third

195

parts are spelt *Fyt.* Only the *Cambridge* MS is consistent, with the spelling of *Fytte* throughout the three parts.

The first *Fytte* of the ballad describes the meeting of Thomas and the *Fairy Queen,* followed by the journey to the Fairy kingdom. The second *Fytte* describes the return to the *Eldon* tree, followed by the request from Thomas for a token of their meeting. The third *Fytte* details the prophecies, as told to Thomas by the Fairy Queen.

The variance in spelling has little significance, other than to illustrate the inaccuracy, and the inconsistency of the early transcribers' works.

One example of the same word being misspelt in the various MS is the following; the *Cotton* MS has the spelling *halyndon hill,* the *Lansdowne* MS, *helydowne hill,* the *Thornton, Eldone,* and the *Cambridge, ledyn/Eldyn.* The assumption being, that the battle in question was the battle of *Halidon hill,* where, during the S*econd War of Independence,* on the19th July 1333, the Scots were heavily defeated by the English. Since many of the Scottish nobles were killed during this battle, the English confidently assumed that the wars would be over; the military power-force of the Scots having been annihilated. Following the seizure of Perth from Baliol, James and Simon Fraser were slain at the battle of *Halidon Hill.*

Preserved in *MS Harl., 2253 (if 127, col.2),* which dates from the early fourteenth century, is the reply from Thomas when the *Countess of Dunbar* asks him when the wars between Scotland and England will cease.

The words are as follows,

La countesse de Donbar demanda a Thomas de
Essedoune quant la guere descoce prendreit fyn. e yl la
repoundy e dyt,

The reply:

"When man as mad akyng of a capped man;
When mon is leuere opermoncs pyng pen owen;
When londyonys forest, ant forest ys felde;
When hares kindles ope herston;
When Wyt7 Willie werres togedere;
When mon makes stables of kyrkes, and steles castles
wyp styes;
When rokesbourh nys no burgh ant market is at
Forwyleye;
When pe alde is gan ant pen ewe is come p don (or don)
nopt;
When bambourne is donged Wyp dedemen;
When men ledes men in ropes to buyen & to sellen;
When a quarter of whaty whete is changed for a colt of
ten markes;
When prude prikes & pees is leyd in prisoun;
When a scot ne may hym hude ase hare in forme p pe
englysshe ne sal hym fynde;
When rypt ant Wrong ascentep to gedere;
When laddes weddep louedis;
When scottes flen so faste p for faute of ship, hy drownep
hem selue;
Whenne shal pis be? Nouper in pine tyme ne in myne;
Ah comen & gon wip inne twenty winter ant on."

The text is written in a manner which is consistent with

the manuscripts of the time; the spelling being inconsistent and capital letters being wrongly used mid sentence. As a rule the letter *t* is substituted by the letter *p*, however this is not always the case. The letter *v* is used in place of *u* at the beginning of a word, and the letter *y* is usually substituted by the letter *p*.

Dr Murray copied the words and layout exactly as he found them in the manuscripts. He also translated the above prophecy, with a short explanation, which I quote here;

The Countess of Dunbar asked Thomas of Erceldoune when the Scottish Wars would end, and he answered saying;

"When people have (man has) made a king of a capped man;
When another man's thing is dearer to one than his own;
When Loudyon (London?) is Forest and Forest is field;
When hares litter on the hearth-stone;
When wit and will war together;
When people make stables of churches, and set castles with styes;
When Roxburgh is no burgh and market is at Forwylee;
When the old is gone and the new is come that is worth (or do) nought;
When Bannockburn is dunged with dead men;
When people lead men in ropes to buy and sell;
When a quarter of 'indifferent' wheat is exchanged for a colt of 10 merks;
When pride rides on horseback, and peace is put in prison;

When a Scot cannot hide like a hare in form that the English shall not find him;
When right and wrong assent together; when lads marry ladies;
When Scots flee so fast, that for the want of ships, they drown themselves;
When shall this be? Neither in your time nor in mine;
But (shall) come and go within twenty winters and one."
The *Bannockburn* was "*dunged with dead men*" at the battle in 1314. *Roxburgh Castle* was the birthplace of King Alexander III. *Roxburgh* was one of the first of the major Scottish burghs, created during the reign of King David1. The thriving township, which flourished near the junction of the rivers *Tweed* and *Teviot*, simply disappeared in the sixteenth century. In later years, the site became the venue for the market of Kelso's *St. James's fair*.

In Thomas's time, the *lads* were the sons of the farm servants, the *ladies* were the daughters of the nobility. The *Countess of Dunbar* referred to in this case, was the wife of the 7th Earl, a friend and neighbour of Thomas. This was not the same Countess of Dunbar - wife of the 8th Earl - who tried, unsuccessfully, to defend the castle at the Battle of Dunbar in 1296. Nor was it *Black Agnes* (daughter of Randolph), the *Countess of Dunbar* who defended the same castle against the English invasion in 1338, and whose fate Thomas requested from the Fairy Queen.

I have compiled the complete *Romance* and *Prophecies*, collated from the five *incomplete* manuscripts. As far as possible I have used the Thornton manuscript; however, since each of the manuscripts is illegible in parts, and

199

the text is completely missing in all five at one point, I have switched between the MSS throughout. At the end of this chapter I have given a brief explanation of the variations in the content of each manuscript.

The article entitled *'Tomas Off Ersselsdowne'* occupies nine pages in the Thornton Manuscript and begins at the top of leaf 149; the version in the Thornton MS being the only one to begin with a prologue. *The Prologue* occupies lines 1 to 24 and is entitled "Tomas Off Ersseldowne"

Tomas Off Ersseldowne

1.   *Lystyns, lordyngs, bothe grete & smale,*
2.   *And takis gude tente what j will saye:*
3.   *I sall zow telle als trewe a tale,*
4.   *Als euer was herde by nyghte or daye:*
5.   *And þe maste meruelle ffor owttyne naye,*
6.   *That euer was herde by-fore or syene,*
7.   *And per-fore priestly j zow praye,*
8.   *That ze will of zoure talking blyne.*
9.   *It es an hard thing for to saye,*
10.   *Of doghety dedis þat hase bene done;*
   Of felle feghtyngs & batells sere;
11.   *And how þat þir knyghtis hase wonne þair schone.*
12.   *Bot jhesu crist þat syttis in trone,*
13.   *Safe ynglysche mene both ferre & nere;*
14.   *And j sall telle zow tyte and sone,*
16.   *Of Batells donne sythene many a zere;*
17.   *And of batells þat done sall bee;*
18.   *In whate place, and howe, and whare;*
19.   *Wha sall takk þe flyghte and flee,*

200

20. *And whethir partye sall hafe þe were;*
21. *Wha sall takk þe heghere gree,*
22. *And wha sall dye and by-leue thare:*
23. *Bot jhesu crist, þat dyed on tre,*
24. *Saue jynglysche mene whare-so þay fare.*

[Fytte The First]

25. Als j me wente þis Endres daye,
26. ffull faste in mynd makand my mone,
27. In a mery mornynge of Maye
28. By huntle bankkes my self alone,
29. I herde þe jaye & þe throstyll coke
30. The Mawys menyde hir of hir songe,
31. Þe wodewale beryde als a belle
32. That alle þe wode a-bowte me ronge.
33. Allonne in longynge thus als j laye,
34. Vnder-nethe a semly tree,
35. I was war of a lady gay,
36. Come ryding ouyr a fayre le.
37. If j solde sytt to domesdaye
38. With my tonge to wrobbe and wrye,
39. Certanely þat lady gaye,
40. Neuer bese scho askryede for mee.
41. Hir palfrae was a dappill graye.
42. The forest Molde that any might be;
43. Here sadell bright as any day
44. Set with pereles to þe knee,
45. And furthermore of hir Aray,
46. Swylke one ne saghe j neuer none;
47. Als dose þe sonne on someres daye
48. þat faire lady hir selfe scho schone.

201

49. Hir selle it was of roelle bone,
50. ffull seemly was þat syghte to see,
51. Stefly set with precious stones
52. And compaste all with crapotee,
53. Stones of Oryente, grete plente;
54. Hir hare abowte hir hede it hange;
55. Scho rade ouer þat lange lee,
56. A whylle scho blewe, a-noþer scho sange,
57. Hir garthes of nobyll sylke þay were,
58. The bukylls were of Berelle stone,
59. Hir steraps were of crystalle clere,
60. And all with perelle ouer-by-gone.
61. Hir payetrelle was of jrale fyne,
62. Hir cropoure was of Orphare;
63. And als clere golde hir brydill it schone,
64. One aythir syde hange belles three.
65. She led iij greyhoundis in a leesche,
66. viij rachis be hir fete ran;
67. To speke with hir wold I not seesse;
68. Hir lire was white as any swan.
69. fforsothe, Lordyngis, as I yow tell,
70. Thus was þis lady fayre began;
71. Scho bare an horne abowte hir hales,
72. And vnder hir belte full many a flone,
73. Thomas laye & saw þat syghte,
74. Vnder-nethe ane seemly tree;
75. He sayd "zonder es marye moste of myghte,
76. Þat bare þat childe þat dyede for mee.
77. Bot if j speke with zone lady bryghte,
78. I hope myne herte will bryste in three!
79. Now sall j go with all my myghte,
80. Hir for to mete at Eldoune tree."

81. Thomas rathely vpe he rase,
82. And he rane ouer *p*at Mountayne hye;
83. Gyff it be als the storye sayes,
84. He hir mette at Eldone tree.
85. He knelde downe appone his knee,
86. Vnder-nethe *p*at grenewode spraye;
87. And sayd, "lufly ladye! rewe one mee ,
88. Qwene of heuene als *p*ou wele maye!"
89. Then spake *p*at lady Milde of thoghte;
90. "Thomas! late swylke wordes bee;
91. Qwene of heuene ne am *j* noghte,
92. ffor *j* tuke neuer so heghe degree.
93. Bote *j* ame of ane o*p*er countree,
94. If *j* be payrelde moste of prysse;
95. I ryde aftyre this wylde fee,
96. My raches rynnys at my devyse."
97. "If *p*ou be parelde moste of prysse,
98. And here rydis thus in thy folye,
99. Of lufe, lady, als *p*ou erte wysse,
100. *p*ou gyffe me Leue to lye the bye!"
101. Scho sayde, "*p*ou mane, *p*at ware folye,
102. I praye *p*e, Thomas,*p*ou late me bee;
103. ffor *j* saye *p*e full sekirlye,
104. *p*at synne will for-doo all my beaute."
105. "Now, luffly ladye, rewe one mee,
106. And *j* will euer more with the duelle;
107. Here my trouthe *j* will the plyghte,
108. Whethir *p*ou will in heune or helle."
109. ------------ " *p*ou might lye me by,
110. Vnder-nethe *p*is grene-wode spraye,
111. ------------ telle to morrowe full hastely,
112. *p*at *p*ou hade layne by a lady gay.

203

113. ------------- I mote lygge by *p*e,
114. Vnder-nethe *p*is grene wode tre,
115. ------------- ll *p*e golde in crystyenty,
116. sulde *p*ou neuyr be wryede for me."
117. "Man of Molde! *p*ou will me marre,
118. Bot zitt *p*ou sall hafe all thy will;
119. And trowe it wele, *p*ou chewys *p*e were,
120. ffor alle my beaute will *p*ou spylle."
121. Downe *p*ane lyghte *p*at Lady btyghte,
122. Vnder-nethe *p*at grene wode spraye;
123. And, als the storye tellis full ryghte,
124. Seuene sythis by hir he laye,
125. Scho sayd, " mane, the lykes thy playe;
126. Whate byrde in boure may delle with the?
127. Thou merrys me all *p*is longe daye,
128. I praye the, Thomas, late me bee!"
129. Thomas stode vpe in *p*at stede,
130. And he by-helde *p*at lady gaye;
131. Hir hare it hange all ouer hir hede,
132. Hir eghne semede owte, *p*at are were graye.
133. And alle *p*e rich clothynge was a-waye,
134. *p*at he by-fore sawe in *p*at stede;
135. Hir a schanke blake, hir *o*per graye,
136. And all hir body lyke the lede.
137. Thomas laye & sawe *p*at syghte,
138. Vnder-nethe *p*at grenewod tree;
139. *P*an said Thomas,"allas! allas!
140. In faythe *p*is es a dullfull syghte;
141. How arte *p*ou fayde *p*us in *p*e face,
142. *p*at schone by-fore als *p*e sonne so bryghte."
143. On euery side he lokyde abowete,
144. He sau he might no whare fle;

145. Scho woxe so grym and so stowte,
146. The Dewyll he wende she had be,
147. In the Name of the trynite,
148. He coniuryde here anon Ryght,
149. That she shulde not come hymn ere,
150. But wende away of his sight.
151. She said, " Thomas, this is no need,
152. For fende of hell am I none;
153. For the now am I grete desese,
154. And suffer paynis many one.
155. this xij Mones þou shalt with me gang,
156. And se the maner of my lyffe;
157. for thy trowche thou hast me tane,
158. Ayene þat may ye make no stryfe.
159. Take thy leue of sone and Mone,
160. And als at lefe þat grewes on tree;
161. This twelmoneth sall þou with me gone
162. And Medill-erthe sall þou none see."
163. He knelyd downe appone his knee,
164. Vnder-nethe þat grenewod spraye;
165. And sayd, "luffly lady! rewe on mee,
166. Mylde qwene of heuen, als þou beste maye,
167. Allas! he sayd, "& wa es mee!
168. I trowe my dedis wyll wirke me care;
169. My saulle, jhese, by-teche j the,
170. Whedir-some þat euer my banes sall fare."
171. Scho ledde hym jn at Eldone hill,
172. Vnder-nethe a derne lee;
173. Whare it was dirke als mydnyght myrke,
174. And euer þe water till his knee.
175. The montenans of dayes three,
176. He herd bot swoghynge of þe flode;

205

177. At þe laste, he sayde, "full wa is mee!
178. Almaste j dye, for fawte of f[ode.]"
179. Scho led hym in-till a faire herbere,
180. Whare frwte was g[ro] wan [d gret plentee;]
181. Pere and appill, both ryppe þay were,
182. The date, and als the damasee;
183. Þe fygge, and als so þe wyneberye;
184. The nyghtgales byggande an þair neste;
185. þe papeioyes faste abowte gane flye;
186. And throstylls sange wolde hafe no reste.
187. He pressede to pulle frowyte with his hande,
188. Als mane for fude þat was nere faint;
189. Scho sayd, "Thomas! þou late þame stande,
190. Or ells þe fende the will atteynt.
191. If þou it plokk, sothely to saye,
192. Thi saule gose to þe fyre of helle;
193. It commes neuer owte or domesdaye
194. Bot þer jn payne ay for to duelle.
195. Thomas, sothely, j the hyghte,
196. Come lygge thyne hede downe on my knee,
197. And [þou] sall se þe fayreste syghte,
198. Þat euer sawe mane of thi contree."
199. He did in hye als scho hym bade;
200. Appone hir knee his hede he layde,
201. ffor hir to paye he was full glade,
202. And þane þat lady to hym sayde;
203. " Seese þou nowe ȝone faire waye,
204. Þat Lygges ouer ȝone heghe mountayne?
205. ȝone es þe waye to heuene for aye,
206. Whene synfull sawles are passede þer [payne,
207. Seese þou nowe ȝone oþer waye,
208. þat lygges lawe by-nethe ȝone rysse?

206

209.	Zone es *pe* waye *pe* soothe to saye,
210.	Vn-to *pe* joye of paradyse.
211.	Seese *pou* zitt zone thirde waye,
212.	*P*at ligges vnder zone grene playne?
213.	zone es *pew aye*, with tene and traye,
214.	Whare synfull saulis suffirris *p*aire payne,
215.	Bot seese *pou* nowe zone ferthe waye,
216.	*p*at lygges ouer zone depe delle?
217.	Zone es *pe* waye, so waylawaye,
218.	Vn-to *pe* birande fyre of helle.
219.	Seese *pou* zitt zone faire castell,
220.	[*p*at standis ouer] zone heghe hill?
221.	Of towne & towre, it beris *pe* belle;
222.	In erthe es none lyke it vn-till.
223.	ffor sothe, Thomas, zone es myne awenne,
224.	And *pe* kynges of this Countree ;
225.	Bot me ware be leuer be hanged and drawene ,
226.	Or *p*at he wyste *pou* laye me by,
227.	When *pou* commes to zone castelle gaye,
228.	I pray *pe* curtase mane to bee;
229.	And whate so any mane to *pe saye,*
230.	*L*uke *pou* answere none botte mee.
231.	My lorde es seruede at ylk a mese,
232.	With thritty knyghttis faire & free;
233.	I sall saye syttande at the desse,
234.	I tuke thi speche by-zonde the see."
235.	Thomas still als stane he stude,
236.	And he by-helde *p*at lady gaye;
237.	Scho come agayne als faire & gude,
238.	And also ryche one hir palfraye.
239.	Thomas said, " lady, wele is me,
240.	that euer I baide this day;

241. nowe ye bene so fayre and white,
242. By fore ye war so blake and gray!
243. I pray you that ye wyll me say,
244. lady, yf thy wyll be,
245. why ye war so blake and gray?
246. ye said it was be cause of me.""
247. "For soothe, and I had not been so,
248. Sertayne soothe I shall the tell;
249. Me had been as good to goo,
250. To the brynnyng fyre of hell."
251. Hir grewehundis fillide with dere blode;
252. Hir raches couplede by my faye;
253. Scho blewe hir horne, with mayne & mode,
254. Vn-to *p*e castelle scho tuke *pew aye.*
255. In-to *p*e haulle sothely scho went;
256. Thomas foloued at hir hande;
257. Than ladyes come, both faire & gent,
258. With curtassye to hir knelande.
259. Harpe & fethill bothe *p*ay fande,
260. Getterne, and als so *p*e sawtrye;
261. Lutte and rybybe bothe gangande,
262. And all manere of mynstralsye.
263. *P*e moste meruelle *p*at Thomas thoghte,
264. Whene *p*at he stode appone *p*e flore;
265. ffor feffty hertis jn were broghte,
266. *p*at were bothe grete and store.
267. Raches laye lapande in *p*e blode,
268. Cokes come with dryssynge knife;
269. Thay brittened *p*ame als *p*ay were wode,
270. Reuelle amanges *p*ame was full ryfe.
271. Knyghtis dawnesede by three and three,
272. There was revelle, gamene, and playe;

273. Luffy ladyes faire and free,
274. That satte and sange one riche araye.
275. Thomas duellide in that solace
276. More *p*ane j *z*owe saye parde;
277. Till one daye, so hafe I grace,
278. My luffly lady sayde to mee:
279. "Do buske, the Thomas, *p*e buse agayne;
280. ffor *p*ou may here no lengare be;
281. Hye the faste with myghte and mayne,
282. I sall the brynge till Eldone tree."
283. Thomas sayde *p*ayne with heuy chere,
284. "Luffly lady, nowe late me bee,
285. ffor certis, lady, *j* hafe bene here
286. Noghte bot *p*e space of dayes three!"
287. "ffor soothe, Thomas, als *j* *p*e telle,
288. *p*ou hase bene here thre zere & more;
289. Bot langere here *p*ou may noghte duelle,
290. The skylle *j* sall *p*e telle whare-fore:
291. To morne, of helle *p*e foulle fende.
292. Amange this folke will feche his fee;
293. And *p*ou arte mekill mane and hende,
294. I trowe full wele he wolde chese the.
295. ffor alle *p*e golde *p*at euer may bee,
296. ffro hethyne vn-to *p*e worldis ende,
297. *p*ou bese neuer be-trayede for mee;
298. *p*ere-fore with me j rede thou wende."
299. Scho broghte hym agayne to Eldone tree,
300. Vndir-nethe *p*at grenewod spraye;
301. In huntlee bannkes es mery to bee,
302. Whare fowles synges bothe nyght & daye.
303. "fferre owtt in *z*one Mountane graye,
304. Thomas, my fawkone bygges a neste;

209

305. A fawconne es an Erlis praye,
306. ffor-thi in na place may he reste.
307. ffare wele, Thomas, j wend my waye,
308. ffor me by-houys ouer thir bntiss browne."
309. loo here a fytt more es to saye,
310. All of Thomas of Erselldowne.

[Fytt The Seconde]

311. "Fare wele, Thomas, j wende my waye,
312. I may no lengare stande with the!"
313. "Gyff me a tokynyge, lady gaye,
314. That j may saye j spake with the."
315. " To harpe or carpe, whare-so þou gose,
316. Thomas, þou sall hafe þe chose sothely."
317. And he saide, "harpynge kepe j none;
318. ffor tonge es chefe of mynstrelsye."
319. "If þou will spelle, or tales telle,
320. Thomas, þou sall neuer lesynge lye,
321. Whare euer þou fare, by frythe or felle,
322. I praye the, speke none euyll of me!
323. ffare wele, Thomas, with-owttyne gyle,
324. I may no lengare duelle with the."
325. "Lufly lady, habyde a while,
326. And telle þou me of some ferly!"
327. "Thomas, herkyne what j the saye:
328. Whene a tree rote es dede,
329. The leues fadis þane & wytis a-waye;
330. & froyte it beris nane þane, white ne rede.
331. Of þe baylliolfe blod so sall it falle:
332. It sall be lyke a rotyne tree;
333. The comyns, & þe Barclays alle,

210

334. The Russells, & *pe* ffresells free,
335. All sall *pay* fade, and wyte a-waye;
336. Na ferly if *pat* froyte than dye.
337. And mekill bale sall after spraye,
338. Whare joye & blysse was wonte [to bee;]
339. ffare wele, Thomas, j wende m[y waye]
340. I may no langer stand w[ith the]"
341. "Now lufly lady gud [and gay]
342. Telle me zitt of some ferly!"
343. "Whatkyns ferlys, Thomas gude,
344. Solde j *pe* telle, and thi wills bee?"
345. "Telle me of this gentill blode,
346. Wha sall thrife, and wha sall thee:
347. Wha sall be kynge, wha sall be none,
348. And wha sall welde this northe counter?
349. Wha sall flee, & wha sall be tane,
350. And whare thir batells donne sall bee?"
351. "Thomas, of a Batelle j sall *pe* telle,
352. *pat* sall be done righte sone at wille:
353. Beryns sall mete bothe fers & felle,
354. And freschely fighte at Eldone hille.
355. The Bretons blode sall vndir fete,
356. *pe* Bruyse blode sall wyne *pe* spraye;
357. Sex thowsande ynglysche, wele *pou* wete,
358. Sall there be slayne, *pat* jlk daye.
359. ffare wele, Thomas, j wende my waye;
360. To stande with the, me think full jrke.
361. Of a batell j will the saye,
362. *pat* sall be done at fawkirke:
363. Baners sall stande, bothe lang and lange;
364. Trowe this wele, with mode and mayne;
365. The bruysse blode sall vndir gane,

211

366.	Seuene thowsande scottis *p*er sall be slayne.
367.	ffare wele, Thomas, j pray *p*e sesse;
368.	No lengare here *p*ou tarye mee;
369.	My grewhundis , *p*ay breke *p*aire lesse,
370.	And my raches *p*aire copills in three.
371.	Loo! Whare *p*e dere, by twa and twa,
372.	Haldis ouer zone Montane heghe."
373.	Thomas said, "god schilde *p*ou gaa!
374.	Bott telle me zitt of some ferly."
375.	holde *p*i greyhoundis in *p*e h[onde,]
376.	And coupill *p*i raches to a [tre;]
377.	And lat *p*e dere reyke ouer *p*e londe;
378.	there is a herde in holtely."
379.	["Of a] batelle, j sall the saye,
380.	[That sall] gare ladyse morne in mode;
381.	At Bankes bourne, both water & claye
382.	Sall be mengyde with mannes blode:
383.	Stedis sall stombill with tresoune,
384.	Bothe Baye & broune, grysselle and graye;
385.	Gentill knyghtis sall stombill downe,
386.	Thorowe *p*e takynge of a wykkide way.
387.	*p*e Bretons blode sall vndir falle;
388.	The Bryusse blode sall wyne *p*e spraye;
389.	Sex thowsand ynglysche, grete & smalee,
390.	Sall there be slane, *p*at jlk a daye.
391.	Than sall scottland kyngles stande;
392.	Trow it wele, *p*at j the saye!
393.	A tercelet, of the same lande,
394.	To bretane sall take *p*e redy waye,
395.	And take tercelettis grete and graye,
396.	With hym owte of his awene contre;
397.	Thay sall wende on an ryche array,

212

398.	And come agayne by land ans see.
399.	He sall stroye the northe contree,
400.	Mare and lesse hym by-forne;
401.	Ladyse sall saye, allas! & walowaye!
402.	þat euer þat Royalle blode was borne.
403.	He sall ryse vpe at kynke horne,
404.	And tye þe chippis vn-to þe sande.
405.	At dipplynge more, appone þe Morne,
406.	Lordis will thynke full lange to stande;
407.	By-twix depplynge and the dales,
408.	The water þat rynnes one rede claye-
409.	There sall be slayne, for sothe, Thomas,
410.	Eleune thowsandez scottis, þat nyghte & daye.
411.	Thay sall take a townne of great renownne,
412.	þat standis nere the water of Taye;
413.	þe ffadir & þe sone sall be dongene downe,
414.	And with strakis strange be slaynea-waye.
415.	Whene þay hafe wonne þat walled towne,
416.	And ylke mane hase cheude þayre chance,
417.	Than sall thir Bretons make þame bowne,
418.	And fare forthe to þe werre of fraunce.
419.	Than sall scotland kyng-lesse stande,
420.	And be lefte, Thomas, als j the saye;
421.	Than sall a kyng be chosene, so zynge,
422.	That kane no lawes lede þar faye;
423.	Dauid, with care he sall wende awaye.
424.	Lordis & ladyse, more ans Myne,
425.	Sall come appone a rich araye,
426.	And crowne hym at the towne of skyme,
427.	Appone an certane solempe daye.
428.	Beryns balde, both zonge and alde,
429.	Sall till hym drawe with-owttyne naye;

430. Euyne he sall to ynglande ryde,
431. Este and weste als lygges the waye.
432. & take a towne with greate pride,
433. & let *pe* menn be slaine awaye.
434. Be-twixe a parke and an abbaye,
435. A palesse and a paresche kyrk,
436. Thare sall *zour* kynge faill of his praye,
437. And of his lyfe be wonder jrke.
438. He sall be tane, so wonder sare,
439. So *pat* a-way he sall noghte flee;
440. Hys nebbe sall rynne, or he thens fare,
441. *pe* redeblode tryklelande vn-to his kn[ee].
442. He shall, throwght a fals fode,
443. Be betrayde of his owne londe;
444. And whithir it torne to ewyll or good;
445. & he shall bide in a ravens hand,
446. the ravin sall *pe* Goshawke wynne,
447. if his fethers be neuer so black;
448. & leide him stayte to London,
449. *per* shall your fawcone fynde his make.
450. *pe* ravin shall his fethers shake,
451. & take tarslettes gaye & greate,
452. With him, owte of his awne contre,
453. & *pe* kinge shall him Mr make,
454. In *pe* northe to do owttraye.
455. And whene he es mane moste of Mayne,
456. And hopis beste *pane* for to spede,
457. On a ley lande sall he be slayne,
458. Be-syde a waye for-owttyne drede.
459. Sythene sall selle Scotland, par me faye,
460. ffulle and fere, full many ane,
461. ffor to make a certane paye;

214

462. Bot ende of it sall neuer come nane.
463. And þane sall Scotland kyngles stande;
464. Trowe this wele, þat j telle the!
465. Thre tercelettis of þe same lande
466. Sall stryfe to bygg & browke þe tree.
467. He sall bygg & browke the tree,
468. That hase no flyghte to fley a-waye;
469. Robert steward kyng shal be
470. Of Scotland, and Regne mony A day.
471. A cheuanteyne then shall ryse with pride,
472. of all Scotland, and bere the floure;
473. Thay sall with pryde to y[n]gland ryde,
474. Este & weste als lygges þe waye.
475. Haly kyrke bese sett be-syde,
476. Relygyous byrnede on a fyre;
477. Sythene sall þay to a castelle gl[yde],
478. And schewe þame þare with mykell ire.
479. By-syde a well & a weare,
480. A withwell & a slyke stone,
481. þer shall ij cheftans mete in fere,
482. the on shall doughtles be slayne.
483. That other cheftan shall be tane,
484. The brusse blud shall with him fle,
485. & leade him to a worthi towne;
486. and close him in a castell light,
487. theare to be with greate renowne.
488. Farewell, I wend my waye;
489. me behoves ouer yonder bent so brown."
490. here endeth þe ij fytt, I saye,
491. of sir Thomas of Arseldon.

492. "Now, luffly lady, gentle and hende,
493. Telle me, ʒif it thi willis bee,
494. Of thyes Batells, how þay schall ende,
495. And whate schalle worthe of this northe countre?"
496. "This worlde, Thomas, sothely to telle,
497. Es noghte bot wandrethe & woghe!
498. Of a batelle j will the telle,
499. That schall be donne at spynkarde cloughe:
500. The Bretons blode schalle vndir falle,
501. The bruyse blode schalle wyne þe spraye;
502. Sex thowsande ynglysche, grete & smalle,
503. Salle thare be slayne þat nyghte & daye.
504. The rerewarde sall noghte weite, parfaye,
505. Of that jlke dulfulle dede;
506. Thay sall make a grete journaye,
507. Dayes tene with-owttyne drede.
508. And of a batelle j will þe telle,
509. That sall be donne now sone at will:
510. Beryns sall mete, bothe ferse & felle,
511. And freschely fyghte at pentland hyll.
512. By-twyx Semberry & pentlande,
513. þe haulle þat standis appone þe red claye-
514. there shalbe slayne xij thowsand,
515. forsothe, of scottes þat night & daye.
516. thei shall take a walled towne,
517. the father & þe sonne bene slayne awaye;
518. knightes shall wynne þer warsone,
519. thurghe dynt of swerd for euer & aye.
520. when þei haue wonne the wallid towne,
521. and euery mann chose his chaunce,

216

522.	the bretons þen shall make them bowne,
523.	and forthe to þe warres of Fraunce.
524.	thei shalbe in fraunce full Thomas,
525.	I saye, iij yeares & mare;
526.	and dynge downe towerz & castells stronge,
527.	betwixt Seiton & þe seye;
528.	the bretons shalbe greaves amonge,
529.	the other este at Barwik fre.
530.	Fforryours further sall flee,
531.	On a Sondaye, by-fore þe masse,
532.	Seuene thowsandes sothely sall be slayne,
533.	One aythir partye, more and lesse.
534.	ffor þer sall be no baneres presse,
535.	Bot ferre in sondir sall thay bee;
536.	Carefull sall be þe after mese,
537.	By-twixe Cetone and þe See.
538.	Of þe brusse, bothe moare & les.
539.	Schippis sall stande appone þe Sande,
540.	Wayffande with þe Sees fame;
541.	Thre зere and mare, þan sall þay stande,
542.	Or any beryne come foche þame hame.
543.	Stedis awaye Maysterles sall flynge,
544.	Ouer þe Mountans too and fraa;
545.	Thaire sadills one paire bakkis sall hynge,
546.	Vn-to þe garthis be rotyne in twaa.
547.	зitt sall þay hewe one alle þe daye,
548.	Vn-to þe sonne be sett nere weste;
549.	Bot þer es no wighte þat зitt wiete mayre,
550.	Wheþer of thayme sall hafe þe beste.
551.	That sall plante downe þaire thare,
552.	Worthi mene al nyghte sall dye;
553.	Bot one þe Morne þer sall be care,

217

554. ffor now *p*er side sall hafe *p*e gree.
555. Than sall *p*ay take a trew, and swere,
556. ffor thre *z*ere & more, j vnderstande,
557. *p*at nane of *p*ame sall o*p*er dere,
558. [Now *p*er] by See ne *z*itt by lande.
559. Betwin ij Saint mary dayes,
560. when *p*e tyme waxethe longe,
561. then sall thei mete, & bannerz raise,
562. on claydon moore, bothe styf & stronge.
563. Gladysmore, *p*at gladis vs all,
564. This is begynyng of our gle;
565. gret sorrow *p*en shall fall,
566. Wher rest and pees were wont to be.
567. iij crowned kinges, with dyntis sore,
568. shalbe slayne, & vnder be.
569. a Raven shall comme ouer *p*e moore;
570. and after him a crowe shalle flee,
571. to seke *p*e moore, without reste,
572. after a crosse is made of stone,
573. ouer hill & dale, bothe easte & weste;
574. Bot wiete wele, Thomas, he sall fynd nan[e].
575. He sall lyghte, whare *p*e crosse solde bee,
576. And holde his nebbe vp to the skye;
577. And drynke of gentill blode and free;
578. *p*ane ladys, waylowaye, sall crye.
579. Ther sall a lorde come to *p*at werre,
580. *p*at sall be of full grete renown[ne];
581. And in his Banere sall he bere,
582. Triste it wele, a rede lyone.
583. Thar sall ano*p*er come to *p*at werr[e],
584. *P*at sall fyghte full fayrein [   ]
585. And in his banere sall he ber[e]

218

586. A Schippe with an ankyre of golde.
587. Zitt sall an oþer come to þat were,
588. þat es noghte knawene by northe n[e southe];
589. And in his Banere sall he bere
590. A wolfe with a nakede childe in his mo[uthe].
591. Zitt sall þe ferthe lordecome to þat w[erre],
592. Þat sall grete Maystries after ma[ke];
593. And in his B[anere sa]ll he b[er]e
594. The bere ....

Eleven lines missing here from all five MSS.

605. freely þei shall fight þat daye,
606. to þat þe sonne be sett neare weste;
607. none of them shall witt, I saye,
608. wither partie shall haue þe beste.
609. a basted shall comme owte of a fforreste,
610. in sothe England borne shalbe-
611. he shall wynne peg re for þe beste,
612. & all þe land after bretens shalbe.
613. then he shall into Enfland ryde,
614. easte weste, as we heare sayne.
615. And holde A parlament of moche pryde,
616. That neuer no parlament by fore was seyne.
617. all false lawes he shall laye downe,
618. þat ar begonne in þat contre;
619. trewthe to do, he shalbe bone,
620. & all þe land, after bretens shalbe.
621. thomas! trowe þat I the tell,
622. that it be so, eueriche worde.
623. of a battell I shall the spell,
624. that shalbe done at sandyford:

219

625. ney *p*e forde *p*er is a braye,
626. and ney *p*e braye *p*er is a well;
627. a stone *p*er is, a lytell fraye,
628. & so *p*er is, *p*e soothe to tell.
629. thowe may trowe this, euery wurde-
630. growand *p*er be okes iij; [3]
631. that is called the sandyford,
632. *p*er the laste battell done shalbe.
633. Remnerdes & Clyffordes bolde shalbe,
634. In Bruse land iij yeares & mare,
635. & dynge downe towerz & castellz high;
636. to do owtraye thei shall not spare.
637. *p*e basted shall get him power stronge,
638. all *p*e fyue leishe lande-
639. there shall not on him bodword brynge,
640. as I am for to vnderstand.
641. pe basted shall die in *p*e holly lande;
642. Ihesu Criste! *P*at mykell maye,
643. his sowle *p*ou take into *p*i hande,
644. when he is deade & layed in claye!
645. & as she tolde, at the laste,
646. *P*e teares fell ouer hir eyen graye.
647. "Ladye, or you wepe so faste,
648. take your leave & goo your waye!"
649. " I wepe not for my waye wyndinge,
650. but for ladyes, faire & fre,
651. when lordes bene deade, without leasynge,
652. shall wedd yomen of poore degree.
653. he shall have steades in stabull fedd;
654. a hawke to bare vpon his hand;
655. a lovly lady to his bedd;
656. his elders before him had no land!

220

657. farewell, Thomas, well the be!
658. for all this daye thowe wilt me marr."
659. "nowe, lovly lady, tell thowe me,
660. Of blak annes of Dvnbar."
661. And why she haue given me þe warre,
662. And put me in hir prison depe;
663. ffor I wolde dwel with hir,
664. And kepe hir ploos and hir she[pe]."
665. " of blak annes comme neuer gode,
666. Therefore, maye she neuer the:
667. For all hir welthe, & worldes gode,
668. in london shall she slayne be.
669. the greateste merchaunte of hir blud,
670. in a dike shall he dye;
671. houndes of him shall take þer fode,
672. mawger all þer kynne & he."
673. thomas, drere mann was he,
674. teares fell ouer his eyen so graye,
675. "nowe, lovly lady, tell þou me,
676. if we shall parte for euer & aye?"
677. "naye!" she saide, "Thomas parde,
678. when thowe sitteste in Arseldon,
679. to hontley bankis þou take þe waye;
680. þer shall I sykerly to the recomme.
681. Thomas, I wende my waye,
682. I may no langer stande with þe,
683. þe pray tel neuyr frendes at home of me."
684. "I shall reken, wheare euer I goo,
685. To beare the price of curtese.
686. [For tu]nge es wele, & tunge es waa,
687. [And tun]ge es chefe of Mynstrallsye."
688. Tonge is water & tonge is wyne,

221

689. [Tonge is che]fe of melody;
690. & tong is thyng *p*at fast wil bynd."
691. [*p*en went] forth *p*at lady gay,
692. vpon hyr wayes for to w[ende]
693. [Scho ble]we hir horne on hir palfraye,
694. [And left]e Thomas vndir-nethe a tre;
695. [To Helmesd]ale scho tuke the waye;
696. [And thus] departed scho and hee!
697. [Of swilke] an hird mane wolde j here,
698. [*p*at couth] Me telle of swilk ferly.
699. [Ihesu], corounde with a crowne of brere,
700. [Bry]nge vs to his heuene So hyee!
                    amene, amene.

                Explicit Thomas of Erseledownne

Lines 1 to 24 are found in the *Thornton* MS alone, and
form a prologue or introduction to the tale.
Lines 25 to 311 contain the first fytte, which, in the main,
describes the circumstances whereby Thomas first caught
sight of the Fairy Queen, the journey to her kingdom, and
the return to the Eildon tree.
Lines 25 to 34 are taken from the *Thornton* manuscript
and are consistent with the three other MSS.
In lines 35 and 36 some of the words are missing from the
Thornton MS, therefore in this instance I have used the
wording from the *Cambridge* MS.
Lines 37 to 41 are again taken from the *Thornton* MS, and
in all four MSS the wording is similar.
Lines 42 to 45 are taken from the *Lansdowne* MS, these
four lines being missing in the three other MSS. Lines 46
to 64 are taken from the *Thornton*.

Lines 57 to 92 are incomplete in the *Cotton* MS. Lines 64 to 71 are taken from the *Cambridge* MS; this being the only MS with the lines complete.

Lines 72 to 108 are taken from the *Thornton;* the wording is comparable in all the MSS at this point.

Lines 109 to 116 are taken from the *Cotton* MS, again this being the only MS with these lines included, however they are imperfect, with words being omitted in a few of the lines.

Lines 117 to 142 are taken from the *Thornton* MS. Lines 143 to 156 are missing from the *Thornton, Cotton* and *Cambridge* and are contained in the *Lansdowne* MS alone. Lines 157 to 236 are taken from the *Thornton* MS. Part of this section of the Cotton MS is fragmented, but the details of the journey are similarly described in all four editions. All MSS are in agreement that they travel for three days, until they reach the *fair herbere,* and wade through water, not blood, to the knee.

Lines 237 to 250 are taken from the *Lansdowne* MS, these lines being missing from the other three. Lines 251 to 310 - the end of the first fytte - are from the Thornton. Lines 301 to 306 are interesting, yet confusing; *"In huntlee bannkes es mery to bee, Whare fowles synges bothe nyght & daye."* The words could imply that the sound of the monks singing can be heard at night, and the sound of birdsong can be heard during the day; the abbey at Melrose being quite near to Huntly Banks. Dr Murray, in his analysis, could offer no explanation for the significance of lines 303 to 306. I have also tried - unsuccessfully - to make sense of the words; therefore, I fear the true meaning must remain lost in the mists of time. The *Thornton, Lansdowne* and *Cambridge* all agree

223

with the words, *fawkone, facon,* or *fowkyn,* which are believed to mean *falcon.* The *Thornton* contradicts, by using the words, an *Erlis praye;* these lines being missing from the *Cotton.* The *Lansdowne* and *Cambridge* both use the words *"the herons pray,"* the words in the *Lansdowne* are *"therefore in no place may she Rest,"* as opposed to *"ffor-thi in na place may he rest,"* in the *Thornton.*

The second Fytte begins at Line 311. Here, Thomas asks the Fairy Queen for a token of their meeting, he then asks to be told *some ferly.* The entire second fytte contains predictions of future battles, naming the locations and the outcomes. At this point, two additional lines appear at the start of the Sloane MS which are not in the other four MSS. The words are *"Heare begynethe pe ij fytt I saye of Sir thomas of Arseldon."*

The Sloane 2578 begins on leaf 6 with *Fytt* 2; this MS contains the prophecies alone, without the ballad. Lines 311 to 374 are taken from the *Thornton* MS, the *Cotton* and *Lansdowne* at this point having many words, or entire lines missing.

Lines 333 to 337, naming the *Comyns, Barclays, Russels* and *Ffresells* (Frasers), relate to the prominent families of the time. The *Comyns* and *Frasers* took different sides during the war between Scotland and England while David II was a minor. David Comyn, the dispossessed Earl of Athol, was appointed Viceroy of Scotland by King Edward III in 1335. When Edward Balliol invaded Scotland in 1332, David Comyn was one of his right-hand men; he was slain soon after in the forest of *Kilblane* by Sir Andrew Moray. *Barbour* quotes one of the prophecies of Thomas as referring to this battle. Walter Comyn was slain at the *Battle of Annan* in 1332; his brother Thomas was executed soon after. The family of the Frasers' were also prominent at many battles, and are named in the history books of the period. Alexander Fraser was a commander at Dupplin in 1332. James and Simon Fraser were both slain at the battle of *Halidon Hill* in 1333, after capturing Perth from Balliol. The role the Frasers played in Scotland's history is mentioned in more detail in Chapter 10. The Barclays are also mentioned in the history books covering this period. In 1345, David de Berklay was responsible for the death of William Bullock, an English ecclesiastic of the period. Sir Walter de Berklay was involved in the plot against Robert Bruce, being tried before the *Black Parliament* of 1320. According to the *'Annals of Fordun,'* Andrew Barclay was executed on October 1st 1322, after being convicted of treachery.

Line 354 in the *Thornton MS* includes the word, *Eldone*, whereas the *Cambridge MS* has *ledyn*. The *Cotton* and *Lansdowne* have *halyndon* and *helydowne* respectively. This prophecy is thought to relate to the battle of *Halidon Hill*, which took place in 1333; this being the case, the two earliest MS have transcribed it incorrectly. Similarly, in lines 355 to 357, the *Thornton* incorrectly predicts the outcome of this battle (if indeed it relates to Halidon hill), with the *Breton's* (English) *blode* losing, and the *Bruyse* (Scottish) *blode* winning the battle. The *Thornton* predicts that six thousand *ynglysche* shall be slain, whereas the Sloane and Cambridge agree that the *scottysshe* or *scottes* shall be slain, but disagree on the number. The discrepancies in the details of the prophecies in each of the five MSS are quite obvious from here onwards.

In lines 361 to 366, all five MSS agree on the battle of Falkirk, however the *Cambridge, Cotton,* and *Lansdowne* have written, incorrectly, that the Scots will win the battle. The *Sloane* and *Lansdowne* include the words fowse *kyrk* and *faw Chirch*, respectively.

The next prophecy, occupying lines 379 to 391, refers to the battle of *Bannockburn*, which took place in June 1314. All five MSS are in agreement here, stating that *"sex thousand ynglysche grete and smallee"* shall be slain.

The tactics of Bruce, whereby he dug pits, and concealed them with turf to trap the unsuspecting enemy, are referred to in lines 383 to 386 *"steades shall stvmbull with treason, with blak & browne, grysell & graye, & gentill knightes shall tvmbull downe, thurghe taking of a wicked waye."*

From this point, I have used the *Thornon* MS, until lines 375 to 379, these lines being in the *Cambridge* MS alone. Lines 379 to line 431 are again taken from the *Thornton* MS, but lines 432 and 433 are from the *Sloane* MS, since these lines are missing from the *Thornton*. *"Than sall scottland kyngles stande,"* these words refer to the death of King Robert Bruce who died in1329, leaving a six year old son, and Scotland without a King. Lines 393 to 414 pertain to the *Battle of Dupplin* and the capture of the *townne of grete renownne* - Perth, in 1332.

In the *Cambridge* MS, lines 388 to 416 are missing entirely, however, the other four MSS agree that the *tercelet* (young falcon), *Edward Baliol* will lay claim to the throne of Scotland. With the backing of King Edward III, Baliol takes with him the dispossessed lords; *the tercelettis grete and graye, Henry Percy, Lord Wake, Henry Beaumont,* and *David Comyn,* to name a few. They come ashore at *kynke horne* (Kinghorn), in 1332. The *Sloane* MS has *kynkborne,* the *Lansdowne* has *kynges horne,* while the *Cotton* has *kynche horn.* It was here that the Scots, led by *Alexander Seton,* were slaughtered on the sands. At *Dupplin Moor,* by the River Earn (which flows over red sandstone), they took the Scots by surprise, resulting in another mass slaughter. They advanced on Perth the following day, where *"pe ffadir & pe sone sall be dongene downe, and with strakis strange be slaynea-waye."*

The *Lansdowne* MS states that *"there shalbe slayne v thousand Englishmen that night and day,"* whereas the *Thornton* states that *"There sall be slayne, for sothe, Thomas, Eleuene thowsandez scottis, pat nyghte & daye."* The *Sloane* states *"per shalbe slayne, forsothe, Thomas, X1 thowsand scottes, pat night & daye."*

Line 418, *"And fare forthe to pe were of Fraunce"* refers to the wars of France in 1337, when King Edward III, thinking that Scotland was subdued under the rule of Balliol, declared war, and subsequently invaded France in 1339.

Up to line 431, I have used the *Thornton* MS; however, the prophecies are not in the correct chronological order. The coronation of David II took place at Scone on November 24th 1331, before he left for France. He returned from exile in 1341, landing at Inverbervie. Lines 427 and 428 appear in the *Lansdowne* MS alone, *"Bornes blode shall wend to Rome, To get lyve of the pope yf they may."* A papal bull was sent from Rome to anoint David II on June 13th 1329, six days after the death of his father, King Robert I (*The Bruce*).

Lines 432 and 433 are taken from the *Sloane* MS; these being missing from the other four MSS. Lines 434 to 441 are taken from the *Thornton* MS, however, lines 442 to 452 are either fragmented in parts, or missing entirely in

227

this MS.

Since they are missing from the other MSS, I have used the *Lansdowne* MS for lines 442 and 443. Lines 444 to 453 are taken from the *Sloane* MS, only the *Sloane* and *Lansdowne* are complete at this point; each account being consistent with the other. The lines refer to the invasion of England by King David II. This occurred in 1346, five years after his return from exile in France. He took "*a towne with greate pryde*" - the town of Hexham - but was defeated at Beaurepair. Severely wounded, he was captured at Nevill's Cross near Durham and taken to London. The *fals fode,* are the *High Steward of Scotland* and the *Earl of March,* both of whom betrayed King David II by escaping from the battlefield with their division; they were later accused of failing to support their King.

The words, "*your fawcone fynde his make,*" are taken from the Sloane MS; five lines are missing from the *Thornton* MS, while the lines in the *Cambridge* and *Cotton* are illegible at this point. The word used in the *Lansdowne* is *goshawke* instead of *fawcone,* but the meaning is the same. The words refer to David II finding his *mate/make,* or *consort* in Joanna, sister of King Edward III.

Lines 451 to 468 are taken from the *Thornton* MS, lines 451 to line 458 are thought to refer to the slaughter of the *Knight of Liddesdale,* Sir William Douglas, who was killed in the *Ettrick Forest* in1353 by one of his kinsmen, after switching allegiance to the English side. Lines 459 to 468 describe the vast amount of money raised by the people of Scotland, through the sale of wool, to pay the King's ransom. King David II was released from imprisonment in London after partial payment of the fee.

Lines 469 to 485 are taken from the *Lansdowne* MS, eight

lines of the *Thornton* being fragmented at this point, with ten lines being missing entirely. The *Sloane* also has six lines missing, while the *Cotton* has unfinished sentences, rendering it impossible to decipher.

Line 469 states that *"Robert steward kyng shalbe"* - Robert II, nephew of King David II, was the first monarch of the *House of Stewart;* following the death of King David II, he became King of Scotland on 26th March 1371.

Line 471 to line 485 refer to the *Cheuanteyne* or *Cheftan,* this being the Earl of Douglas. In 1338, he and his supporters rode into England, plundering and pillaging, leaving everything, including religious houses, ablaze in their wake, especially in the county of Durham. They rode to Newcastle, and challenged Henry (Hotspur) Percy, the eldest son of the 1st Earl of Northumberland. However, the brave Douglas was eventually slain in a marsh at Otterburn. Hotspur was then captured and taken to Scotland. Lines 490 and 491 are from the *Sloane* MS.

The third fytte consists of Lines 492 to 700. As with the second fytte, there are many discrepancies between the five manuscripts, and many parts missing from each. The third fytte continues to tell of more battles to come, and ends with Thomas asking the lady if they will ever meet again.

Lines 492 to 515 are taken from the *Thornton* MS. The first six lines are missing from both the *Sloane* and the *Cambridge.*The first of this part describes a battle which will take place at *spynkard cloughe.* It is written as *Spenkard slough* in the *Sloane, spincar clow* in the Lansdowne, *spynyard hill* in the Cambridge, and *spynkar cl* in the *Cotton.* Apart from the variations in the spelling, the manuscripts disagree on the outcome of this battle.

229

The *Thornton, Sloane,* and *Lansdowne* maintain that the Scots, or *Brusse blode,* will win the battle, while the *Cotton* and *Cambridge* contradict, by predicting the English or *Bretyns blode* shall win. It is uncertain which battle this referred to, but has been regarded latterly as pertaining to the battle of Pinkie Cleugh. The *Thornton* and *Sloane* both agree that the *rereward* or *reareward* shall not take part in this *dulfulle dede,* but shall journey for ten days without fear. However, the Lansdowne contradicts this by saying "*the forward shall not wit, parfey, Certeyn of that dolfull dede.*" The Cambridge has four lines missing at this point, while the *Cotton* repeats the line "*Fare wele, Thomas I wend my way, I may no langer stand*"......

Lines 508 to 515 in the *Thornton* speak of a battle which will be fought at *pentland hyll,* By-twyx *Semberry* & *pentlande.* The *Sloane* calls the hill *Eldon, betwin Edynburgh* & *Pentland,* the *Lansdowne* has the words *Bytwix Eden brought and the Pent- the hall that stond on the Rede glay,* while the *Cotton* has *by twys edynburgh* & *pentlande.* They are all consistent here, with the inclusion of the words *hill* or *hall* that stands on the red clay, where eleven thousand *scottes* or *scotis mene, shall be slayne that nyghte* & *daye;* possibly referring to the invasion of Scotland by King Richard II in 1385, or the invasion by King Henry 1V in 1400, followed by the siege of Edinburgh.

Since there are thirteen lines missing from the *Thornton* MS, and eleven from the *Cambridge* at this point, I have used the *Lansdowne* MS until line 527. The words in lines 520 to 523 are a repetition of lines 415 to 418 in the second fytte. The four MSS are consistent in the description of a battle which will take place: *betwixt Seiton & pe seye,* the *englyshe shall ly in craggis amonge.* Variations in the spellings occur between the manuscripts; however, it is thought to refer to the town of Berwick. The *Thornton* has *barboke,* the *Sloane Barwik,* while the *Lansdowne* has *barkle.* The wording in the *Cambridge* is completely irrelevant here, while the *Cotton* mentions the *frenshe* in the corresponding line. However, all agree that *Seuene thowsandes,* according to the *Thornton,* and *v thowsand* according to the other four MSS, shall be slain on either side. *"No baners shall be raised, ffor per sall be no beneres presse, but farr in sonder shall thei be."* Neither side shall claim victory, but many men on either side shall be massacred.

Lines 537 to 562 are taken from the *Sloane* MS, since the lines are fragmented in part in the *Thornton* and *Cotton,* and partly missing in the *Lansdowne* and *Cambridge.* The words describe the dearth of men after this battle, and the sense of desolation which will ensue. *"Ships shall stand upon the sand, tossing in the* foam, *three years as I understand, with no-one to bring them home. Horses, masterless shall ride, to the mountains to and fro, saddles on their backs will hang, until the girths rot their sides in two."* The only two legible manuscripts at this point are the *Sloane* and the *Cambridge;* both state that a truce shall be declared by either side. The truce shall last for three years or more, until once again the banners will be raised on *claydon* or *gleydes moore.* It is uncertain which battle this refers to since Gladsmuir or Gledsmoor is mentioned many times in prophecies relating to Scotland and England. According to the prophecy, there will be great sorrow after this battle, *"Kings will be slain and the*

231

Ladys shall cry welawey."
Lines 563 to 578 are taken from the *Cambridge* MS, these lines being missing from the *Lansdowne and Cotton,* fragmented in the *Thornton,* while lines 577 to 604 are not included in the *Sloane* MS. The words in the *Cambridge* are *rauen* and *schrew,* while the *Sloane* has the words *Raven* and *crowe.* The raven and crow shall search the moor for a cross made out of stone, they will search over hill and dale, but will find none. *"He shall light wheare the crosse shuld be, & holde his nebbe into pe skye; & drynk of gentill blode and free."*

Lines 579 to 594 are contained in the *Thornton* alone, the words tell of a lord of *grete renown[ne]* who will come to the war displaying a *rede lyone* on his *Banere.* The following lines tell of the other lords who will come to the battle, they are not named, but described by their *armorial bearings; A Schippe with an ankyre of gold, A wolfe with a nakede childe in his mo[uthe,] The bere...........* Lines 577 to 604 are missing from all MSS except the *Thornton;* however, line 594 beginning with the words, *The bere* is incomplete in this MS. From line 595 to line 608, only the first two letters of each word appears; four lines being missing entirely at the bottom of this column. From line 612 to line 672, the leaf has been torn out of the *Thornton* MS.

Lines 605 to 614 are taken from the *Sloane* MS, however, this MS disagrees with the birthplace of the *basted,* or *bastarde,* who shall come from a *fforreste.* The words in the *Sloane* are, *"a basted shall comme owte of a fforreste, in soothe England borne shalbe"*- the words in the *Cambridge* are, *"A bastarde shal cum fro a forest - Not in ynglond borne shall he be,"* while the words in the

Lansdowne are, *"A basterd shall come out of the west, And there he shall wyne the gre."* The lines in the *Cotton* are fragmented here, the legible words being *forest*, and *in south yngland born sal be.* All four MSS agree that he shall ride into England, "shall *lay down* false laws, *hold a parliament where no parliament was ever seen, and become leader of all Britain."* Since two lines, 615 and 616, are missing from the *Sloane*, I have used the *Lansdowne* MS here.

Lines 617 to 660 are taken from the Sloane MS, these lines describe *"the last great battle which shall be done at Sandyford."* The word *Sandyford* is written as *Sawdyngford* in the Lansdowne MS. The *Lansdowne* MS ends abruptly at line 629 in the middle of its description of the battle's location, however, so far as it goes, it agrees with the description given in the other three MSS. The *Sloane* and *Cotton* include the name *Clyffordes*, and while the *Sloane* also includes *Remnerdes*, this word is fragmented in the *Cotton* MS. According to the prophecy, these people, whoever they may refer to, shall be in *"bruces land 3 years and more,"* and shall *"dynge down towers & castells high."* At this point the events in the *Cambridge* MS are out of sequence with the *Sloane* and *Cotton*. The *bastarde* shall be strong in power, he will kill all his foes, and then he will die in the Holy Land.

In the *Cambridge* MS, this occurs before the battle at Sandyford, the lady then sheds tears after describing the last battle. Whereas, in the *Sloane* and *Cotton* MSS, the battle is described in greater detail, after which, the *"basted shall die in the holly lande."* The lady then weeps for all the *"ladyes faire & fre"* who will be left without husbands. Opinions vary as to which battle *Sandyford*

233

refs to since the name also crops up in English prophecies.

Thomas then asks the fate of Black Agnes of Dunbar, the lines from 659 to 672 are from the *Cambridge* MS. The *Cotton* MS refers to Black Agnes as *"the sothely lady at arsyldoun".* Black Agnes famously defended the castle at Dunbar against the attack by the English in 1338; almost forty years after Thomas had befriended *"the sothely lady at arsyldoun"* - the wife of Earl Patrick III, Countess of Dunbar in the late 13ᵗʰ century.

Since Thomas lived in the period before that of Black Agnes, he would not have been aquainted with this particular Countess of Dunbar, and it would seem that there is some confusion between the Countess of Dunbar who was alive in 1338, and the Countess who was captured by the English at the Battle of Dunbar, in 1296.

The lady tells Thomas of the fate of *'Black Agnes'* at the hands of the English, at which point the three MSS describe his reaction. According to the Sloane *"thomas, drere man was he, teares fell ouer his eyen so graye,"* the Cambridge *"pen Thomas, a sory man was he, pe terys ran out of his een gray,"* the Cotton *"a drery man was he, pe teres ran of his eyn grey."*

Lines 673 to 680 are from the *Sloane* MS. They are missing from the *Thornton* MS, however, they are consistent in the *Cotton* and *Cambridge MSS*. These seven lines tell of Thomas's question to the lady *"if we shall parte for euer & aye"* and her answer, *"naye!"* she saide, *"when thou sitteste in Arseldon, to hontley bankis pou take pe waye."*

Lines 681 to 693 are missing from the *Cambridge*, while lines 687 to 695 are missing from the *Sloane*. Lines 681 to

683 are contained in the *Cotton* alone, lines 684 and 685 are taken from the *Sloane*, since they are missing from the *Cambridge* and fragmented in the *Cotton* and *Thornton*. Lines 686 and 687 are taken from the *Thornton*, while lines 688 to 692 are taken from the *Cotton*; these lines being missing from the others. Lines 693 to 700 are taken from the *Thornton*, the *Cambridge* and *Cotton* being the only other manuscripts to continue to the end of the tale. The *Sloane* MS finishes on line 696 with the words "*and thus departid she & he!*"

Although the words in lines 697 and 698 are fragmented in the *Cotton*, they are similar to the wording in the *Thornton* and the *Cambridge*, "*Of such a woman wold I here, That couth telle me of such ferly!*" The final two lines in the three MSS are consistent, "*Ihesu, crowned with thorne so clere, Bring vs to thi hall on hye!*"

It has been suggested that the second and third fyttes, which contain the prophecies, were, at one time, not included as part of the Romance. Robert Jamieson, who edited the poem in his "*Popular Ballads and Songs,*" was of the opinion that the ballad itself was of a much more "*fanciful*" and "*elegant* style," compared with the style of the prophecies. Professor Child, in his "*English and Scottish Ballads*" (London 1861), maintained that the second and third fyttes, which contain the prophecies, are the work of another, inferior, hand. James A.H. Murray disagrees with both, arguing that fytte one could hardly "*stand alone*" without the prophecies contained in the second and third fyttes.

There is a continuation of the theme of Thomas and the Fairy Queen throughout the three fyttes, which leads me to believe that the three fyttes are the complete work of

235

the same person. The first fytte, in my opinion, is the one least altered, the prophecies, included in Fytte two and three, have been grossly misinterpreted, due mainly to the dialect being misunderstood by the later scribes; it would also explain the major discrepancies between the extant manuscripts.

Taking into account that the earliest manuscript - of which we have written evidence - dates from the mid-fifteenth century, more than one hundred years after Thomas's lifetime, it is almost certain that even this early edition is not entirely accurate. That aside, were it not for each of those invaluable manuscripts, an important part of our literary heritage would be lost forever.

....

Chapter 10

The Late Thirteenth Century

During his reign, King Alexander III became a strong and powerful monarch; his untimely death saw the start of the bloodiest period in the history of the wars between Scotland and England. The first Scottish War of Independence began in 1296, and lasted until 1328, ending when the *'Treaty of Edinburgh/Northampton'* was signed. The second Scottish War of independence began in 1332, and ended in 1357, with the *'Treaty of Berwick.'* The area known as *'The Merse'* was the scene of the worst atrocities inflicted on the people of Scotland by the English army during these wars. During the first of the wars, Berwick, being in Scottish hands at this time, suffered constant invasions. Cross-border raids of butchery and arson ravaged the land until the Battle of Bannockburn in 1314. Although this battle was a milestone in Scotland's long and turbulent history, the wars continued for many centuries to come.

On the throne of England when the first war began was King Edward 1. He was called *"The Hammer of the Scots"* and not without good reason. Due to his great size and stature, he was also known by the name of *"Longshanks"*. It is apparent that Thomas was still alive at this time, and by all accounts had knowledge of the future events which would inevitably unfold. Without the powerful leadership of King Alexander III, the country was now an easy target for the might and power of the English army.

Since the three children from his first marriage

predeceased him, King Alexander's unborn child was the rightful heir to the throne. However, according to historical accounts, it was doubtful if his young bride was indeed pregnant. Some reports tell that Queen Yolande gave birth to a stillborn child in the month of November 1286, eight months after the King's death. Regardless of the truth of either report, the fact remained that there was no rightful heir to the Scottish throne. King Alexander's young granddaughter Margaret (*modern Gaelic Mairead*), also known as the *Maid of Norway*, was only three years old at the time of King Alexander's death. The child was the daughter of King Eric II of Norway, and Margaret, daughter of King Alexander III. The child's mother died in 1283, reports that she died while giving birth to her daughter Margaret, have not been proven.

Sir *Simon Fraser* was one of the Barons of the *Scottish Parliament* which met at *Birgham* on March 14th 1290 to arrange the conveyance of the young Maid of Norway across the sea to Scotland. The plan being, that the young *Maid of Norway,* now age seven, would sail to Scotland to be crowned as the new *Queen of Scotland.* King Edward 1 had guaranteed that there would be peace between the two nations if the new *Queen of Scotland* married the future *King of England,* the five year old Edward II. The treaty, in which he made this vow, was known as the *Treaty of Birgham* - signed on *July 18th* 1290.

Alas, this was not to be, on the voyage between Bergen and Edinburgh, the ship carrying the future Queen of Scotland was caught up in a severe storm, forcing it to come ashore at South Ronaldsay - one of the Orkney

Islands off the north coast of Scotland. Here, the little *Maid of Norway* died.

King Alexander III (*Alasdair mac Alasdair*), was the last *Gaelic* king to rule Scotland; the death of his granddaughter brought to an end the direct line of the *House of Canmore* which had ruled Scotland for over two centuries. The prosperous *Kingdom of Scotland,* having flourished for almost two centuries since the reign of King David 1, also came to an end following her death. Due to the continuing wars with England, the development of the Scottish nation, both in intellectual and literary terms, was abruptly halted. The Abbeys, once the seats of learning, were desecrated, forcing the scholars to lay down their quills and pick up swords. Young men, who should have been cultivating the fields, were slain as their workplaces became battlefields. Severe winters, which saw temperatures plummet, killed much of the live-stock, crops failed, and famine was rife; the country of Scotland was in turmoil.

In the period known as the interregnum, the first being between 1290 and 1292, four '*Guardians of Scotland'* were appointed to maintain order and stability. During this time, many of the Scottish nobles swore allegiance to the English King. Sir Simon Fraser swore allegiance to King Edward 1 on June 14th 1290. On June 13th 1291, many more followed suit, kissing the ground at *Norham Castle* on the English side of the border. Sir Simon Fraser, like his father before him, swore allegiance to the English King, on July 23rd 1291.

Following the death of the Maid of Norway, fourteen rivals vied for the throne of Scotland. In 1292, the claimants to the throne met King Edward I at Norham

Castle to discuss succession; King Edward chose John Balliol. King Edward I of England was slowly but surely manipulating the monarchy of the Kingdom of Scotland. On November 30th 1292, *John Balliol* was crowned King of Scotland at *Scone.*

With the future Queen dead and John Balliol the ruling monarch of Scotland, King Edward I abrogated the *Treaty of Birgham,* or, as it was also known, the *Treaty of Salisbury;* signed at Salisbury in 1289, and at Birgham in Berwickshire in 1290. Under the terms of the treaty, the marriage was arranged between Margaret, granddaughter of King Alexander III, and Edward, son of the present king of England; it also bound King Edward to observe and honour the independence of Scotland.

The abrogation of the treaty, combined with a Scottish King who was firmly under the control of his superior English counterpart, created a time of great unrest and confusion in Scotland. Many of the wealthy landowners in Scotland sought to secure their own positions, being aware of King Edward's power and John Baliol's weakness. The division between the wealthy nobles and the lower classes grew ever wider at this time. King Edward's arrogance incurred the wrath of the Scottish lower classes. His rule, of making the Scots plead before the English parliament as the final court of appeal, was not met with approval or subservience. When it became obvious that King Edward I intended to usurp the Scottish parliament, Sir Simon Fraser (the son), swore allegiance to the Scottish cause in 1296, four years after the accession of John Baliol.

In April of that year, King Edward and his army sacked

the town of Berwick. According to the *Lanercost Chronicles* "*As I was composing my limbs to rest I saw an angel with a drawn sword brandishing it against the bookcase in the library.*" The compiler of the story had this vision, "*after mass on the Lords Day in 1296.*" He goes on to say "*I myself beheld an immense number of men told off to bury the bodies of the fallen. I saw with my own eyes the nefarius pillaging, incredibly swift, of the books, vestments and materials of the Friars.*"

The Countess of Dunbar, on hearing of the atrocity, and with the knowledge that the English army was fast approaching Dunbar castle, closed the castle gates. Her husband, the 8th Earl of Dunbar was fighting alongside the English King - against the Scots. The English army eventually reached Dunbar, where, on April 27th 1296, the *Battle of Dunbar* took place. Following this battle, the *Countess of Dunbar* and Sir Simon Fraser were taken prisoner. The Scottish army, made up of 40,000 foot soldiers and 1,500 horsemen, many of them being from the Ettrick forest, was defeated, giving King Edward I supremacy over Scotland. The sacking of Berwick, still in Scottish hands at the time, saw the slaughter of almost every man, woman, and child in the town.

Had the marriage of *Margaret* and the young *Edward II* gone ahead as planned, the *Union of the Crowns,* as predicted by Thomas, would have taken place in his lifetime instead of almost four centuries later; Scotland's history may then have taken an entirely different course. In 1296, a man by the name of *John Rymer,* a Berwickshire freeholder, swore allegiance to King Edward 1, as did *Friar Thomas,* the Master of the *Trinity*

241

House of Soltra. John Rymer was no relation to Thome Rymor of Ercildoune.

A second interregnum, which began in this year, lasted for ten years, until 1306, when once again *'Guardians of Scotland'* were appointed; William Wallace being one of them. It was around this time, in 1296, that the young William Wallace instigated a rebellion against the English invaders, nonetheless, the invasions continued.

It is known that Thomas frequented the castle of his neighbour, the Earl of Dunbar in Ercildune; however, it is also known that Thomas, nearing the end of his life, became friendly with William Wallace. It would appear that Thomas, faced with the decision of his allegiance, chose to side with the Scots. The Scottish bid for lasting freedom from the English invasions was now being led by William Wallace. It can only be assumed that the friendship between Thomas and the present Earl of Dunbar came to an end when the Earl swore allegiance to King Edward 1st of England.

These mystical, alluring lands, which inspired Thomas to write his poetry, and the *Cumbric Britons* fought so bravely to retain, were once again witnessing scenes of bloodshed and carnage. The wars continued for many years and changed Scotland for all time. It was during this period, between 1296, and 1300, that Thomas simply vanished without trace.

The 7th Earl, with whom Thomas had a close affinity, died in 1289, his son Patrick 1V (8th Earl), succeeded him. It has been suggested that Thomas, being regarded as a traitor by the 8th Earl of March and Dunbar, was killed by his agents. According to the writers of the time, Thomas had a close bond with the 7th Earl's wife; the

Countess of Dunbar described in the *Cotton MS* prophecy as *"the Sothely Lady at Arsyldoun."*

In his book, Dr Murray suggests that Thomas may have retired to live out his life as a recluse at Fail monastery in Ayrshire. His theory being, that if Blind Harry was correct when he wrote *"Thomas usyt offt to that religious place,"* this would explain his seven year disappearance from Ercildoune. He suggests further, that Thomas, weary and dispirited by the wars ravaging his country, put his affairs in order by disposing of his assets, before disappearing to end his days in the sanctuary of Fail monastery. I have deliberated over this theory, but question the lack of any such inclusion in the chronicles of Fail monastery.

The Soltra Charter states *"Thomas de Ercildoun, filius et heres (son and heir) of Thome Rymour de Ercildoun, conveys by charter to the Trinity House of Soltra, all the lands which he held by inheritance in the village of Ercildoun."* The fact that his lands and property were gifted to the *Monks of Soltra,* rather than to the *Friars of Fail,* would seem to suggest that it was not Thomas the father who made the bequest. Had this been the case, the charitable organisation of Fail monastery, where Thomas spent much of his time, would surely have taken precedence over Soltra.

It has been generally accepted that the date of the *Soltra Charter,* when the *Rhymer's Tower and Lands* were signed over to the monastery, was November 2nd 1299, *"after the feast of the apostles Simon and Jude."* If the account of *Blind Harry* is correct with regard to Thomas meeting William Wallace, Thomas was still alive in 1297. Mr *Pinkerton's* claim that Thomas lived until 1300, is not impossible, since the year of birth is estimated to be c1220/25

The following transcript of the *'Soltra Charter'* is taken from the book entitled 'The Romance and Prophecies of Thomas of Erceldoune.' Dr. Murray, the editor, states that the document has been printed many times, the date having been quoted at least twenty times, each editor giving the date as *nonagesimo nono,* 1299. In the following transcript, the date is given as *nonagesimo quarto,* 1294. It is obvious that Thomas, the son and heir, could not have bequeathed his inheritance to Soltra before his Father's death.

Below is the transcript from the *Cartulary of the Trinity House of Soltra,* Advocates Library, W.4 14;

Ersylton

Omnibus has literas visuris vel audituris Thomas de Ercildoun filius heres Thome Rymour de Ercildoun, Salutem in Domino, Noueritis me per fustum et baculum in Pleno judicio resignasse ac per presentes quietum clamasse pro me et heredibus meis Magistro domus Sancta Trinitatis de Soltre et fratibus eiusdem domus totam terram meam cum omnibus pertinentis suis quam in tenemento de Ercildoun hereditarie tenui Renunciando de cetero pro me et heredibus meis omni jure et clameo que ego seu antecessores mei in eadem terra alioque tempare de preterito habuimus siue de futuro habere poterimus. In cuius rei testimonium presentibus literis sigillum meum apposui Data apud Ercildoun die Martis proximo post festum Sanctorum apostolorum Symonis et Jude Anno Domini Millessimo cc Nonogesimo quarto.

244

(1294)

Loosely translated, the charter states that Thomas de Ercildoun, son and heir of Thome Rymour de Ercildoun, bequeaths his home and all the lands which he holds by inheritance, renouncing in the future, for himself and his heirs, any right or claim to the land which belonged to his ancestors.

Despite the victory for the Scots at Bannockburn, as prophesied the subsequent English monarchs continued their raids into Scotland. Following one of the many raids on the much besieged town of Berwick, the castle at Dunbar was once again under attack, the date being 13th January 1338. The Countess of Dunbar at this time was Agnes, daughter of *Randolph* Earl of Moray. Her nick-name of *Black Agnes* was thought to be due to her dark complexion and black hair. Her husband, the 9th Earl of Dunbar, was absent from the castle, fighting another battle in the north. The English army, led by the Earl of Salisbury, considered the seige of Dunbar castle, inhabited mainly by women at the time, to be an easy conquest. The expectation being, that after the initial bombardment of the castle with rocks and lead shot, the Countess would surrender. The Earl of Salisbury and his army had underestimated the fortitude of Black Agnes and her staff. Undeterred, the Countess sent her maids - dressed in their best clothes – onto the castle ramparts, and in full view of the English army they, derisively, removed the debris with their lace hankerchiefs.

Black Agnes and her servants outwitted and belittled the renowned leadership of the Earl of Salisbury for five months and were successful in defending the castle and its occupants. Supplies for the besieged castle's occupants were brought by boat, unseen by the landward army, and delivered through a submerged doorway. Eventually, disheartened by their futile attempts to gain access to the castle, and weakened by the lack of food, the siege was abandoned.

The town of *Berwick,* one of the first of the Scottish burghs, and later the county town of Berwickshire, was on the receiving end of many of the atrocities inflicted on Scotland by the English armies. It was unfortunate to be in a key position, having a port, and also being situated on the border between the two countries. Berwick was sacked by the English many times, captured, and re-taken by the Scots, until 1482, when it was re-taken and finally held by the English. Today it is approximately two miles south of the Scottish Border.

The final disappearance of Thomas, in keeping with much of his lifetime, is shrouded in mystery. The tale, famous in folklore, details the circumstances in which he disappeared. Thomas, while hosting a banquet in his tower at Ercildoune, was told of a white hart and hind calmly parading the streets of the village. Thomas rose from the table, left the tower, followed the animals across the Leader River into the forest, never to be seen again.

In his ballad, Sir Walter Scott wrote the words which were supposedly uttered by Thomas when told of the two deer coming in from the forest, *"My sand is run, my thread is spun, this sign regardeth me."*

White deer are very rare, in Celtic mythology they are believed to be *Fairies* in one of their many forms of disguise.

246

According to the legend, Thomas had waited a lifetime for such a sign; he believed that his beloved Fairy Queen had finally called him. Now, they could be reunited forever in the land of everlasting life. From that day to this, Thomas, in mortal form, was never seen again.

Some said to hill, and some to glen,
Their wondrous course had been,
Bur ne'er in haunts o' living men,
Again was Thomas seen."

Sir Walter Scott

....

Chapter 11

Ercildoune becomes Earlston

The hamlet of Ercildoune continued to grow and expand, eventually merging with the houses at the east end, the part once known as the 'Earl's Toun.' The name of Ercildoune ceased to be used and the village became known as *Earlstoun*, later becoming Earlston. For many centuries following Thomas's final departure from his tower, Earlstoun continued to be a place of great importance, and was visited regularly by reigning monarchs. On the night of 8th September 1513, King James 1V and his army *'campit ae nicht at Ersilton'* en route from Edinburgh to the fateful *Battle of Flodden*. In 1745, during the *Jacobite Rebellion, Charles Edward Stuart*, otherwise kown as *Bonnie Prince Charlie,* stayed in Earlstoun on his way to Berwick.

The 'Battle of Flodden,' which was fought near the village of Branxton, just a few miles south of the Scottish border, was a catastrophic defeat for the Scottish army. The tragic loss of countrymen, many coming from the Ettrick Forest in the lowland region, dealt a huge blow to the morale of the Scottish army. It also left a vastly depleted army of Scottish soldiers.

A haunting poem called *"The Floe'rs o' the Forest"* was written by Jean Elliot in the 18th century to commemorate the *Battle of Flodden.* Now known as a popular air, it is played as a lament on many occasions to this day.

Mary Stuart, *Queen of Scots,* stayed briefly at Cowdenknowes while en route from *Craigmillar Castle* to meet her lover, *Bothwell,* at *Hermitage Castle* his Borders stronghold near Newcastleton. *James Hepburn,* fourth *Earl of Bothwell,* was suspected of being an accessory to the murder of *Lord Darnley,* Mary's husband. When Mary and Bothwell married in 1567, Bothwell became her third husband. A tree in the grounds of Cowdenknowes House is said to have been planted by *Mary, Queen of Scots.* The bedroom in which she slept was known for many years as the *'The Queen's Room.'* Sir Walter Scott also frequented Cowdenknowes, a traditional ballad known as *The Broom o' the Cowdenknowes* is included in *The Minstrelsy of the Scottish Border.* A copy of the pastoral air, with lyrics, was published by *Mr Herd* in 1772; this beautiful song is still frequently sung as a traditional air.

In the 17th century, a large proportion of the lands in and around Earlston formed part of the estate of Cowdenknowes, included in the estate were the Rhymer's Tower and lands. In a document dated1630, the *teinds, or tithes* of one tenth of the income from the Rhymer's lands was paid to the church as a tax, the teinds were exhausted c1830. Cowdenknowes continued to be a place of great esteem for many centuries, despite the curse of Thomas. The broom, which covered the estate for many miles around, was like a forest. It was reputed to be thirteen feet in height, apparently a man could ride through it on horseback without being seen, and its yellow blossom was said to be a sight to behold. The forest of broom remained for many years, until the estate lands were cultivated for pasture and crops.

Between 1834 and 1837, the Tenant of the Rhymer's Mill and mill lands was a man by the name of John

250

Hyslop. He paid a rent of £72.00 to the estate of Cowdenknowes for a three year period. The tenant of the Rhymer's Tower, between the years of 1835 and1837, was a man called James Richardson. His rent for the two year period was £5.00; this also being payable to the estate of Cowdenknowes. The holdings of the feu duty payable on the *Rhymers lands* at this time were held by *The Governors of Trinity Hospital* at the rate of 13s.4d per annum.

A curious story, from the nineteenth century, tells of a man who resided in the tower during the eighteenth century; however, there are two conflicting accounts of this story. According to the account by Sir Walter Scott, *"the veneration paid to the dwelling place of Thomas even attached itself in some degree to a person, who, within the memory of man, chose to set up his residence in the ruins of Learmont's tower. The name of this man was Murray, a kind of herbalist; who, by dint of some knowledge in simples, the possession of a musical clock, an electric machine, and a stuffed alligator, added to a supposed communication with Thomas the Rhymer, lived for many years in very good credit as a wizard."* However, contradicting the account by Sir Walter Scott, Dr Robert Chambers, in a note in *"Popular Rhymes"*, pronounces this account a strange distortion and mystification of the fact, that a respectable and enlightened physician, namely Mr Patrick Murray, who *"pursued various studies of a philosophical kind, not common in Scotland during the eighteenth century,and is known as the author of some medical works, lived in the tower of Thomas of Ercildoune, then a comfortable mansion,"* and adds, *"when we find a single age, and*

251

that the latest and most enlightened, so strangely distort and mystify the character of a philosophical country surgeon, can we doubt that five hundred years have played still stranger tricks with the history and character of Thomas the Rhymer."

When Thomas lived in Ercildune in the early thirteenth century, the estate of Cowdenknowes was in the possession of the *Lindsays,* thereafter, the family of *Douglas* owned the lands. From the sixteenth century onwards, the estate was in the possession of the *Homes.* A tale, told by a local man in the early 1800's, links the home of Thomas to the house of Cowdenknowes. The story tells of red sandstone corbels from a fireplace being found by locals while clearing brushwood from the old quarry behind the *Black Hill.* The corbels were said to be an exact replica of the existing fireplace in the *Rhymer's Tower.* The man went on to say that the corbels were taken to Cowdenknowes House for safekeeping; the mansion house of Cowdenknowes is situated very near to the foot of the Black Hill. The ownership of the house of Cowdenknowes has changed many times since the early nineteeth century, therefore the location of the old fireplace corbels at the present time is not known.

In 1834, the estate of Cowdenknowes, including a considerable amount of land, went on the market. Included in the estate were lands in Earlston and Redpath, among these lands were the Rhymer's Mill, the Rhymer's Tower and all adjacent lands. The Rhymer's Mill at this time was not the *Tweed Mill,* which was built later and also called *Rhymer's Mill,* but the old *Meal Mill,* which was of a much earlier date, and included an old

252

water-wheel. In the early 1800's, the owner of the Rhymer's Mill was a man by the name of Whale; his name, engraved on a sandstone lintel, is preserved at Rhymer's Mill engineering works to this day.

In the mid-nineteenth century, while draining a peatbog for the laying of the new railway line, a two-handed sword was recovered from the depths of the mire. Due to the style of the handle, the sword was said to date from the period of the thirteenth century. The land from which it was recovered belonged to a local resident, namely Mr George Noble. The sword was reputed to have been bought by another local man by the name of Robert Learmont. Robert was the last man to claim direct descendancy from Thomas the Rhymer, and according to local rumour, wished to keep the sword which, it was thought, may have belonged to 'The Rhymer.'

For nearly five hundred years the sword was preserved and concealed in the peaty ground, the old track, which Thomas used when he visited the castle of the Earls of Dunbar, ran alongside the peatbog. The sword was reported to have been in a pristine condition when found, unfortunately, like Thomas, it has vanished into thin air, with no-one knowing its present location. It is not outwith the bounds of possibility that the body of Thomas was also concealed in this watery grave.

An old map of Earlston, dated 1862, names this piece of ground as *Halcombe Haugh,* however, a later map dated 1865, marks the station and the route of the railway on the same site. In 1834, the land known as *Halcombe Haugh* was part of the estate of Cowdenknowes. A man by the name of James Sheills paid an annual rent of £5 and 5 shillings to the estate of Cowdenknowes for this piece of land. This was the same James Sheills who recounted the demise of the *Earlston Thorn Tree* and quoted its description so graphically.

I believe the name *'Halcombe'* to be the modern name for the area known in Thomas's time as the *Hawke's Kaim*. *Kaim* is the old Scots word for *comb* and *Hawk* has connections with the old *Hawking* ground of the Earl of Dunbar. The street at this location is now known as *'Halcombe Crescent'*.

A small thatched cottage, thought to be at least four hundred years old, still exists in Earlston; the thatch is protected by a corrugated tin roof. The cottage was once known as *Flauchter's Cottage, or* more recently *Fluther's Field Cottage.* A *'Flauchter spade'* in the *Scots* dictionary is defined as being a *'turf-cutter.'* I am reliably informed by Mr Alex Blair, a fourth generation resident of the village, that as a young boy he heard tales about the old man who lived in the cottage - *the Flauchter* - going out to the bog to cut the peat. Alex also recalls his ancestors using the marshy ground as a quoit rink; one of his ancestors lived in the old thatched cottage at the time.

The site of the Earl of Dunbar's castle is beside the primary school, near the east end of Earlston. No visible remains of the castle exist today, however, a level piece of ground beside the Turrford burn, near to where the castle once stood, was known for many years as *The Butts;* butts is the old Scots word for *archery ground.* Arrow heads, dating from the thirteenth century, were unearthed at this site during the construction of the *gas-works* in the early nineteenth century.

The ruins of an ancient tower, which for many centuries

has been known as *Rhymer's Tower,* situated near the banks of the river Leader, is all that remains of the ancestral home of the Learmonts. There is little to see nowadays except for a remnant of the west and north walls. Had it not been for a forward-thinking group in the nineteenth century, these two walls may not have survived.

Locals tell of stones being taken from the tower over a prolonged period during the nineteenth century; these allegedly being used in other constructions. All that remained of the tower was gradually disappearing piece by piece in front of their eyes. At this time, local and national heritage was of little importance, tourism was virtually non-existent.

The remaining fragment of the Lairds of Leamonts' once impressive residence was saved from indubitable annihilation by the *Edinburgh and Border Counties Association.* The association bought the tower, enabling the last forlorn remnants of the once grand tower to be saved for posterity. A grand celebration was held in Earlston on the 2nd August 1894, shops and businesses closed for the day, and a carnival atmosphere ensued. It is astounding that even in the nineteenth century, nearly six hundred years after his death such adulation was felt for Thomas in his home town. A sandstone tablet on the west wall of the ruin is inscribed with the following words, these being included in the poem written by Sir Walter Scott

"Farewell my Father's ancient tower
A long farewell" said he;
The scene of pleasure, pomp or power,

thou never more shalt be".

The plaque was erected by the *Edinburgh and Border Counties Association* on obtaining ownership of the ruin and adjoining lands on Friday 2nd August 1894.

The tablet, designed by D.W. Stevenson R.S.A., was unveiled by Mr Wallace Bruce, United States Consul in Edinburgh at the time.

An extract from a *Geophysical Survey* carried out in 1908 by *Glasgow University Archaeological Research Division*, on behalf of *Historic Scotland*, states "*the southwest wall stands at a height of around 20ft, it was originally rectangular in plan, and had a frontage of 23ft, and walls 4ft thick." "The lower chamber has been vaulted.*"

The results of the survey revealed that the present ruin is that of a peel tower of a later date, probably sixteenth century; however, it has long been recognised as being part of the original home which once belonged to the family of *Thomas the Rhymer*.

The ruin was granted a '*Category B listed building status'* by Historic Scotland on June 9th 1971.

Despite the ruinous condition of the remains, it continues to stir the imagination, remind us of our heritage and attract the curious visitor. For over one hundred years, the tower has been in its present state; no-one within the last five generations can remember it being any different, except for it once being ivy covered. The ivy was removed in the early twentieth century to preserve the stonework; sadly the ruin is now almost hidden from view by the expansion of local businesses. In 1966, the responsibilty for the safe-keeping of the

256

tower ruins was transferred by deed to the *Rhymer's Tower Trustees*.

The site of the *Eildon Tree* was marked for many years by a large, irregular shaped whinstone boulder. Whinstone, a molten lava deposit, was once quarried locally. The whereabouts of the original boulder, which was of considerable size, remains a mystery. Recent searches, using various types of detectors, proved unsuccessful. A replacement stone was erected in 1929 by the Melrose Literary Society. It was first placed in situ on the south side, in close proximity to the road, and stood there for many years. The same stone was re-erected in an elevated position on the opposite side of the road, slightly further back from the road-side, in 1970.

In 1998, a group, founded by Val Miller from Melrose, created a visitor attraction at this location using the site of a disused electricity sub-station. Here, visitors can read the tale of Thomas's meeting with the Fairy Queen from the interpretation panel. A stone tablet, inscribed with one of Thomas's predictions relevant to the area, is also on view; the site is easily accessible, and sign-posted from the A6091 near Melrose. The road, on which the Eildon Tree Stone is situated, is well known in the locality as the "*Bogle Burn*" road; it now forms part of the popular '*Four Abbeys Cycle Route*.'

The original site of the Eildon Tree is thought to be approximately half a mile further up the slope, towards the north Eildon from the existing viewpoint. The "*Huntlee Bankis*," where Thomas first caught a glimpse of the lady riding down the "*faire long ley*," has been identified as being the same distance west towards

257

Melrose from the site of the tree. A field lower down the slope, next to the road, is named as *"Monks Meadow."* A little further up the slope is *"Huntly Brae"* and to the west is the *"Corse Rig,"* *"Gallows Hill"* and *"Bowers Brae."* From this vantage point at *Huntly Brae,* the site of the Eildon Tree can be clearly seen across the hillside. The B*ogle Burn* (Goblin Brook), still *trickles* down the Eildon slopes, slightly further south from this spot. The word *trickles* is relevant today, however, in the thirteenth century, which had more rainfall than the present day, it would carry considerably more water.

The inscription on the headstone is as follows,

> *"This stone marks the site of the Eildon Tree,*
> *Where legend says Thomas The Rhymer*
> *Met the Queen of the Fairies*
> *And where he was inspired to utter*
> *The first notes of the Scottish Muse."*

The relevant words of Thomas's prophecy are inscribed on a stone tablet, which can also be seen at the viewpoint

> *"At Eldon tree if you shall be*
> *A brigg ower Tweed you there may see."*

The first road bridge to span the river Tweed at Leaderfoot was built in 1780. Nearly a century later, 1865, saw the construction of a viaduct to convey trains to Berwick on a branch of the old Waverley Line. Both bridges were built with locally sourced red sandstone, and local stonemasons were employed in their construction.

The viaduct consists of nineteen arches, today, although it no longer carries a railway, it is still regarded as a local landmark worthy of a visit. A *new* (concrete) road bridge was built in 1973, and the three contrasting adjacent bridges are an awe-inspiring sight to behold, not to mention fulfilling yet another of '*True Thomas'* prophecies.

A stone tablet on the east wall of the present parish church reads *"Auld Rymr Race Lyees in this place."* The tablet is not the original, but a replica of the original bearing the same inscription. For many years, the original stone tablet was situated in the cemetery of one of the older churches which stood on the same site; the stone being transferred to the *new church* in 1736. The original stone was desecrated by an inebriated member of the *Waterstone* family in 1782; apparently he took issue with the location of the headstone in the local churchyard. However, the local minister of the time compelled him to replace the inscribed stone. This was duly done, but the lettering was of a more modern style than the original. The stone was then transferred to the present Victorian style, red sandstone church in 1892; it is now encased in glass.

Although there was a Roman Catholic Church in Ercildune in Thomas's time - from 1070 until 1560 - there is no record or local knowledge of the location of the original stone prior to 1736. Apparently there was a Celtic Church in Ercildune from 600AD until 1070.

Thomas's prophecies continued to come to fruition for many centuries after his disappearance, this serving only to strengthen his credibility and spread his fame.

. . . .

Chapter 12

The Legacy

For many centuries after his departure from the land of
mortals, Thomas's tale was upheld by his kinsmen; his
name spoken with reverence and wonder. A chapbook
containing his prophecies was kept in almost every
farmhouse in Scotland and consulted regularly. The
prophecies of Thomas were consulted before ensuing
battles, not least during the Jacobite rebellions in 1715,
and 1745. The little hamlet of Ercildune in the Merse
was famously known as being the place of his birth. The
legend of Thomas of Ercildune was known throughout
Scotland, his name, as well known in the north of
Scotland and the Western Isles as it was in his southern
homelands. Thomas, being hailed "*The Gaelic Messiah,*"
was to the *Gaelic* tradition what King Arthur was to the
Cymric tradition. The Gaels believed him not to be dead,
but, like King Arthur, merely awaiting the call to return
and save his kinsmen.

The *Cymry* believed King Arthur to be invincible, having
been transported temporarily to an unknown mysterious
place from where he would return and lead them to
victory; "*A mystery to the world is the grave of Arthur;*"
likewise is the grave of *Thomas of Ercildoune.* He did not
die, there is no record of his death, or of his place of
burial, but, similar to King Arthur, he was simply
transported from this world to '*dree his weird*' in
another. In old Gaelic traditions, the belief was that
Thomas would one day return to be "*The Saviour of the
Gaels*"

261

The following quote refers not only to King Arthur, but also to Thomas of Ercildoune:

"Whether The Vale of Avalon or the Halls of the Eildons, holds them who cannot die, they will come again to earth to the ultimate power of the righteous, which is immortal in man."

In Gaelic tradition, the ghost of Thomas was said to frequent horse-fairs on the lookout for suitable horses to complete his complement *"When that day comes he will return to earth and there will be a great battle fought on the Clyde."* On the island of Mull, off the west coast of Scotland, it was believed that one of the horses would come from the meadow of *Kengharair*, which is near Dervaig.

During his lifetime, Thomas was a man unwittingly caught up in the politics of his country, a country which had aspired to being a secure and stable nation under the leadership of King Alexander III. The period following the death of the king must have brought great fear and anxiety, not only to Thomas, but to the majority of the population of Scotland. My perception of Thomas is that he was a humanitarian, but also a patriot. As such, his wish would be for the continuation of a stable and peaceful country, united in its allegiance to a Scottish monarch. His foresight into the future however, would portray an entirely different picture.

The politics of the time were anything but straightforward, made even more complicated by the lack of a rightful heir to the Scottish throne. The division between the nobles and the commoners grew ever wider as many of the nobles, once having links to the Saxons, switched their allegiance to King Edward1.

The existing evidence shows Thomas to be an educated man; however, after his return from his seven year absence he went about his daily life uttering strange, ambiguous words, of which only he knew the meaning. Many of his rhyming prophecies were not written down, but passed orally from one person to the other. Thomas was not particularly creditworthy as a seer in his own lifetime, at least not until the night of 19th March 1286, by which time he was nearing the end of his time on earth. Even then, the words spoken to the Earl of Dunbar were ambiguous; the prediction of a strong wind blowing across Scotland the following day gave no indication that the King would meet his death.

The date of 24th June 1314, which heralded the famous victory for the Scots at *Bannockburn,* will be remembered in Scottish history for all time. The Battle of Bannockburn took place a relatively short time after Thomas was seen for the last time in his native Ercildune. The battle was won by the Scots, the location, and the manner in which it was won, all having been correctly predicted by Thomas. Within a few years of his disappearance from this world, in this instance only fifteen years, the legend of *Thomas the Rhymer* was beginning to gather momentum. The adulation of his fellow countrymen continued to grow as, one by one, his prophecies continued to come to fruition. His credibility as a prophet increased as more of his ambiguous words began to make sense. His fame reached a peak around the seventeenth century, by which time the writers were said to have embellished and exaggerated his legend.

The mystique of Thomas, combined with his unearthly image, served only to enhance this legend.

263

It is certainly the case that the tale of Thomas has *"grown wings"* with the passing years, making it very difficult to separate truth from fiction; the various authors' interpretations of the legend of Thomas differing considerably.

For many centuries, the names of prophets such as Bede, Gildas, and Waldhave, were spoken with the utmost veneration; the prophecies of *Merlin* being the most respected until the time of Thomas of Ercildune. The prophecies of Thomas of Ercildune gradually outshone that of his contemporaries, to the extent that his authority was often quoted to lend greater credence to theirs.

The oldest printed edition yet discovered which contains the prophecies of Merlin, Bede, Gildas, and Thomas the Rhymer, was printed by *Robert Waldegrave*, printer to the *Kings Most Excellent Majesty*, anno 1603; some of the contents were written during the reign of King James 1 of Scotland. The title of this edition being, *"The Whole Prophecie of Scotland, England, and some parts of France and Denmark, prophesied bee meruellous Merling, Beid, Bertlingtoun, Thomas Rymour, Waldhave, Eltraine, Banester and Sibbilla, all according in one, containing many strange and meruellous things."* In the years between 1603 and the beginning of the nineteenth century, the book was reprinted many times.

For over seven hundred years, the tale of the *'Romance of Thomas the Rhymer'* has been the topic of controversial discussions and less than satisfactory conclusions. The *'Ballad of Thomas the Rhymer,'* which is based on the original *'Romance'*, has been edited by many famous authors, most recently by Sir Walter Scott

264

in the nineteenth century; this being included as a traditional ballad in his *'Minstrelsy of the Scottish Border.'* It is believed that the original manuscript of the Romance was in circulation as early as thirty years after the demise of Thomas, c1320; unfortunately, this manuscript, if it still exists, has not been located.

Two lines in the earliest extant manuscripts are proof that an earlier manuscript existed, *"als the story says"* and the line *"als the storye tellis full ryghte;"* the implication being that this copy was transcribed from an older copy.

A copy of the ballad can be found in Mr Jamieson's *'Collection of Scottish Ballads and Songs'.* This copy is entire and kept in the museum of the *Cathedral of Lincoln.* Another copy, kept in *Peterborough,* is not in a good condition. An extract from the ballad can also be found in the *Pinkerton* MS. Also included in the manuscript of Mr Pinkerton, is one of the prophecies ascribed to Thomas,

"There shall the lion lose the gytle
And the libbards bear it clean away.
At pinkyn cleuch there shall be spilt
Much gentle blood that day."

This prophecy told of the *'Battle of Pinkie,'* which took place near Musselburgh, in September 1547. The battle was one of many fought between England and Scotland during *'The Wars of the Rough Wooing.'* Henry VIII of England tried to unite the two countries by marrying *Edward,* to *Mary, Queen of Scots.*

The influence of *Thomas the Rhymer* among

265

connoisseurs of the arts, from the fourteenth century until the present day, is unprecedented. His influence rekindled the ancient *Celtic* traditions which the Anglo-Saxons had tried, but failed, to eradicate. He inspired musicians, poets, and authors, both at home and abroad, and continues to do so today. English writers, including *Rudyard Kipling,* were also influenced by Thomas. *Rudyard Kipling,* poet of the nineteenth century wrote *The Last Rhyme of True Thomas.* His reply to the King,

> *"I hae harpit ye up to the throne of God,*
> *I hae harpit your midmost soul in three,*
> *I hae harpit ye down to the hinges o' hell,*
> *An'–ye–would–make–a– Knight –o'–me!"*

The prophecies of Thomas were documented in *'English Prophetic Writings'* in the fifteenth and sixteenth centuries. There is evidence to suggest that the prophecies of Thomas were known, and heeded, as far afield as Wales and the southernmost extremities of England.

A collection entitled *'The Prophecies of Thomas the Rhymer'* was published both in Latin and English at Edinburgh in 1690/91, and has been reprinted many times.

Thomas is mentioned in works by the early writers, including Fordun, Barbour, Wintoun, Pinkerton, Boece, and Henry the Minstrel. Spanning a period of eight hundred years, innumerable books regarding Thomas the Rhymer have been published, in the present day there is still a market for such literature.

266

The late eighteenth century author and poet, *James Hogg* (1770-1835), otherwise known as the *Ettrick Shepherd,* wrote about Thomas, as did the author and poet *John Leyden* (1775-1811), born in *Denholm* near *Hawick* in the *Scottish Borders.* Another author whose roots go back to the small Scottish Borders village of *Denholm* near *Hawick* is *Sir James Augustus Henry Murray.* He lived during the nineteenth century and was the original editor of the *Oxford English Dictionay.* Dr Murray detailed his collation of five manuscripts, which contain the work of Thomas the Rhymer, in his book entitled *'The Romance and Prophecies of Thomas of Erceldoune.'*

Sir Walter Scott (1771-1832) held Thomas in the highest regard. In *'The Minstrelsy of the Scottish Border'* he devotes a large section to *'The Ballad of Thomas the Rhymer'* with the inclusion of part second and part third, which I have included in this chapter. He also ingeniously weaves Thomas into his final novel *'Castle Dangerous'.* In the novel, the fictitious castle is owned by *'The Douglas'* whose servant is called *Hugonet.* One of Hugonet's many roles is that of minstrel to 'The Douglas' and as such he is a talented bard and violer. Among the Douglas's vast collection of literature is the lays of the *'Bard of Ercildoune.'*

Knowing that the castle is about to be destroyed, Hugonet seeks out from the study, a copy of his favourite work by Thomas of Ercildoune, namely Sir Tristrem. His plan is to take the book to a place of safety, however, as he momentarily places the book down on the desk, it suddenly moves of its own accord. He becomes aware of the shadowy outline of a tall thin

267

man, cloaked in a robe and with long flowing hair. As Hugonet peers at this strange apparition, he notices two shadowy outlines accompanying the man, these being of a hart and hind. Hugonet and the man engage in conversation, during which, the man tells Hugonet he is none other than Thomas of Ercildoune. He proceeds to inform Hugonet that at certain times of the year he has the ability to revisit the scenes of his former life.

Thomas the Rhymer had a profound effect on Sir Walter Scott. As well as including Thomas in many of his works, Sir Walter renamed a glen so that the *'Rhymer's Glen'* would be included in the grounds of his estate of Abbotsford. The glen was formerly known as *Dick's Cleuch,* a remote, but picturesque spot situated at the base of the most westerly Eildon. The said glen was within the boundaries of the estate of Abbotsford, whereas the original *'Rhymer's Glen'* was near the foot of the north Eildon; outwith the estate's boundary. The original 'Rhymer's Glen' was near to the spot where Thomas first saw the Fairy Queen *"come riding down a fair long ley,"* a distance of approximately two miles away. Sir Walter's obsession with Thomas did not end there however; in 1817 he purchased the nearby property, known at the time as *Toftfield,* for a large sum of money. He re-named it *Huntlyburn,* the name of a nearby burn, because of the association with the *Huntly Banks,* where Thomas first saw the lady on the grey horse.

Included in the appendix to the general preface of *Waverley,* is a fragment of an incomplete *'Romance of Thomas the Rhymer.'* Approximately ten pages of the Romance have been written, before it ends abrubtly; Sir

Walter Scott's intention was to write a Romance which centred on the legend of Thomas of Ercildoune. Also included in this volume is the tale of 'Canonbie Dick.' Another tale which is thought to be based on the story of Thomas and the Fairy Queen, is *'The Ballad of The Young Tamlane* or *Tam Lin.'* The ballad tells of the spirit of Tam returning from *Fairyland* for a brief encounter with *Janet* at *Carterhaugh.* Janet subsequently discovers that she is 'with child.' Tam, now disenchanted with his life in Fairyland, wishes to return to the mortal world and spend the remainder of his life with Janet and their child. He enlists Janet's help to break the spell, by which he is bound forever to the Fairy Queen. Janet does exactly what is asked of her and the spell is broken; Tam is restored to the land of mortals. The tale is included in *'The Minstrelsy of the Scottish Border',* and has also been recorded as a folk song. Likewise, *'The Ballad of Thomas the Rhymer'* has been recorded as a folk song by 'Steeleye Span.'

One of Russia's famous poets, *Mikhail Yuryvich Lermontov*, who lived from 1814 until 1841 wrote;

"Beneath the curtain of mist
Beneath a heaven of storms
Among the hills of my Scotland
Lies the grave of Ossian.

Thither flies my weary soul
To breathe its native gale
And from that forgotten grave
A second time to draw its life."

According to his biographer, Mikhail Lermontov was aware of the link between the Russian Lermontovs and the Scottish Learmonts. In the early seventeenth century, George Learmont from Scotland went to *Czarist Russia*, where he settled, married and raised a family. The Russian equivalent of George is *Yuri*, so the descendants of George Learmont from Scotland, would later become the *Yuri Lermontovs* of Russia. The Lermontov clan are proud of their Scottish connection - they have a recognised *Lermontov* tartan - with many of that name keen to trace their Learmont origins. It is testament to his fame and legend that people from around the world have a desire to be associated with the poet and prophet from Ercildoune.

Below is an extract from *Finlay's 'Wallace'*

"Oh! Long shall Scotland sound with Rhymer's name,
For in an unknown cave the seer shall bide.
'Till through the realm gaunt kings and chiefs shall ride,
Wading through floods of carnage, bridle deep;
The cries of terror, and the wailing wide
Shall rouse the prophet from his tranced sleep,
His harp shall ring with woe, and all the land shall weep.

The above was taken from an article in the annual review of 1804 and is included in Scott's works, Vol 1. – Sir Tristrem.

Another inclusion in 'The Minstrelsy of the Scottish Border' by Sir Walter Scott is the following:

Thomas The Rhymer

270

Part Second

When seven years were come and gane,
The sun blinked fair on pool and stream;
And Thomas lay on Huntlie bank,
Like one awakened from a dream.

He heard the trampling of a steed,
He saw the flash of armour flee,
And he beheld a gallant knight,
Come riding down by the Eildon tree.

He was a stalwart knight, and strong;
Of giant make he 'peared to be;
He stirr'd his horse, as he were wode,
Wi' gilded spurs, of faushion free.

Says- "Well met, well met, true Thomas!
Some uncouth ferlies show to me."
Says- "Christ thee save, Cospatrick brave!
Thrice welcome, good Dunbar, to me!"

"Light down, light down, Cospatrick brave,
And I will show you curse's three,
Shall gar fair Scotland greet and grane,
And change the green to the black livery."

"A storm shall roar this very hour,
From Rosse's Hills to Solway sea."
"Ye lied, ye lied, ye warlock hoar!
For the sun shines sweet on fauld and lea."

271

He put his hand on the earlie's head;
He shewed him a rock, beside the sea,
Where a king lay stiff, beneath his steed,
And steel-dight nobles wiped their e'e.

"The neist curse lights on Branxton hills;
By Flodden's high and heathery side,
Shall wave a banner, red as blude,
And chieftains throng wi' meikle pride.

"A Scottish king shall come full keen;
The ruddy lion beareth he;
A feather'd arrow sharp, I ween,
Shall make him wink and warre to see."

"When he is bloody, and all to bledde,
Thus to his men he still shall say-
'For God's sake, turn your back again,
And give yon southern folk a fray!
Why should I lose, the right is mine?
My doom is not to die this day."

"Yet turn ye to the eastern hand,
And woe and wonder ye shall see;
How forty thousand spearmen stand,
Where yon rank river meets the sea."

"There shall the lion lose the gylte,
And the libbards bear it clean away;
At Pinkie Cleuch there shall be spilt
Much gentle blood that day."

"Enough, enough, of curse and ban;
Some blessings shew thou now to me,
Or, by the faith o' my bodie," Corspatrick said,
"Ye shall rue the day ye e'er saw me!"

"The first of blessings I shall thee shew
Is by the burn, that's call'd of bread;
Where Saxon men shall tine the bow,
And find their arrows lack the head."

"Beside that brigg, out ower the burn,
Where the water bickereth bright and sheen,
Shall many a falling courser spurn,
And knights shall die in battle keen."

"Beside a headless cross of stone,
The libbards there shall lose the gree;
The raven shall come, the erne shall go,
And drink the Saxon blood sae free.

The cross of stone they shall not know,
So thick the corses there shall be."

"But tell me now," said brave Dunbar,
"True Thomas, tell now unto me,
What man shall rule the isle of Britain,
Even from the north to the southern sea?"

"A French Queen shall bear the son,
Shall rule all Britain to the sea;
He of the Bruce's blood shall come,
As near as in the ninth degree."

"The waters worship shall his race;
Likewise the waves of the farthest sea;
For they shall ride ower ocean wide,
With hempen bridles and horse of tree."

The *"horse of tree"* referred to the wooden boats which would eventually sail the oceans. The *"hempen bridles"* refer to the ropes and canvas, made from hemp, which were used to manouver the sailing boats. The French Queen was Mary, 'Queen of Scots', and her son James V1 who became King of a united Scotland and England following the 'Union of the Crowns' in 1603.
The following poem is also included in *'The Minstrelsy of the Scottish Border.'*

Thomas The Rhymer

Part Third - modern

When seven years more were come and gone,
Was war through Scotland spread,
And Ruberslaw shew'd high Dunyon,
His beacon blazing red.

Then all by bonny Coldingknow,
Pitched palliouns took their room,
And crested helms, and spears a rowe,
Glanced gaily through the broom.

The Leader, rolling to the Tweed,
Resounds the ensenzie;

They roused the deer from Caddenhead,
To distant Torwoodlee.

The feast was spread in Ercildoune,
In Learmont's high and ancient hall;
And there were Knights of great renown,
And ladies, laced in pall.

Nor lacked they, while they sat at dine,
The music, nor the tale,
Nor goblets of the blood-red wine,
Nor mantling quaighs of ale.

True Thomas rose, with harp in hand,
When as the feast was done;
(In minstrel strife, in Fairy Land,
The elfin harp he won.)

Hush'd were the throng, both limb and tongue,
And harpers for envy pale;
And armed lords lean'd on their swords,
And hearken'd to the tale.

In numbers high, the witching tale
The prophet pour'd along;
No after bard might e'er avail
Those numbers to prolong.

Yet fragments of the lofty strain
Float down the tide of years,
As buoyant on the stormy main
A parted wreck appears.

He sung King Arthur's table round;
The warrior of the lake;
How courteous Gawaine met the wound,
And bled for ladies sake.

But Chief, in gentle Tristrem's praise,
The notes melodious swell;
Was none excelled, in Arthur's days,
The Knight of Lionelle.

For Marke, his cowardly uncle's right,
A venomed wound he bore:
When fierce Morholde he slew in fight,
Upon the Irish shore.

No art the poison might withstand;
No medicine could be found,
Till lovely Isolde's lilye hand
Had probed the rankling wound.

With gentle hand and soothing tongue,
She bore the leech's part;
And, while she o'er his sick-bed hung,
He paid her with his heart.

O fatal was the gift, I ween!
For, doom'd in evil tide,
The maid must be rude Cornwall's Queen,
His cowardly uncle's bride.

Their loves, their woes, the gifted bard
In fairy tissues wove;

276

Where lords and knights, and ladies bright,
In gay confusion strove,

The Garde Joyeuse, amid the tale,
High rear'd its glittering head;
And Avalon's enchanted vale
In all its wonders spread.

Brangwain was there, and Segramore,
And fiend-born Merlin's gramarye;
Of that famed wizar's mighty lore,
O who could sing but he?

Through many a maze the winning song
In changeful passion led,
Till bent at length the listening throng
O'er Tristrem's dying bed.

His ancient wounds their scars expand,
With agony his heart is wrung:
O where is Isolde's lilye hand,
And where her soothing tongue?

She comes! She comes! –like flash of fame
Can lovers' footsteps fly:
She comes! She comes!- she only came
To see her Tristrem die.

She saw him die: her latest sigh
Joined in a kiss his parting breath:
The gentlest pair that Britain bare,
United are in death.

There paused the harp: its lingering sound
  Died slowly on the ear;
The silent guests still bent around,
  For still they seem'd to hear.

Then woe broke forth in murmurs weak,
  Nor ladies heaved alone the sigh;
But, half ashamed, the rugged cheek
  Did many a gauntlet dry.

On Leader's stream, and Learmont's tower,
  The mists of evening close;
In camp, in castle, or in bower,
  Each warrior sought repose.

Lord Douglas, in his lofty tent,
  Dream'd o'er the woeful tale;
When footsteps light, across the bent,
  The warrior's ears assail.

He starts, he wakes "What, Richard, ho!
  Arise my page, arise!
What ventures wight, at dead of night,
  Dare step where Douglas lies!"

Then forth they rushed: by Leader's tide,
  A wondrous sight they see-
A hart and hind pace side by side,
  As white as snow on Fairnalie.

Beneath the moon, with gesture proud,
  They stately move, and slow;

Nor scare they at the gathering crowd,
Who marvel as they go.

To Learmont's tower a message sped,
As fast as page might run;
And Thomas started from his bed,
And soon his cloaths did on.

First he woxe pale, and then woxe red;
Never a word he spake but three;-
"My sand is run; my thread is spun;
This sign regardeth me."

The elfin harp his neck around,
In minstrel guise, he hung;
And on the wind, in doleful sound,
Its dying accents rung.

Then forth he went; yet turned him oft
To view his ancient hall;
On the grey tower, in lustre soft,
The autumn moon-beams fall.

And Leader's waves, like silver sheen,
Danced shimmering in the ray:
In deepening mass, at distance seen,
Broad Soltra's mountains lay.

"Farewell, my father's ancient tower!
A long farewell, said he;
The scene of pleasure, pomp, or power,
Thou never more shalt be."

"To Learmont's name no foot of earth
Shall here again belong,
And, on thy hospitable hearth,
The hare shall have her young."

"Adieu! Adieu! Again he cried,"
All as he turned him roun'-
"Farewell to Leader's silver tide!
Farewell to Ercildoune."

The hart and hind approached the place,
As lingering yet he stood;
And there, before Lord Douglas' face,
With them he cross'd the flood.

Lord Douglas leap'd on his berry-brown steed,
And Spur'd him the Leader o'er;
But, though he rode with lightning speed,
He never saw them more.

Some said to hill, and some to glen,
Their wondrous course had been:
But ne'er in haunts of living men
Again was Thomas seen.

A story from Australia links two *'Ercildounes'* and two
'Thomas Learmonths.'
In 1835, Thomas and Somerville Learmonth aged
seventeen and sixteen respectively, were sent to Victoria
by their father to find land suitable for sheep rearing.
Their father, previously a successful Edinburgh
merchant, moved first to Calcutta, before finally settling

in Hobart, Tasmania. The two young brothers eventually found land near Ballarat at the foot of Mount Ercildoun, and began to rear sheep on a spread of 20,000 acres. One of their first tasks was to build their living accommodation; this being in the style of a Scottish baronial mansion. According to notes by Sir Alan Currie who bought Ercildoune homestead in 1921, the house was started in 1840 and completed in 1858, with many additional extensions built during that time.

Due to the strong character of the young Learmont boys, their hard work and diligence saw the spread prosper and grow. In 1849, the now 75,000 acre spread was licensed to John, Thomas, and Sommerville Learmont. At this time they were regarded as the best and most knowledgeable sheep-rearers in Australia. However, luck turned against the Leamont family, and one disaster followed by another eventually took their toll. First, Thomas returned to the land of his birth, then, following his death, some of his descendants followed suit. Thomas Learmont from Ercildoune Australia is interred in the family plot at Warriston cemetery in Edinburgh.

This branch of the Learmont family claimed to be descended from Thomas Learmont who once lived in *Ercildoune in the Merse*. A stone, taken from the original *Rhymer's Tower* in Ercildoune Scotland, is incorporated in a replica tower which is situated in the garden grounds of the present homestead at Ercildoune, Australia. John and Christine Dever bought the run down homestead in 1999; thereafter they began the huge task of restoring the former sheep-station and mansion to their former glory. The Learmont family motto, *'Dum Spiro Spero'* (While I Breath I Hope), was uncovered on the arch in the entrance hall during restoration work. Information on the life of *Thomas the Rhymer* of *Ercildoune* forms part of the history of the homestead. Although it is now a private residence, Ercildoune Homestead is listed as a *Cultural Heritage Centre* by the *Australian National Trust.*

The furore surrounding Thomas the Rhymer has diminished slightly in the last century, however, the associated intrigue and curiosity still bubbes away under the surface. The accuracy and credibility of Thomas's predictions influenced courses of action, which in turn shaped Scotland's history; the importance of which cannot be overestimated.

The rhyming tale of Thomas's journey to the otherworld and his subsequent gift of prophecy, worked both for and against him. There are some who, because of this tale, still regard Thomas merely as a *"figure of fantasy,"* nothing could be further from the truth. On the other hand, it is mainly due to this tale of fantasy that the legend of Thomas the Rhymer has survived for nearly eight centuries.

Thomas the Rhymer continues to intrigue and influence the modern writers of today. A historical novel entitled 'True Thomas' was written by Nigel Tranter and published in 1982. A collectors' book entitled 'The Journey of Thomas the Rhymer' by Angela Lemaire, was printed in the autumn of 2000, by *The Old Stile Press.*

I too have paid homage to his immortal memory by recently composing two poems dedicated to Thomas of Ercildoune.

The first is entitled 'Thomas of Ercildoune,' and the second is entitled 'Thomas, My Companion.' The third

282

poem in the sequence is taken from a small collection of *lays,* all of which were composed by residents of Earlston in the twentieth century.

The booklet is entitled *'Lays From Leaderside'* and was compiled by the Rev. W.S. Crockett D.D. Edinburgh, Minister of Tweedsmuir, being printed in 1928 for the *Masonic Bazaar of the Lodge of Ercildoune* No.1119. Unfortunately, the poem which I have included entitled *'A Visit From The Rhymer,'* is anonymous.

Thomas of Ercildoune

Yer name lives on in Earlston,
Yince kent as Ercildoune,
Mony are the years that's passed
Syne last ye saw yer toon.
The 'Black Hill' stands aloft as aye,
Dourly lookin' doon,
Yer ruined tower stands forlorn
Gawpin' tae sun an' moon.

As poet an' prophet, few surpassed,
Yer words kent far an' wide.
"A brigg ower Tweed at Leaderfoot-
Haigs aye in Bemersyde."
Yer name revered wi' Kings an' Carle,
Soon yer legend grew.
'True Thomas," ye couldnae speak a lie,
An' a' yer words cam' true.

Ae nicht while feastin' wi' yer kin
Yer Queen ye went tae find,

283

When doon the streets o' Ercildoune
Paraded hart an' hind.
Ye quietly rose an' made yer way
Across the Leader river,
Followed the beasts tae forests deep,
An' disappeared forever.

Ye'd waited lang for sic a sign
Tae return an' serve yer Queen.
An' o' yer face upon this earth
Nae sicht wis ever seen.
Some say ye drooned in swirlin' tide -
The Leader ran high that nicht.
But ne'er again in a' the land
Wis there ever ony sicht.

But come again tae Earlston,
As legend says ye will;
Changes, aye yer sure tae see,
But ye'll be welcome still.
For a' the years that's come an' gone,
Yer toonfolks aye the same;
We sing the praise o' Earlston
An' proudly say its name.

•••••••••••

Thomas, My Companion

'Twas on a cold October morn,
That I walked from Ercildoune,

284

The place that's now called Earlston,
Well known as 'Rhymer's Toun.'

As I sauntered round the lee
Of Black Hill's rugged side,
The breeze was but a whisper,
A hawk o'erhead did glide.

I felt that I was not alone,
I sensed someone was near,
'Though not a soul was there in sight,
Nor footsteps did I hear.

I climbed the Black Hill's lofty peak,
The land was cloaked in green,
My eyes beheld the wonder
Of natures' perfect scene.

By Scott's View and Bemerside
I slowly made my way,
And all the while two shadows
I saw in sun-light's ray.

As the triple peaks came into view,
I heard a gentle sigh,
Yet, as I glanced from whence it came,
Not a soul was there nearby.

I gazed down where 'Old Melrose'
Once overlooked the Tweed-
Where monks would kneel in prayer,
In reverence to their Creed.

285

The sun was setting in the west
O'er Eildon's peaks of three -
Where Thomas met the Fairy Queen
At Eildons' magic tree.

By Gledswood and Ri'path dean,
I made my way back home -
Past Craighouse Cap and Park Farm,
Where 'The Rhymer' once did roam.

The "Bonnie Broom o' Cowdenknowes,"
Alas, it is no more,
But Leader's sweet and silver tide,
Still gently flows to shore.

The warbling sound of birdsong,
In sweet melodic tune,
Drifted through the trees,
As I reached dear Ercildoune.

My companion was 'True Thomas',
He'd walked with me a while,
And as he took his leave,
I'm sure I saw him smile.

It seems he comes to visit,
On the eve of Hallowe'en
To check out his old haunts,
And view his favourite scene.

He'll 'dree his weird' wi' the fairy folk,
For ever and a day,

286

But ay his heart is in Ercildune,
Where once he was blessed to stay.

....

A Visit From The Rhymer

(Anon)

The other day a queer auld man
Cam' daund'rin' hrough the toun,
His coat was o' the brichtest green,
And gowden were his shoon.
The folk turned out to see him pass,
And as he ga'ed alang;
"An' is this Ercildoune?" he asked,
An' aye he said or sang;
"Doon the rainbow hae I slid,
An' wi' the sunbeams run,
That ance again my feet might tread
My native Ercildoune."
He gazed upon the Rhymer's Tower,
An' passers-by could see
The bricht tear wet his furrow'd cheek
An' dim his glancin' e'e.
He leaned upon his silver staff
An' muttered deep an' lang,
An' as he turned to leave the spot
He sadly said or sang;
"Oh, where is now the bonniest ha'

287

That e'er the sun shone on?
An' where the friends that graced the feast
Langsyne in Ercildoune?
He wandered down by Cowdenknowes,
The Leader wimpled clear,
The zephyrs played among the trees,
The birds sang in his ear,
The bricht sun, burstin' frae the cloud,
The green leaves shone amang
But wistfu' still the auld man looked
An' sadly said or sang;
"Where is the broom, the bonny broom,
Bricht wavin' in the sun,
Whose beauty gladdened oft mine eye
Seen here from Ercildoune?
He climbed the Black Hill's rugged side,
An' standin' on its crest,
Gazed far out owre the spreadin' Merse,
An' far intae the West-
To Bemersyde, and Huntly Burn,
An' to the Eildon Tree,
But aye he crooned his dolefu' sang,
The bricht tear in his e'e;
"Oh, what to me this smilin' land,
The trophies man has won,
When these but make my feet unkenned
An' strange in Ercildoune?
As sunk the sun o'er Soutra Hill,
Some bairns amang the broom
At Carolside a wee man saw
(As legend paints Prince Thoom)
Astride upon a butterfly,

An' as he soared away
Aboon the trees and up the lift
They heard him sing or say;
"Doon the rainbow hae I slid,
And wi' the sunbeams run,
Alas, to find nae hame for me
Remains at Ercildoune!"

Anon.

And so the mystery goes on, the truth, like the facts regarding the life of Thomas, will remain forever elusive. His mysterious life, and equally mysterious disappearance, will continue to be the subject of intrigue and speculation for many centuries to come; or, at least until the following questions are answered.

Did he retire to live out his days as a recluse at Fail monastery?
Was he murdered by one of his many enemies during the terrible, bloody times following the death of his friend King Alexander III?
Did his body lie for five centuries, within a few yards of his home, in the peatbog of the Hawke Kaim?
Or is he with his beloved Fairy Queen, deep beneath the mystical *Eildon Hills*, awaiting the call to return and save his kinsfolk, as the Gaels believed?

To preserve the name and legend of *'The Rhymer'* for future generations, *The Friends of Thomas Group* Earlston was formed in 2007. New signs were erected at the entrances to Earlston, denoting the village as being

The Home of Thomas the Rhymer and information leaflets, containing fact and folklore relevant to Thomas, were distributed to various local outlets.

....

Glossary

Aye	always
Aythir	either/both
Bale	fire/signal fire
Baners	banners
Bannock	a cake of home made bread
Bent	moor-land/coarse grass
Beryns/bernys	barons/nobles/chieftains
Bygge	build
By-teche	commit/deliver
Bod-word	message
Boune	ready
Bonnie	pretty/attractive
Braye	slope/incline
Breton's blood	Englishmen
Brucy's blood	Scotsmen
Bryttened	cut up/broke down
Busk	dress
Bygg	build
Carp	speal/relate
Chance	perk/booty
Chief	intimate
Chese	choose
Cheude	achieved
Cheuanteyne/Cheftan	refers to the Earl of Douglas
Claydon/donne moore	Dunse moor
Crapotee	a flawed precious stone
Crawhillside	Carolside near Earlston
Crystenty	Christendom
Damasee	Damson
Dere/derian	to hurt or harm

Derne	concealed/secret
Desse	the raised dias/top seat
Devise	speech/command
Ding	beat/thrash
Drede/dreid	dread/fear
Drie/dree	endure
Dullful/Doleful	sad
Dyng	overcome/defeat
Dynts	a blow, with force
Dyke	ditch
Eldoune tree	eildon tree
Erders	earthly
Enders	by-gone
Fast	haste
Fawte	failure/want
Fee	possessions
Fell	astute/ferocious
Fell	open hill
Fere	friend/companion
Ferly	a strange thing or event
Fers	fierce
Flone/Flane	arrow
Fode	a brood
Free	single/unmarried
Frith	firth/estuary
Frythe	enclosed field
Gay	pretty
Garthes	girths or garters
Gente	handsome/elegant
Gleydes more	the moor of the gleydes or kites
God schilde	God forbid

Goshawke	refers to David II
Gree	supremacy
Grete	great
Grew hound	greyhound/greek hound
Halse	neck
Harp	dispute/quarrel
Hethyne	hence
Herbere	garden
Hert	heart
Hertis	harts/female deer
Hende	gentle/skilful
Holt/ely	woodland
It bearis the belle	surpasses all others
Jalouse	deduce/suspect
Kirk	church
Lesynge	falsehood/lie
Lever	rather
Lire	complexion
Lygges	lies
Magrat/maugret	in spite of
Maun/mayne	accomplish/control
Mavys	Mavis/songthrush
Medill-erthe	the earth
Mekill	lowly/common
Mirk	dark/obscure
Mode	courage
Mone/moan	be aware of
Montenans	amount
More and Myne	greater and lesser
Neb	nose
Outray/owtraye	to treat disgracefully
Palfrey	horse

Paye	to pacify/satisfy
Presse	charge/assault
Psaltery	ancient stringed instrument
Rachet	tracker dog/scent hound
Rede	advise
Rewell	haughty/proud
Roelle bone	material saddles were made from
Rysse	twig/brushwood
Shawe	wood/copse
Schalle	shall
Skyme	Scone
Sembery	Edinburgh
Semble	assembly/conflict
Skylle	the faculty of reason
Sore	hard/tough
Speir	enquire
Spraye	spread out
Stane	stone
Sted	place/location
Stern/e	star
Sooth	trust/honesty
Soothe	truth
Spede	speed/succeed
Spelle	discourse
Syne	afterwards
Teen/tene	grief/sorrow
Tercelet	young falcon
Tercelletis	lords
Thre zere	three years
Thristle-cock	missel thrush
To-morn	tomorrow morning/*the morn*

Traye/trane	trouble
Trewe/trewis	truce
Trowe	believe
Wandrethe	misfortune/sorrow
War	aware
Welloway/wayloway	alas/lamentation
Wend	go/proceed/continue
Whatkyns	what kind of
Wyneberry	currant/grape
Wodewale	wood-lark
Worthe	become
Wryede	accused

Also published by Llanerch:

OLD SCOTTISH CUSTOMS
E J Guthrie

BUSHED AND BRIARS
Folk Songs Collected by
Ralph Vaughan Williams
edited by Roy Palmer

BESOM MAKER
Heywood Summer

105 SONGS OF OCCUPATION FROM THE
WESTERN ISLES OF SCOTLAND
Frances Tolmie

TOMBS OF THE KINGS
John Marsden

TALIESIN POEMS
Meirion Pennar

THE GODODDIN OF ANEIRIN
Steve Short

ORIGINS OF PICTISH SYMBOLISM
Earl of Southesk

ARTHUR & THE BRITONS IN WALES & SCOTLAND
W F Skene

TWO CELTIC SAINTS
The Lives of NINIAN and KENTIGERN
Ailred and Jocelinus

SHETLAND FOLKLORE
John Spence

STARTING TO READ MEDIEVAL LATIN
David Gosden

THE COMPLETE COLLECTION OF IRISH MUSIC
George Petrie

IRISH & SCOTTISH GAELIC NAMES OF
HERBS, PLANTS, TREES, etc.
Edmund Hogan

A GARLAND OF COUNTRY SONG
Sabine Baring Gould

CHINESE TALES OF VAMPIRES, BEASTS, GENIES & MEN
Leon Wieger and Derek Bryce

BALLADS AND SONGS OF BRITTANY
By Tom Taylor

GESTO COLLECTION OF HIGHLAND MUSIC
Francis Tolmie

FOLKLORE OF THE SCOTTISH LOCHS & SPRINGS
James M Macinlay

LIVES OF THE SCOTTISH SAINTS
W Metcalf

JOHN OF FORDUN'S CHRONICLE OF
THE SCOTTISH NATION
W F Skene

For a complete list of small-press editions and facsmilie reprints
of books on traditions, music, Celtic interest, early history, archery
mysticism, Anglo-Saxon interest and Literature of Llanerch Press Ltd
publications, please visit our website:
www.llanerchpress.com
or alternatively write to:
Llanerch Press Ltd, Little Court, 48 Rectory Road
Burnham-on-Sea, Somerset. TA8 2BZ